Mrs Guppy Takes A Flight

A Scandal of Victorian Spiritualism

www.nwp.co.uk

First published by
Neil Wilson Publishing Ltd
www.nwp.co.uk

ISBN: 978-1-906000-87-5
Ebook ISBN: 978-1-906000-75-2

Frontispiece: 'Miss Elizabeth Nicholl'

CONTENTS

Acknowledgements

Stephanie Bilton and Nicholas Connell have been the most generous and skilled of colleagues, leaving me in my ivory tower, and searching far and wide for genealogical and archival material to form the backbone of this book. My husband, Richard Whittington-Egan, offered me the use of his splendid collection of occult and psychic books and papers. I remember that he used to take me, years ago, to the Society for Psychical Research, of which he was a member. As ever, he has been my inspiration.

List of Illustrations

Preface

Into the Cabinet

MANY MOONS AGO, IN THE high Victorian era, Mrs Guppy, the famous medium, was enjoying a sparkling success. Over the rooftops of Bloomsbury she sailed, was infused through lathe and plaster, and clambered on to tables in the darkness, magicking down showers of apports.

Night after night, once the lights were extinguished, and the damped fires had died in the grates, the séance could begin in plush and mahogany drawing-rooms. The O of her mouth in speaking trances was a portal to the spirit world. Her lidded eyes were flickering sensors. The floating paper trumpets were channels to catch the direct voices of the departed. Curtained cabinets were entrances to the unknown land.

There, in the thrilling, breathing gloom, decked out in a merging black gown, portly – not ethereal – Mrs Guppy silently, deftly, tripped her own fantastic dance in little, pointy, soft, boots. Definitely invisible, for none ever spotted her, and very nearly noiseless – once, she set a chandelier a-tinkling – she glided behind the bowed heads of her awestruck sitters, and dispensed upon the table a cornucopia of gifts and symbols, apports from the spirits: animal, vegetable and mineral.

At the moment of revelation, when the taper was lit, and the guests blinked, the display was dazzling, a joyous rainbow of colours and textures; set pieces of fruit in patterns and pyramids, fresh flowers, be-dewed, in and out of season, tall plants, deracinated or entire. The smell of London loam clogged the heavy air of shuttered rooms closed against the light. Chunks of snow stained the tablecloths.

Not all that rained down was inanimate, by any means. For

those of a nervous or phobic disposition, there was a measure of apprehension. Slithery fauna were apt to appear, eels alive and wriggling, bewildered starfish, and lobsters not yet red. Occasionally, the medium tucked into the apported fruit. Wings swooped and birds burbled; doves were released. Lights darted and twinkled. Auditory effects, tactile feelings, stroking, prickling, oriental smells, made temporary schizophrenics of solid citizens. To and fro in the impenetrable murk the medium crept, sprinkling divine perfumes on the grateful believers and apportioning real jewels – rubies and opals. She was a sensation.

* * *

Sadly, though, she was a fake medium, or a cheat, as they called it then, deliberately and in full consciousness employing techniques and devices in order to deceive others that she was in contact with the dead. She was lucky, or exceptionally talented: no lurking sceptic ever managed to expose her, to put up the light prematurely, snatch off a veil, or disclose a mask or waxen body part, as was happening to her rivals. If she had been caught, she would have bluffed it out, and survived, if somewhat tarnished. Although she could be bold and apparently reckless, basic prudence stopped her from overreaching her powers. She was clever, friendly and perceptive, skilled at planning and preparation, always learning and watching, secretly rehearsing.

She lived a double life, concealing her false self even from those who were close to her, and that was vital for her survival. It was lonely, but she had learnt to be tough and as time passed she had the company of those fellow practitioners who were similarly engaged.

If the constant stress of subterfuge, the fear of public failure, bore heavily upon her, she did not show it. Her mental health was excellent – no neuroses for Mrs Guppy. She was placid, stately and Juno-esque, soft-toned in her trance utterances, but she could become powerful in her office, an imposing presence. Sometimes a rumbunctious, chaffing persona emerged and was a little over the top for genteel spinsters to tolerate.

The fact is that Mrs Guppy was not a lady: she was an opportunist of the actress type with natural dramatic ability. Upwardly mobile describes her perfectly. It is well accepted that, after food on the table, personal advancement, respectability, was the ultimate gain attached to mediumship for lower-class women whose options were limited. Successful mediums were treated with deference and delicacy, with a kind of reverence, taken up as 'friends' by their betters. The way to improve your status was to remain an amateur, not soliciting or accepting professional fees for sittings. To attain position, some other form of ancillary support, such as marriage, had to be sought. A rich patron might suffice. Then, if you had the nerve, soon you could be out in society, queening it in the best salons, the admired centrepiece of an elaborate charade. Importance, respect, gifts, hospitality, were laid at your feet but, of course, it was an artificial situation, and when you failed to impress, you found yourself living in oblivion in some backstreet in Battersea. Daniel Dunglas Home, the doyen of them all, dined with the Tsar and married his high-born goddaughter.

The age was sick with desire to hold on to the belief in the life everlasting. Evolution had not wiped out the entire Christian structure and many clergy were able to arrive at an accommodation. Victorian scientists were no different in their yearning for the hope of survival in which they had been brought up. Although they were self-styled as materialistic, and also hard, gloriously inventive, and cruelly experimental in vivisection, some of the brightest minds were drawn to the séance tables, where, thinking that they were applying the strictest scientific methodology, their level of credulity still amazes. They accepted the central practice of séances – the prevailing darkness, the cloak and facilitator of the multifarious special effects.

Not recognizing their own emotional needs, some of these men of science, once drawn in, sought to justify their presence by professing their utmost objectivity. Alfred Russel Wallace, who was, of course, the great evolutionary naturalist, duped through and through by Mrs Guppy, solemnly identified the species of her apports in a vain attempt to validate the phenomena. He believed in her absolutely.

The séances in people's homes, with refreshments laid on, were pleasurable social gatherings, eagerly looked forward to, often with a comforting nucleus of regular sitters. A favoured medium was a part of the group, and new psychics were welcomed and assessed. An unwritten code of conduct, in those early days, usually protected the medium from too rigorous investigation: there were some divagations from polite acceptance of all that took place. It was known that fakes were abroad, but it was thought that private mediums were beyond reproach. Even when the recently bereaved were present, the séances were by no means occasions of sorrow; the sitters experienced a communal sense of pleasurable anticipation followed by joy. Just as the Established Church buries the dead in the hope of eternal life, so the séances, often conducted in a semi-sacerdotal mode (although not so by Mrs Guppy, who was not up to it) appeared to be triumphs of ratification of that belief.

The experience was addictive, with some seeking out sittings several times a week. Mrs Guppy gave hundreds of séances. It did not matter that the happenings were often quite repetitive. The holy grail of spiritualism – the materialisation of the spirit form, to walk and talk and embrace – evolved gradually. It was perilous, an extreme endeavour. An instant lapse could destroy a hard-won reputation, except that spiritualists were so convinced that they were apt to explain away failure as the influence of bad spirits, or simply understandable fatigue or stress. It was often noted that a medium, even stalwart Mrs Guppy, could appear to be 'nervous' during a complicated piece of action. Some took to alcohol, but not Mrs Guppy.

As her 'powers' increased, she came to her apotheosis in the June of 1871, with a feat of levitation which captivated the nation. The image of the fat lady flying across London caused admiration and derision in equal measure. Portly in her billowing *déshabille*, bearing a quill pen and an account book, like a parodic figure of justice, she floated from her house in Highbury to a séance in progress in Bloomsbury. They called her 'Venus in transit', she was pictured with wispy sylphs upholding her, she was a comet in slow motion, and she was celebrated in *Punch*:

There is a lady, Mrs Guppy –
Mark, shallow scientific puppy! –
The heaviest she in London, marry,
Her, spirits three long miles did carry.

Upon a table down they set her,
Within closed doors. What! you know better,
And we're all dupes and self-deceivers?
Yah! Sadducees and unbelievers!

Her likeness, in what we might call a group photograph of mediums (see picture 13, page 206) shows an expression intended to be spiritual. Another marvellous studio portrait (see frontispiece) reveals her lack of refinement, her undeniable obesity, but also the prettiness which attracted men. It is a surprise that her hair and colouring seem to be fair, which is disarming. One would have expected a witch's dark sheen. She clutches, defiantly, a large black fan. Her clothes are good. She is beguiling, an unlikely magician. When she was beginning her career, she was seen by a leading spiritualist, Benjamin Coleman, as an 'unusually tall and powerfully made woman, without a trace of the signs of mediumship about her, though, as her father tells me, she is of an excitable and nervous temperament.' We shall hear more of her 'father' in due course.

Mrs Guppy was often characterised in terms of her weight. *Plus ça change.* We cannot be sure that she was thick-skinned about it. (The late Dr Eric Dingwall, psychic expert, told the author's husband that her weight, variously assessed as between 17 and 20 stone, was in fact 20 stone.) Often referred to now as a matronly figure, she was, in her early celebrity, still a young woman, with marriage and children ahead of her. Alfred Russel Wallace, who knew her well at that time, said that she was 'very stout and heavy.' This disability, as it were, inhibited her capacity for acrobatic manoeuvres or for frisking like a gossamer spirit, because her bulk would have been laughably recognisable.

As time went on, forced to hone her repertoire and put on ever more spectacular performances – for rivals were springing up with bells and castanets – she was not above adopting co-conspirators and risking a flaw in her bubble of secrecy. These could be professionals. She did not do much harm and she gave comfort to many even if that was not at all her motivation. Mediumship was her career. There were no lamentable letdowns, such as the ghastly scene when the Fox sisters in America confessed that their rappings had been produced by movement of their own bones, and the bereaved, betrayed, wept in the aisles. Some thought that she was a kind person and various indications support that view. Some laughed, as scepticism grew sharper, and some had always laughed, with *Punch*.

In the end, as the century lengthened, after the period of innocence, psychic research became deadly serious and dull, with no fun. Hapless mediums were to be tested in laboratories, gritting their teeth as they were subjected to searches, ignominiously stripped down to their underpinnings, and probed in their very orifices like convicts on entry to some vile penitentiary. Quite early on, Mrs Guppy, too, was placed in a position where she was obliged to submit to mild violation and stand in the back parlour all vulnerable and fleshy in her trendy Jaeger combinations. Her own house was the easiest setting for her manifestations, but she was brave and willing to perform outside the 'home circle'. Gradually, her psychic renderings were seen to be explicable and her reputation faded without gross scandal.

In her palmy days, at the beginnings of the British craze for spiritualism she was a maker of miracles and her name is still remembered. Her private life, obscured to those who believed in her, was curious and based on fundamental lies.

1

The Sculptor's Apprentice

MRS GUPPY WAS A GREAT pretender, an arch deceiver, both in her mediumship and in her version of her family history and upbringing. A fairy-tale background enhanced the mystery of a psychic: being orphaned or adopted, abandoned on a mountainside like Oedipus, or homeless like a Dickensian waif, invited sympathy and set you apart. The earlier the susceptibility to spirit voices, visions and disturbances, the deeper the adult powers. A hint of higher social class sealed the imposture. This was the pedigree, patented by the great DD Home, who very nearly always baffled. He was supposed to be kin to the Earls of Home, through his illegitimate father, William. Actually, Peter Lamont, in *The First Psychic*, has some good support for this claim. Adopted by a childless aunt at a tender age, and later whisked away from Scotland to America, he began to have supernatural experiences as a young boy, heralded by a phantasm of the dead, according to his autobiography, *Incidents in My Life*. No doubt Mrs Guppy eagerly perused that effusion.

In her case, she was already living a lie, *for reasons of respectability*, before she adapted it to buttress her psychic career. In 1870, when she was aged 32, in the presence of her husband, Mr Samuel Guppy, she granted an interview to an admiring representative of the *Spiritualist* (issue of September 15th). The resulting mythologised version of her wondrous life to date has unfortunately persisted as a biographical Bible, right into the 21st century, pervading works of reference, not only those of spiritualistic persuasion. The bogus family history could lead to some extraordinary interpretations. Dr Nandor Fodor, who was a psychologist with a strong psychoanalytical bent, mused that, 'she was an orphan, although she grew up with a father fixation, grandfather stepping into the place of the original parent.' (*Mind over Space*, 1962)

Back in 1870 the readers lapped up the information that, 'Miss Ann Nicholl was born in London, of youthful parents, in the year 1838. Her father and mother both died before she was 11 months old, and her grandfather, Mr Nicholl, sculptor, of Grafton Street, took charge of the little orphan, brought her up, and educated her.

'Mr Nicholl was a sculptor of considerable eminence and ability. He designed and executed the statuary which adorns the front of St. George's Hall, Liverpool ... On the retirement of Flaxman as modeller to the King, and to Messrs. Rundell and Budge, Mr Flaxman recommended Mr Nicholl as his successor, and he held the appointment for twenty-five years. While under the care of her grandfather, Miss Nicholl learnt the art of sculpture, and became clever in the use of the hammer and chisel; she likewise learnt electrotyping and photography.'

These inventions, more venial than heinous, perhaps, which wiped out her real and living parents and raised her social class by notches, were implicitly accepted by her close associates, but never did she foresee that by magical genealogical methods of another century her lineage could be traced back to the third generation and was a humble one.

The facts are that she was born Elizabeth or Eliza White, on January 22nd, 1838, in the Lanes, Horncastle, Lincolnshire. Sometimes her intimates called her 'Lizzie', but 'Ann' and also 'Agnes', which have crept into commentaries, are wrong.

Elizabeth's parents were not especially youthful: they were Charles Taylor White, who was born in Sculcoates, Hull, in about 1801, and Sarah Vickers, born in 1810 in Metheringham, rural Lincolnshire. There were six children of the marriage: Susannah, Charles Taylor, Elizabeth, Sarah, Mary Jane, and George Henry. The first three were born in Horncastle, the last in Hull.

There certainly was a 'Mr Nicholl, sculptor', and his full name was William Grinsell Nicholl, but he was not Elizabeth's grandfather, nor was he related to her in any way. The Taylor White and Nicholl lines show no convergence. However, there was a veridical relationship of some kind between Elizabeth and the sculptor. In 1861, they were both living at 57 Teddington Low Road, Hampton Wick, near the River Thames where it loops. He was described as a married man of 64, and Elizabeth White, 23, was his daughter, not his granddaughter. They were alone; no servants were listed. In false explanation of the difference in sur-name – for she did not dare to claim 'Nicholl', Elizabeth had said that she was *married*.

In fact, Nicholl had plenty of genuine daughters of his own, and a wife *vivante*, Emma, who was definitely not Elizabeth's mother, nor her grandmother. He did not always live *en famille*. The necessity for a lofty studio to accommodate his large statues might have been the reason for the separation. The situation was fluid.

Nicholl had married Emma Elizabeth Nicholson (born in Marylebone in 1803) in April, 1821. Seven children were born: Emma, Charlotte, Sarah, Emily, Thomas, Margaret and William. In 1841, when Emma had produced the first six children, Nicholl was in Cambridge and Emma and the family were at Grafton Street, West London. By 1861, when, as we have seen, Nicholl and Elizabeth White had formed an ambiguous ménage in Teddington, Emma and her family were miles away, at Harrington Road, North Marylebone. On the surface, this is a peculiar state of affairs. If Nicholl simply and innocently, out of professional necessity, and the artistic desire to be in a beautiful area, was maintaining two establishments, why was there a young woman living with him and claiming to be his married daughter for the purpose of the census? The implication is obvious. Elizabeth White was his mistress. What other explanation is there for the subterfuge?

Possibly she had gone to him as a domestic servant, or model, or both. Nicholl was noted for the 'chunkiness' of his sculptural forms. The *Observer* art critic, for example, wrote unpleasantly of his sculpture exhibited at the Royal Academy in the summer of 1831, 'Satan is tottering to another fall. This colossal figure gave way in the middle, and has been propped behind, which was wrong. Had it fallen, never to rise again, "It would have been well," for it is an ungainly thing, the head poor in expression, and the figure out of proportion.'

At some stage, Elizabeth had left her home in the north to seek her fortune in London. She could well have gone into domestic service. Her elder sister, Susannah, was already placed by the age of 16 as a general servant, at 26 John Street, Bridlington, Yorkshire. Her employers were Richard Monk, a cow keeper, and his spinster sister. It does not sound like an enticing prospect. It is impossible even to guess how many jobs Elizabeth had had before she surfaced in 1861 at Hampton Wick. Servants tended to move on in search of better conditions.

There is a clue, a link, in the information which she fed to the *Spiritualist*: when she was aged 17 – i.e. in 1855 – she was living with her 'grandfather' at No. 1 Gloucester Crescent, Regent's Park, but at No. 2, not No. 1, according to the *Guardian* of July 5th, 1858. There was a report of a fatal explosion at the Atlas Iron Works in Manchester, when the boiler of a locomotive with unusually thick plates, ordered by the Russian Government, blew up under testing. There was gross carnage: a severed head was carried to the roof of a building nearly 60 yards away. Among the seven dead was Thomas Grinsell Nicholl, gentleman apprentice, son of Mr W Nicholl, sculptor, of No. 2, Gloucester Crescent. This was Nicholl's eldest son, born in 1836. Perhaps Elizabeth had been the sculptor's servant at Gloucester Crescent. She might have forgotten the exact address, or chosen not to give it, or perhaps Nicholl had changed houses; that is not at all inconceivable. Or, more romantically, he had eyed his neighbour's buxom servant about her duties.

William Grinsell Nicholl was a man of far more standing than Elizabeth White could ever have hoped to catch, but, of course, there was no chance of marriage, and concealment was necessary. Born in Marylebone in 1796, he studied at the Royal Academy, and exhibited there until 1861. Among his works are the Fitzwilliam Museum pediment, panels for the Oxford and Cambridge Club, and the four massive sandstone lions on the steps in front of St George's Hall in Liverpool. Favoured by the architect, CR Cockerell, he was the principal ornamental sculptor for the Ashmolean, Oxford, and he executed the sculpture for Cockerell's imposing Freemasons' Hall in Great Queen Street, London. Not exactly famous, he accomplished a plenitude of strong, solid work, often as executant rather than designer.

Frederick Cockerell became a Freemason, a member of the Grand Lodge, and was appointed to the high office of grand superintendent of works. It is therefore quite possible that Nicholl went in with him, and was even more concerned not to cause gossip, since the moral teaching of the Craft stressed the importance of moral laws and the imperative to rule and subdue the passions. The Hall was conceived in 1861 and completed in 1866, covering the period of the household in Hampton Wick. If, notionally, there had been another, innocent reason for concealing Elizabeth's real status, such as a queasiness about his living alone, not a bachelor, with an unmarried, young, woman servant, this idea completely fails when, as we shall see, he accompanies her into society, at séances, while keeping up the front of being her father.

Improvements and polish might indeed have come to Elizabeth under the sculptor's roof, with a Pygmalion effect, but they were not attached to her real childhood, which was demonstrably spent with her own family in Horncastle and Hull. Horncastle, her birthplace in 1838, a small market town of Roman origins, surrounded by the flat Wolds of Lincolnshire, can have left no formative memories. Charles and Sarah White brought up only their first two children in the network of congested, almost medieval streets known as the Lanes, but by 1841 Charles had moved his family away to the wretched area of dockside Hull.

Charles Taylor White changed from one uninspired avocation to another. His great-grandfather was a 'tanner.' When between jobs, Charles styled himself as 'independent'. On Elizabeth's birth, and marriage, certificates he appears as 'gentleman', but no real gentleman would have settled in slums or allowed his daughters out to domestic service. Elizabeth's siblings went on to live very ordinary lives. Her next sister, Sarah, married John Cobley, a basket maker, and they had seven children, staying in Hull and then moving out to Grimsby.

In 1840, Charles tried his hand at running a rough public house, just off the Humber Dock. This dubious establishment was the Hamburgh Tavern, at No. 25 Blanket Row, an alehouse tied to Worthingtons. Charles took over from an insolvent, James White, not traced to be a relative: it was quite a common surname in Hull. Some half-dozen public houses were mapped in that same thoroughfare: they changed hands and names regularly. The photograph of the Hamburgh, (see picture 2, page 203) chillingly reminiscent of the landscape of Jack the Ripper's Whitechapel, shows, therefore, one of Elizabeth White's childhood homes, a far cry from her genteel fantasies. Previously signed the Hand of Providence, then the Billy Boy, the Lamb and the Tam O'Shanter, it breathes a bad reputation.

Packed in between the dwellings and courts were a large police station, the noisy Kingston Chain Works, and a steam sawmill. It was not a good place to bring up children, and cholera thrived in the murky, contaminated water supplies. In 1849, a direful strain of Asiatic cholera was brought into Hull. It lasted for three months and carried off 1,860 people. The gravediggers delved by night and day, and the cholera plot at the Hull cemetery looked like a ploughed field. The hearse toiled to remove the stricken poor from all quarters of the town and public places were deserted.

It was an area to escape from – as Elizabeth triumphantly achieved – but her father had been born in the Sculcoates part of Hull, and must have been drawn to it, always in search of occupation. It was there that he died, in 1874. We do not know if he was aware of Elizabeth's false claims of parenthood, or if she kept in touch with the family.

There is a glimpse of three-year-old Elizabeth in the census of 1841, when the Whites were all listed in a painfully narrow, crowded passage named Little Lane, which was close to the South End Graving Dock. Mariners, labourers, tailors, porters, and a customs officer were their very near neighbours. Charles' father, also Charles, was in the household, and both were set down as 'independent'. In 1851, when Elizabeth was 13, they were domiciled in Brewery Place, and Charles was a 'Rail Broker'. In 1861, with Elizabeth long removed to her glamorous life in London, they were at No. 1 Paradise Place, and Charles was a commercial traveller, the métier which he kept up at least until 1871, when he reached 70. For extra income, they had a 'paying boarder,' a three-year-old child from Lincoln, named Elizabeth Foreman.

Irretrievably cast from her Hull-ish origins, Elizabeth was forced to consider her prospects. She was marking time in the sculptor's studio, and, in true Pre-Raphaelite fashion, as a mistress, absorbing arts of her own, but she was ambitious. She was in her early twenties and he was 41 years older. How much longer would he last? It seems inconceivable that Emma Nicholl was unaware that an ample young woman from the north was associating with her husband and calling herself his daughter, but the years did eventually reunite the bipartite Nicholl family, and by 1871 they were together at 2 Bell Terrace, Churchfield Road, Acton and that was where, on December 8th, the sculptor died, his life's work done, commemorated by sandstone lions. His Will was proved by his only surviving son, William, a bachelor and a clerk to the Great Western Railway Company, and his effects were 'under £200'.

It was in about the year of 1866, that, according to the *Spiritualist* chronicle, 'Miss Nicholl resolved for several reasons of a private nature, to perfect herself in photography and painting. She therefore made an arrangement with Mr and Mrs Sims, photographers, who resided at Westbourne Grove. A strong friendship sprang up between Mrs Sims (Frances or Fanny) and Miss Nicholl; the former knew something about spiritualism, and so did Mr Sims, who, however, had a rooted repugnance to the whole subject.'

Here, then, is the connection, the cross-over, with spiritualism. Already, in the *Spiritualist* feature, Elizabeth has established a DD Home-like history of her early psychic proclivities, which also serves to embroider her bogus middle-class tapestry:

Her first symptoms of mediumship appeared at a time when she and her friends knew nothing about spiritualism; and it was that particular phase of see-ing-mediumship which is very naturally often mis-taken by doctors and the general public for a species of mental derangement. When she was about nine years of age, she began to see spirits enter the room in which she was sitting; sometimes she saw them looking in through the windows. They appeared to open and shut doors, or to come through the wood of the door; sometimes they trooped into the room in such numbers that they appeared to fill it, and to occupy every available seat, causing her such terror that she became nearly frantic. These ghostly visitors were dressed in both modern and ancient costumes, and some of them, to use her own words, were 'very funny, old-fashioned people.'

By day and by night Miss Nicholl was troubled by her fantastic visitors, who, however, seemed to be friendly and good sort of people. Her grandfather reasoned with her and laughed at her alternately, in the endeavour to make her free herself from the hal-lucination, and finally he placed her under the care of Dr. Smedley, the superintendent of the baths at Matlock.[1]

Neither cold water applications, nor plenty of exer-cise on foot and horseback in the open air, relieved Miss Nicholl from her imaginary visionary friends; but while at the baths she said nothing to others about what she saw, as she did not wish to be consid-ered a witch, or a lady suffering from aberration of

[1] There was a famous John Smedley (1803-74) not, in fact, a doctor, a wealthy indus-trialist and philanthropist, who built a large and successful hydro at Matlock Bath, Derbyshire, in 1853. Guesses about this fairly safe piece of specificity might include: she had worked at the spa in some lowly capacity on her way down to London; or Nicholl had indeed taken her there for a break – from his own arduous occupation.

8

intellect. Although her grandfather sometimes laughed at her visions, a circumstance occurred one night which somewhat startled him. At the time she was seventeen years of age, they lived at No. 1 Gloucester Crescent, Regent's Park, and Dr Riding, of Euston Square, had been selected by her grandfather as her medical attendant. One night Miss Nicholl and her brother went to the theatre.[2]

Mr Nicholl remained at home alone, reading in the drawing-room. In the course of the evening, when all was quiet, he heard the handle of the door move; he looked up, saw the handle turn, and the door open just wide enough for somebody to come in, but nobody entered; then it shut again. He thought that it was the servant, Mary, but, at the same time, wondered why she opened and shut the door without coming. Soon afterwards there was a ring at the street-door bell; he wondered that she did not answer it; a second and third ring followed, so he went down and opened the street-door himself. To his surprise he found that it was Mary who rang the bell. She had a lobster in her hand [that being one of Mrs Guppy's favourite apports] and she apologised to him for making him open the door, and for having forgotten to take the latch-key with her, when she went out to fetch the fish. On being questioned, it was found that she had been absent for an hour. Mr Nicholl, very much startled, told her that somebody had opened and shut the door of the drawing-room only a minute or two before she rang. They then closely searched the house from garret to basement; they found that the back-door was locked, and no living thing anywhere in the house, nor a window open. Mr Nicholl then felt very uncomfortable, and expressed his intention of getting out of

[2] Which brother might this be? Not one of her own brothers, for sure. She could have known the sculptor's two sons.

the house as soon as possible. From this time he modified his tone considerably when speaking to his granddaughter about her visions.

She had, too, told a previous interviewer (Benjamin Coleman) that her family doctor had ordered her head to be shaved and blistered to cure her 'delusions.' The spiritualist press fostered long, circumstantial accounts of this type, considering them more convincing. It is very odd that Elizabeth insists on referring to Nicholl as her grandfather, when he was well known at séances as her father. Her readers must have felt puzzled. Samuel Guppy, who was supporting her during the interview knew that the sculptor was no kin, as will become evident, but he understood the reason and did not contradict his wife in full flow. The narrative continues:

> When Mrs Sims heard about the visions of her pupil, she told her that probably she was a medium, and that she might be able to get manifestations by sitting at a table. She accordingly made one of a circle which was formed, and very loud raps were obtained: she would not believe that she had anything to do with the production of the said raps, but found that when she left the table they ceased, and when she returned to it, they began once more. This first sitting took place about six years ago, and from that hour the visions which had troubled her for so long previously, almost ceased.

Fanny (the wife of Thomas Sims) happened to be Alfred Russel Wallace's sister, and that is how he met his nemesis, an unfortunate conjunction, by no means at the end of his career, which caused grievous damage to his reputation. Officially, as it were, because the *Spritualist* said so, and more especially because Wallace said so, it was Fanny who introduced Elizabeth to the world of spiritualism, and Wallace himself who discovered her and further brought her out. The idea was that mediums in their nascent state had to be 'developed' by another sensitive, not necessarily a full medium, in order to know themselves and attain optimum power.

Wallace was on the friendliest of terms with his sister and her husband. Fanny, born in London in 1816, was an achiever, who, with all her siblings, had been let down by her feckless, non-practising attorney father. She had had to find her own way in life, teaching in Lille and America. In 1851, she married Thomas Sims, from Swansea, ten years younger than she was. He was handsome and artistic, and, like her, had struggled to make a living. There was a strong, early connection with Alfred Russel Wallace: Thomas was the eldest son of the helpful 'Mr Sims' with whom Alfred and his brother, William, had lodged at Neath, Glamorgan, while training to be surveyors.

Self-taught, Thomas Sims was one of the first generation of professional photographers in Great Britain. He set up in Weston-super-Mare in 1847, and, in 1852, contributed to the first British photographic exhibition held by the Society of Arts in London. Always improving, Thomas and Fanny moved up to London in 1853, taking a studio at 44 Upper Albany Street, Regent's Park, with a sideline as booksellers. For a time, they had two studios. In 1855, they transferred to 7 Conduit Street, Regent Street and thence, in 1861, to 15 Newton Road, Paddington. Money was often tight. By 1863, Fanny was advertising for business on her own account: 'Chalk sketches, beautifully finished, made from cartes de visite and other photographs or miniatures. Bust, life size, four guineas; including hands, five guineas. Address Mrs F. Sims, 5 Westbourne Grove Terrace, Bayswater.' (*The Times*, October 31st)

There had been excruciating patent difficulties before 1855, when the famous Fox Talbot, who was attempting to incorporate the wet plate into his patent, had sent in bailiffs and forced Thomas to close his studio because he was refusing to invest in a licence of the gross sum of £350 from Fox Talbot.

Wallace stayed with the Sims' in Upper Albany Street after his return from the Amazon in 1852, and again, on his return from the Malay Archipelago in 1862, at No. 76½ Westbourne Grove.

There, in a large, empty room at the top of the house, he brought together all the collections of fauna which he had reserved for himself. He also displayed a series of the rarest and most beautiful specimens of his birds and butterflies in Thomas' large photographic gallery.

In the spring of 1865, Wallace moved to a small house of his own at No. 9, St Mark's Crescent, Regent's Park, agreeably near the Zoological Gardens. His mother joined him there. 'It was in November, 1866,' he wrote (thus correcting Elizabeth's estimate of these unfortunate events as occurring in about 1864) that my sister discovered that a lady living with her had the power of inducing loud and distinct taps and other curious phenomena; and I now began a series of observations in my own house.' (*Miracles and Modern Spiritualism*, 1875, p.132) In the same volume, (p.162) he expands, 'I knew Miss Nichol [*sic*] before she had ever heard of spiritualism, table-rapping, or anything of the kind, and we first discovered her powers on asking her to sit for experiments in my house. This was in November, 1866, and for some months we had constant sittings, and I was able to watch and test the progress of her development.' It should be noticed that Wallace had been known at that time to be searching amongst all his friends for 'one who had power to produce distinct taps' (*ibid*, p.132) while attending informal séances in a familial setting.

Wallace says that Elizabeth was *living* with the Sims, but that was only temporarily and she was certainly not Fanny's paid companion as has sometimes been surmised, rather grandly. Frances Sims was not of that class, anyway. Elizabeth was domiciled at Hampton Wick at least from 1861, possibly longer, until the end of 1867. Excitedly, Fanny informed the *Spiritual Magazine* (February 1st, 1867) that 'Miss E.N. came to reside with me about three months since, and had at that time never heard of Spiritualism. About six weeks back we sat down to a table with a few other friends, some of whom had slight medium power, and were astonished at hearing distinct raps, which answered our questions exactly in the same manner that the tips of the table had done previously.'

Although the discovery of Elizabeth was the defining event for

Wallace, he had for some time been approaching spiritualism by other routes. In 1844, while teaching at a school in the Midlands, he had become interested in mesmerism, and found that he had the power to send particular boys into a trance. In 1865, Mrs Mary Ann Marshall was recommended to him as a public medium who would show him wondrous things, and he was impressed by her results: 'Accordingly, in September 1865, I began a series of visits to Mrs Marshall, generally accompanied by a friend – a good chemist and mechanic, and of a thoroughly sceptical mind. What we witnessed may be divided into two classes of phenomena – physical and mental.' Darkness was not a requisite.

The alphabet system was employed by Mrs Marshall, with the sitter going over the printed card and being rewarded by taps, until complete 'messages' were obtained. 'When I first received a communication myself,' Wallace wrote, 'I was particularly careful to avoid giving any indication, by going with steady regularity over the letters; yet there was spelt out correctly, first, the place where my brother died, Para; then his Christian name, Herbert; and lastly, at my request, the name of the mutual friend who last saw him, Henry Walter Bates. On this occasion our party of six visited Mrs Marshall for the first time, and my name, as well as those of the rest of the party, except one, were unknown to her. That one was my married sister, whose name was no clue to mine.'

Mary Marshall's small lair, reached by a narrow staircase, above a cabinetmaker's shop in Upper King Street, Bloomsbury, attracted many enquiring minds in the early days of British spiritualism. She had a lot to answer for. She was a first port of call before a journey which could last for a lifetime. Sir William Crookes, the discoverer of thallium, climbed those stairs in 1869, at the beginning of his psychic odyssey, only to be ensnared, famously, by his own Circe, Miss Florence Cook, of Hackney. He had not, in fact, lost his faith in the Creator, but he was troubled by personal loss.

Mrs Guppy and Mrs Marshall seem to have been on amicable terms. Their main difference was that the older woman's livelihood depended on her mediumship. She was lower class and poor. Somatically, they were alike: Mary Marshall, too, was very stout. She 'walked rather lame' and bore a 'kind, good-natured expression.' Make no mistake, she was clever. She had spotted the opportunity to set up as a medium in 1858, when she was some 59-years-old, and there were not many rivals around. In a quieter way than Elizabeth, she had her own following, and developed the confidence to travel to Bristol, or Malvern, to preside over private séances – even with 40 sitters, for a decent remuneration, of course. If she failed to impress in matters of accuracy, she would press on calmly, relying on the general impact of her performance. Operating in bright daylight in a pleasant drawing-room at No. 13 Victoria Place, Clifton, she called forth the spirit of Dante, but 'it was as plain as a pikestaff that the spirits knew as much of Italian as of high Dutch. (*Bristol Mercury*, September 30th, 1865). Her appearance caused unkind comments. A dissatisfied sitter writing to the Glasgow *Daily Herald* (January 25th, 1864) compared her dimensions to David (he meant Daniel) Lambert, 1770-1809, keeper of Leicester gaol, who weighed 52¾ stones at the time of his death.

Mrs Guppy was not prone to failure, but all her performances were all-or-nothing *tours-de-force*. In spite of the unevenness of her results, Mrs Marshall's reputation was high enough for the committee of the London Dialectical Society, established in 1867, to hear oral evidence concerning her séances. The committee of worthy intellectuals held a brief to 'investigate the phenomena alleged to be Spiritual Manifestations, and to report thereupon.' Alfred Russel Wallace was a member. Various mediums were considered, but they were not called in to demonstrate their powers in cold blood; sub-committees went out and held test séances in private houses, where their presence obviously had an inhibitory effect on the mediums, who failed to shine.

DD Home was the star. He came in to the enquiry and willingly answered questions on his own account. He was charismatic, confiding, fascinating.

> In a trance I see spirits connected with persons present. Those spirits take possession of me; my voice is like theirs. I have a particularly mobile face, as you

may see, and I sometimes take a sort of identity with the spirits who are in communication through me. I attribute the mobility of my face, which is not natural, to the spirits. I am most frequently in the air when I am awake. When I am in a trance I frequently take a live coal in my hand. I was sceptical on that point, and on taking one in my hand when awake I raised a blister. I have never been mesmerised, and cannot mesmerise. I have an exceedingly soothing power, an exceedingly gentle way of approaching anyone, whether well or ill, and they like to have me near them. I may say I am exceedingly sick after elongations.[3] While in Paris I saw the figure of my brother, then in the North Sea. I saw his fingers and toes fall off. Six months afterwards tidings came of his having been found dead on the ice, his fingers and toes having fallen off through the effects of scurvy.

Mr and Mrs Guppy were abroad during the enquiry of 1869, but Samuel Guppy was happy to send to the committee his clearly sincere digest of his wife's foreign séances. He could scarcely present himself as an objective observer, but that cannot have occurred to him, so sure as he was of the joint Guppy integrity. Miss Georgiana Houghton (*v. post*) spoke enthusiastically of some of Mrs Guppy's best, previous séances. Mrs Marshall was frequently referred to and one verbal report by Mr Hain Friswell cast a new light on her power over her sitters:

Well, I was once employed by a celebrated journal to get certain facts; I spent ten pounds, twenty pounds, without getting them. While I was going along by Mrs Marshall's, I thought I would look in, and I entered. The table was so crowded that I could not get a place at it, of which I was very glad, for I wanted to be a spectator only, and I sat by the fire. The table moved tremendously and came to me. There

[3] Weird extension of the body or limbs.

was a paper written underneath it; the words were 'Let the scribe come to the table.' I sat at the table. There was a sort of cataleptic seizure of those present, which principally affected the ladies. They foamed at the mouth and shook each other. They then began to talk nonsense and to prophesy.

The investigation by the Dialectical Society could have been an important landmark in the spiritualist movement but it was generally considered too credulous, and the press savaged the final report of 1870. *The Times*, consistently hostile to spiritualism, said that it was 'nothing more than a farrago of impotent conclusions, garnished by a mass of the most monstrous rubbish it has ever been our misfortune to sit in judgement upon.' It was better not to have been too closely associated with the enquiry, and Mrs Guppy did well to be absent. For the general good of the movement, however, neither Mrs Marshall nor Mrs Guppy cared a jot. To women of their background, ethical considerations were of no account.

Mary Marshall's admirers treated her with respect, as they handed over their half-crowns, but there was no pretence and it was obvious to everyone that she was a woman of the working classes. Both she and Elizabeth White had their origins in dockland slums. Mary Ann Marshall was a Londoner, born in February, 1799, in Shadwell, by the cold River Thames, where workers, traders and shops serviced the busy ships, and the rough dwellings were damp and unhealthy. Her father was Jacob Anderson, a mariner. On January 1st, 1832, she married William Marshall, a cooper, at St Saviour's, Southwark. He was 15 years her senior. In 1841, they were living in High Timber Street, just about as close to the north bank of the Thames as you could get. In 1851, they were at 14 Fair Street, Southwark, but by 1861, Mary was widowed, and at 22 Red Lion Street, Holborn.

William and Mary had two children: Emanuel and Ann, who was 12 years old in 1841 and thereafter disappeared from view. Emanuel, born on October 11th, 1832, was the 'young son' or 'young man' referred to in séance reports as an active helper. In

1851, he was a 'whig maker' - a cottage industry. On March 28th, 1865, he married Mary Ann Brody. She was, in fact, his first cousin, the daughter of Mary Marshall's sister, Dorothy, who had married William Brody in 1827. This explains why there were two Mrs Mary Marshalls working together and sometimes separately, an otherwise confusing state of affairs.

Although Mrs Marshall was an important propellant in the forces that carried Wallace deeper into spiritualism, he was not entirely satisfied with her work, and wanted something more. Finding an amateur, young medium in his own sister's home, beyond reproach, by association, struck him like a *coup de foudre*. It was Elizabeth who bowled him over. He made her the mainspring of his total conversion and it was her influence that permeated his mind and stoked his ill-judged rhapsodic writings on the subject. Their relationship was absolutely proper. There were other mediums around, and to come, who were more 'baffling', but as far as Wallace was concerned, she was the enchantress.

It was not that she made any conceptual contribution to his thinking about spiritualism; she was merely the instrument, giving substance, by her manifestations, to what he saw as the objective reality, the truth, and the scientific facts which proved his theories. We can see how he connected science with spiritualism:

> The organic world has been carried on to a high state of development, and has been ever kept in harmony with the forces of external nature, by the grand law of 'survival of the fittest' acting upon ever varying organisations. In the spiritual world, the law of the 'progression of the fittest' takes its place, and carries on in unbroken continuity that development of the human mind which has been commenced here.

Other, 'higher' mediums, such as the American, Mrs Emma Hardinge Britten, whose views he quoted approvingly, were in tune with his ideas, but Mrs Guppy was, in a way, for the time being, his property and his creation. He names her repeatedly, just as Conan Doyle included references to her in *The History of*

Spiritualism (1926) and stated that 'Mrs Guppy showed powers which in some directions have never been surpassed.'

He tries, himself, to analyse the progression of his thoughts:

> During twelve years of tropical wanderings, occupied in the study of natural history, I heard occasionally of the strange phenomena said to be occurring in America and Europe under the general names of 'table-turning' and 'spirit-rapping'; and being aware, from my own knowledge of Mesmerism, that there were mysteries connected with the human mind which modern science ignored because it could not explain, I determined to seize the first opportunity on my return home to examine into these matters. It is true, perhaps, that I ought to state that for twenty-five years I had been an utter sceptic as to the existence of any preter-human or super-human intelligences, and that I never for a moment contemplated the possibility that the marvels related by spiritualists could be literally true.

The mental processes which led him to spiritualism are complex, and earnestly debated by scholars. In some way, having established our beastly origins, he proceeded forwards, over the edge, to the idea of 'other and higher existences than ourselves.' He was not returning to the conventional religion of his youth, nor did he become a Christian Spiritualist, which is distinctive in its own right. His intellectual powers were very tenacious, and when he felt driven to investigate an issue, he gave himself to it unreservedly. Once evolution had been established and Darwin's *On the Origin of Species* had been published in 1859, spiritualism poured into the vacuum created in the speculative part of his mind, while at the same time his important scientific works came out – such as *The Malay Archipelago* (1869).

Wallace continued to enquire into the phenomena for the rest of his life, and always considered spiritualism to be a scientific endeavour. He made no claims to having a 'spiritual' aspect, and he scarcely liked even to use the world 'spirit'. It was not a short-lived aberration. There was no 'fit of temporary insanity', although, for sure, his peers did wonder if he had taken leave of his senses. As time went on, Darwin realised that the differences between them were greater than he had imagined.

There is a distinction to be made between the unfathomable cerebration which drove Wallace on from his great, achieved sciences to the false idol of Mrs Guppy, and the psycho-dynamic elements which clearly present themselves as plausible contributory factors to his entrapment. A 'disappointment in love', as it used to be called, when it carried off melancholic women to asylums, with the sudden loss of the expectation of sexual fulfilment, was the most discernible of his personal losses and traumata. The incident bears the advantage of being described by Wallace himself, in a letter to Darwin, (January 20th, 1865):

> For the last six months I have been doing absolutely nothing and fear I shall not be inclined for work for some time to come. The reason is that I have suffered one of those severe disappointments few men have to endure. I was engaged to be married at Xmas, and had every reason to look forward to happiness, when, at the last moment, when everything was arranged, and even the invitations sent out by the lady's father, all was suddenly broken off! No cause has been given me except mysterious statements of the *impossibility* of our being happy, although *her affection for me remains unchanged.* Of course I can only impute it to some delusion on her part as to the state of her health. You may imagine how this has upset me when I tell you that I never in my life before had met with a woman I could love, and in this case I firmly believe I was most truly loved in return.[4]

Later, in his autobiography, (vol. 1, p.401) Wallace reveals more

[4] Darwin Archive 106/7 (ser.2): 20-21, Cambridge University Library

about the impediment to marriage: 'Miss L' had been harbouring a wild delusion that he had concealed from her a previous engagement to a certain widow, a friend of Wallace's mother. Apparently, then, it was a case of mental illness. 'Miss L' and her family disappeared forthwith, leaving Wallace with 'such intensely painful emotion' never felt by him before or afterwards.

It may be that we should not lightly assume that Wallace had *not* been emotionally upset by the appearance of Darwin's *Origin* just because he said all the right things, was generous and gracious, was delighted that his own insight into Natural Selection, 20 years after Darwin in 1858, had stimulated Darwin into writing the great book, and was glad that he himself had not been taxed with the task of putting the profound and intricate theories into writing. We do not know, as he tried to carve his own future, how much disappointment and regret he had repressed, not admitted to himself, or just kept secret when he saw Darwin's fame so pre-eminent. He was only human.

Wallace was not a lucky man, and he had no personal deity to rage against. Even the brig *Helen* let him down in 1852 when he was returning home from South America. She caught fire in the ocean and all were forced to abandon ship, with the loss of his collections and his precious papers. Meeting Mrs Guppy was bad luck. He thought that it was serendipity but perhaps she deliberately placed herself in his path.

Personal losses naturally incline the bereaved to thoughts of spirits. The death of Wallace's younger brother, Herbert, in 1851, had left him with strong complications of guilt, because he had succumbed to yellow fever after following Wallace to the Amazon. Exposure to tropical climes and diseases eroded health and Wallace suffered repeated attacks of malaria, almost to death, which had weakened him. Although he was brave and resolute, an admirable man, his underlying personality was shy and sensitive. Respected by his academic colleagues, he was still aware of his lack of a university background, and he had a ready sympathy for the poor, and the underdog. 'Miss Nicholl' was unconventional, as he was, and he might have sensed an ambiguity about her background, although he accepted her fabricated pedigree, which was aided by the constant, hovering presence of William Grinsell Nicholl. It was noticed that Wallace was socially insecure, and he had a tendency to blurt things out. He was 'quite unused to good society' (*ipse dixit*) and, in 1863, Lady Lyell, wife of the geologist, found him 'unimpressive'.

The greatest mystery, however, is why the scholar who had looked deeply into the natural world and thought profoundly about evolution, was tricked by Mrs Guppy, blind to her legerdemain and gross conjury. The obvious parallel, of course, is Conan Doyle and the faked 'Cottingley fairies'. Even without a magnifying glass, and he assuredly used one, and took expert advice, which backed him, it is plain to see that the sprites are cut-out artefacts. The explanation, albeit a truism, must be that he *wanted* to see fairies. We probably all understand that, and he was a bereaved man, but Wallace, a scientist in mid-career, is more puzzling. In a moment of profound realization in 1858, stretched on his sickbed, tended by natives on one of the volcanic Spice Islands, he had seen into the truth of Natural Selection, but, back in England, all dressed up in stuffy drawing-rooms, he marvelled at heaps of fruit smuggled from underneath the petticoats of the pretender from Hull.

Whatever the origins of the ludicrous connection between Alfred Russel Wallace and Mrs Elizabeth Guppy, we cannot wish it away. For some sensitive people, personal loss led to the dark consolation of the séance room. The prospect of a barren land and empty skies receded and death lost its sting.

2

Into the Dark

ELIZABETH WAS ON THE MOVE. She was on terms of friendship with the Wallace family, and she had secured entry to a house at the hub of the scientific revolution, where men of note – Charles Darwin, Herbert Spencer, TH Huxley – used to gather for discussion of the deepest gravity. Wallace was also on the move, with his mood lightening. In 1866, he married Annie Mitten, an 18-year-old girl about half his age. It was a green alliance; she was the eldest daughter of his friend, William Mitten, of Hurstpierpoint, Sussex, the English authority on mosses. The séances continued as before, with no objection from Annie. Three children were to be born: Herbert, Violet and William. When Herbert died, aged six, in 1874, Wallace's grief was reminiscent of the better-known grievous loss of Annie Darwin in 1851. He could not speak of what had happened: his eyes would fill with tears.

Elizabeth's closeness to the Wallace family is shown in the way in which her name is offered as a comfort in that most sensitive form of communication – a letter of condolence. Miss Arabella Buckley, Sir Charles Lyell's secretary, wrote to Wallace:

> How wonderful it is how completely spiritualism alters one's idea of death; but I think it increases one's wish to know what they are doing – you have so many friends who can get information for you and I suppose Mrs Guppy having known dear little Bertie would be able to learn a good deal. I wonder who will take care of him and educate him for you.

The Westbourne Grove séances, where Fanny Sims officiated, with a few, chosen, like-minded friends, were centred upon table-rappings, but when Wallace bore his discovery off in triumph to his own home (not to stay there) the second wave of séances at St Mark's Crescent rapidly escalated, perhaps with suspicious speed, to better effects. Fanny had provided Elizabeth with an education in spiritualism. She took the periodicals, and she probably had a small library of spiritualist literature.

Over a period of some six months, in 1866, Wallace observed his new medium and made exhaustive notes. At first, the 'experiments' took place in a well-lighted room, where many fast taps and blows were heard at a large loo table without a cloth, which vibrated to the sounds, as they appeared to be coming from the underneath of the table leaf. 'They will keep good time to a tune whistled by one of the party; they will sometimes, at request, play a very fair tune themselves, or will follow accurately a hand tapping a tune upon the table.' Wallace dismissed the 'absurd and inadequate' explanation that the sounds were caused by the slipping of tendons or the cracking of joints. When a small work table turned and rocked and rose, suspended, resisting force, he admitted that, 'Of course, the first impression is that some one's foot is lifting up the table.' He constructed an apparatus, a cylinder of hoops and lathes, covered with canvas, which, placed outside the table, kept feet and ladies' dresses from contact, but still it rose. Therefore, 'It would appear that there is some new and unknown power here at work.'

Elizabeth became adventurous and took to the darkness. A strong pillar table was all that she needed. It was at a friend's house, this time. A sitter held both her hands. 'First, Miss Nicholl's chair was drawn away from under her, and she was obliged to stand up, my friend still holding both her hands. In a minute or two more I heard a slight sound, such as might be produced by a person placing a wine glass on the table, and at the same time a very slight rustling of clothes and tinkling of the glass pendants of the chandelier. Immediately my friend said, "She is gone from me." A light was at once struck, and we found Miss N. quietly seated in her chair on the centre of the table, her head just touching the chandelier. My friend declared that Miss N. seemed to glide noiselessly out of his hands. Deception was impossible,' Wallace said. The feat was beyond the known laws of nature. 'She was very stout and heavy, and to get her chair on the table, to get upon it herself, in the dark, and noiselessly, and almost instantaneously, with five or six persons close around her, appeared, and still appears to me, knowing her intimately, to be physically impossible.' This was the standard of the constant sittings at which Wallace 'was able to watch and test the progress of her development.'

Winter séances were freezing occasions, with the coals black and damp in the grate, and the sitters shivering in their outdoor clothing. On the evening of February 27th, 1867, the medium had brought the personage known as her father, and Wallace's new wife and her sister were present as onlookers. A subdued gaslight was allowed. A single wine glass was positioned on the floor between Miss Nicholl and her father, and it was, apparently, gently struck, producing a clear ringing sound. Soon, then, the room rang with the chiming of two glasses, delicate, silvery notes. It was as if one were inside the other, with a clang as one dropped in, and yet Wallace was sure that there was only one in the room. They lifted the visible glass on to the table, and the medium and a sitter held it to prevent vibration, but still it tinkled like a glass bell. Then they took an accoustic article – a rude bamboo harp from the Malay Archipelago – one of Wallace's colourful collection of curios – and the strings were twanged, loudly, under the table. When it was raised on to the table, very faint imitative twangs were heard, and 'We were informed by taps in the ordinary way that it was through the peculiar influence of Mr Nicholl that this extraordinary production of imitative musical sounds without any material object was effected.' What is this? Surely the distinguished sculptor was not acting as the medium's assistant? Why would she think it was expedient to introduce this idea? Was it to disarm any suspicion of his rôle? Special psychic powers were not usually imputed to him – a known sceptic according to his contemporaries.

The apports began on December 14th, 1866. That morning,

Fanny Sims had had a message, via Elizabeth, presumably, purporting to be from her dead brother, William Grendle Wallace, surveyor, who had departed unexpectedly at Neath in 1845, aged 36. 'Go into the dark at Alfred's this evening, and I will show that I am with you,' the raps spelled out. Elizabeth and Fanny arrived early for tea at St Mark's Crescent and there were six sitters, all friends. The shutters did not fit properly in the séance room and admitted a little diffused light from the gaslights in the street, so that the apports were faintly seen in the air as they fell.

It was the custom for accounts of successful séances to be submitted to the spiritualist periodicals, and Wallace, enthralled by the new manifestation, sent a report to the *Spiritual Magazine*, where it was published in February 1867, and received a considerable amount of attention. 'Thinking it better to see how we were placed before beginning the séance,' he reported, 'I rose up to turn on the gas, which was down to a blue point, when, just as my hand was reaching it, the medium, who was close to me, cried out and started, saying that something cold and wet was thrown on her face. This caused her to tremble violently, and I took her hand to calm her.' There follows a rare stab of doubt: 'It then struck me this was done to prevent me lighting the gas.'

However, he continued smoothly, 'Obtaining a light, we were all thunderstruck to see the table half covered with flowers and fern leaves, all fresh, cold, and damp with dew, as if they had that moment been brought out of the night air. They were the ordinary winter flowers, which are cultivated in hot houses for table decoration, the stems apparently cut off as if for a bouquet.' Now the botanical breakdown, to validate the event. The recital went rather like a bizarre Christmas jingle: 'Fifteen chrysanthemums, six variegated anemones, four tulips, five orange-berried solanums, six ferns of two sorts, one *Auricula Sinensis*: with nine flowers, thirty-seven stalks in all.'

Who paid for this abundance? Certainly not the spirits. Elizabeth had no visible means of support, but she had a bogus 'father', who, no doubt, did not leave her penniless, and certainly provided her with appropriate clothing. Surely Mr Nicholl did not knowingly press money into her hand to buy a monster bouquet?

Let us, just this once, put forward an analysis of the simple, but successful deception. Wallace himself provides the important clue: 'Miss N. had come early to tea, it being mid-winter, and she had been with us in a very warm gaslit room four hours before the flowers appeared.' It is obvious that Elizabeth would have needed to empty her bladder before beginning the séance; she had been drinking tea, and she would have been in a state of nervous anticipation. All present, or at least most, would have been under the same imperative, and so, at discreet intervals, all proceeded to the water closet. This was Elizabeth's chance for jiggery-pokery, the brief absence that was never referred to, never taken into account, and no doubt she made use of it many times in her career.

She already knew the layout of the house. She had a small slot of time. She, or her agent, would have had to hide the bunch of apports in advance, in a cool or cold place, perhaps in an outhouse or in the bushes. Then, quick, quick, a scurry to retrieve it, take it into the WC out of radar, use a perfume spray primed with some kind of liquid, and stuff the bundle under her skirts. Into the séance room, the light extinguished more or less immediately – Wallace obligingly contributed 'four minutes' – and then she retrieved and cast the apports all fresh up in the air. It is vain to quibble: she concealed her apports, really imports, about her person, and her bulk was in itself a shield and camouflage. We do not need to be impressed by Wallace's insistence that, 'Not a petal was crumpled or broken, not the most delicate point or pinnule of the ferns was out of place.' There were many things that he was not seeing properly, in his state of heightened sensibility.

Elizabeth was not on her own premises: there was no question of a concealed entrance to the room. She was, later, to be in the habit of wandering surreptitiously round her hosts' houses before a séance, or even days previously, in order to abstract useful articles for future use. Servants *were* suborned by mediums, but that was later, if at all, for Elizabeth. Wallace would probably have had only one domestic servant at that time, and that was advantageous to a medium because it was easy to know where she was. While Wallace was of such paramount importance to her, it was unlikely anyway, that she would have put her trust in her own patron's servant.

Elizabeth had successfully launched her new activity – the production of apports – which was to become her trademark. Her fame was founded on flowers and fruit. In those trusting days her popular séances brought colour out of darkness, the symbolic gifts from the spirits were reassuringly tactile, not frightening, and the sitters knew what to expect. Wallace commented that she repeated the phenomena hundreds of times and in many houses and under various conditions. 'Sometimes the flowers have been in vast quantities, heaped upon the table. Often flowers or fruit asked for are brought. A friend of mine asked for a sunflower, and one six feet high fell upon the table, having a large mass of earth about its roots.'

The theory of apports, an old one at that, and certainly not Elizabeth's invention, although she adopted it for all that she was worth, required the sympathetic medium to provide a channel for the objects to pass from the spirits through material barriers and appear on the table intact and as it were reconstituted. It would seem to be a dead end for an aspiring medium, but Elizabeth kept it in her repertoire for years. Historically, according to Frank Podmore (*Mediums of the Nineteenth Century*, Vol. 1, pp.80-81) and Nandor Fodor (*Encyclopaedia of Psychic Science*, pp. 10-16), the phenomena were first witnessed in France in 1819 by Dr GP Billot, when a dove, white as snow, was seen flying about the room with a paper packet in its beak, which was found to exhale a sweet smell. Inside, there were three fragments of sacred bones, glued on to small strips of paper. The occasion was the experimental 'magnetism' of three prophetic people in hypnotic trance. Also present was a blind woman, and at a later session she suddenly cried out that a spray of flowers had landed on her apron. It proved to be a piece of Cretan thyme, which, Podmore commented, exactly foreshadowed Mrs Guppy's feats.

The dove is an intense symbol of Christianity, representing the Holy Ghost or Paraclete, and often seen in paintings showing the phases of the life of Jesus Christ, especially the

Annunciation and the Baptism. A white dove came to a séance in Boston in the earliest days of American spiritualism, and Elizabeth's first recorded dove appeared in 1867. It was vital that the bird was a tamed performer, able to endure confinement, and not prone to panic in the darkened room. Sometimes the medium convulsed, writhed, or cried out in apparent agony as the apport emerged. The Victorians weathered the embarrassing, disinhibited grotesquery in mixed company with surprising sang-froid.

Afire with his new convictions, and in a controlled but simmering emotional state, married at last, Wallace entered on a mission to convert his colleagues, learned men of science. He caused a delicate situation; they cringed, but he was liked and respected, and they did not care to shun him when he begged their attendance at a little séance at St Mark's Crescent. The project was doomed. Elizabeth was nervous and circumspect, but, as ever, relied on her personality to survive the ordeal. It would have been awkward for her to refuse to co-operate. Wallace's deference to her must have disconcerted the visitors before the proceedings even began.

Dr William Benjamin Carpenter (1813-85), naturalist and polymath, was 'above middle height, of quiet and somewhat formal manner, spare, keen-eyed, and tenacious-looking,' and known for his exposure of quackery (*Dictionary of National Biography*). He was not, however, closed to spiritual matters, and regarded miracles as manifestations of a higher order, not as violations of natural order. As for Darwinism, he believed that Natural Selection leaves untouched the evidence of design in creation. He was a Unitarian and used to play the organ at the church in Hampstead. Only a few, tentative raps were heard at the table. 'He knew,' Wallace remarked sadly, 'from my statements that this was a mere nothing to what often occurred, and though I strongly urged him to come at least two or three times more, I never could prevail upon him to come again.' Dr Carpenter had sat motionless and silent and it had been an uncomfortable experience for everyone. Mrs Sims took Elizabeth home.

Professor John Tyndall (1820-93), scientist of great eminence, tried to negotiate terms with Wallace in advance:

> My dear Wallace, your sincerity and desire for the pure truth are perfectly manifest. If I know myself, I am in the same vein. I would ask one question. Supposing I join you, will you undertake to make the effects evident to my senses? Will you allow me to touch the effects with my own hands, see them with my own eyes, and hear them with my own ears? Will you, in short, permit me to act towards your phenomena as I act, successfully act, in other departments of nature? I really wish to see the things able to produce this conviction in a mind like yours, which I have always considered to be of so superior a quality.

Annoyed, Wallace could 'undertake' nothing, and it would be wise for Tyndall to be, at first, a passive spectator, but, 'At the very beginning, he forgot or purposely acted contrary to my advice.' On being asked to sit at the table he refused, saying, 'I never form part of my experiments. I will sit here and look on.' He drew his chair about three feet away. Better rappings occurred than when Dr Carpenter loomed at the table: they were more varied, some mere ticks, others loud slaps or thumps. Tyndall was not impressed and began to joke with Elizabeth, who was, said Wallace, 'always ready for fun.' 'We know all about these raps,' Tyndall, who was an Irishman and quite outgoing, said in a jovial manner. 'Show us something else. I thought I should see something remarkable.' After more chaff with Elizabeth, he said 'Good night.'

Wallace did not care. He pressed on with his investigations, going to many mediums, among them DD Home, and committing himself in the strongest terms: 'Surely these are phenomena about which there can be no mistake. What theories have ever been proposed by our scientific teachers which even attempt to account for them? Delusion it cannot be, for the flowers are real, and can be preserved, and imposture under the conditions described is even less credible.' In 1866, he caused consternation when he published, privately, in 100 copies, a pamphlet, entitled *The Scientific Aspect of the Supernatural*. This was a long essay which had first appeared in the *Fortnightly Review*, where it would have been widely read, and it was incorporated in 1875 in Wallace's passionately argued tract, *Miracles and Modern Spiritualism*, which, as with his autobiography, *My Life: A Record of Events and Opinions* (1905) is permeated by the antic figure of Mrs Guppy.

As she gained in confidence and aspiration, Elizabeth began to venture beyond her 'home circle' to the wider sphere of private séances in good houses. At this stage, she may not have formed the full, conscious intent of making mediumship her life's calling. Boosted by Wallace's belief in her powers, no doubt she was seeing how far she could go. It was very exciting, and Nicholl was encouraging her. She could give it up at any time. There was still the possibility of marriage and children. She decided to diversify. 'Shortly after her mediumship began to attract public attention,' the defining *Spiritualist* feature of September, 1870, reported, 'Miss Nicholl went to the Mesmeric Infirmary, and qualified herself as a lady operator. She worked very hard at her duties in connection with the establishment, and was highly successful in curing the diseases of many of the lady patients. Her evenings were usually devoted to spiritual séances, and at this time her grandfather resided near Hampton Court.'

Such an establishment, a curious temple of alternative medicine, certainly did exist, and similar institutions had sprung up in other big cities such as Edinburgh and Dublin. The inspiration and founder was Dr John Elliotson (1791-1868), who was one of the foremost physicians of his time, an exceptional clinician and teacher, pioneer of the use of the stethoscope and the application of iodine in the treatment of thyroid disorder. However, there is a parallel with the almost spoiled career of Alfred Russel Wallace: he, too, stepped off the main track of scientific thought into a by-way along which he continued with

inflexible, lifelong enthusiasm, alienating his conventional colleagues, while remaining an excellent doctor. He had come to
mesmerism via the cul-de-sac of phrenology. In 1838, he was
forced into resigning his professorship at University College
Hospital, because his wide-ranging mesmeric claims and beliefs,
tinged with supernormal elements, such as clairvoyance and
healing during trance, were unacceptable.

In 1850, he set up the London Mesmeric Infirmary in
Weymouth Street, expressing its aims to be, 'for the alleviation
and cure of diseases, and for the relief and prevention of pain, by
means of mesmerism.' It was popular with a small number of
full-time staff and lay volunteers treating some 300 outpatients a
year. (See Antonio Melechi's *Servants of the Supernatural*, p.97
and *passim* for full account of Dr Elliotson). In 1854, partly due
to the nimbyism of neighbours, the infirmary relocated to
Wimpole Street, whither, in 1867, the young Miss Nicholl made
her dignified journey. It is unlikely that she met Dr Elliotson,
because he was failing by then, but (she claimed) she was taught
by Mr Fradelle. He was a leading mesmerist at the infirmary, and
sometime secretary there. It was said that he 'in all cases pro-
cured interior vision in his patients who prescribed for themselves the medicine which cured them; his speciality was to cure
Epilepsy, Tumours, cancer, and strumous complaints, [swellings
of tubercular or thyroid origin in the neck] and to mesmerize animals, controlling them by his will and curing them.' (*v. Mental
Magic*, 1884)

Wallace knew all about the infirmary, because his dentist,
Theodosius Purland, of 7 Mortimer Street, Cavendish Square,
had helped Dr Elliotson in the setting up of the new establishment in Wimpole Street. He and Wallace were on friendly terms.
An eccentric, Egyptologist and numismatologist, he was, worry-
ingly, totally opposed to chemical anaesthesia, preferring to
employ mesmerism, which, hopefully, came to the rescue.

Incredible claims were made for mesmerism; it was said to
have been successful in curing typhus fever in its last stages, con-
sumption, dropsy, bronchitis, a multiplicity of nervous disorders,
and even surgical cases such as a woman diagnosed with ovarian

tumour. (*v.* Emma Hardinge Britten's *Nineteenth Century Miracles*, pp. 124-5) What was later termed hypnosis was combined with healing techniques such as the laying on of hands, and manual passes. Actual magnets were sometimes applied. Dr Elliotson was, however, absolutely not a charlatan, and the public displays of mesmerised psychiatrically ill and epileptic girls at his home at No. 37 Conduit Street, which are now regarded along the lines of medical abuse of women, and for which he is now remembered, are in the tradition of the great Charcot's public exhibitions of hysterical patients at the Salpêtrière Hospital in Paris.

The lay element of well-meaning middle-class women assisting at the London Mesmeric Infirmary, practising healing in good faith, imports a chaotic air to the proceedings. Mrs Britten stated that 'some of the best Mediums were developed among the poor patients who sought aid at the Mesmeric Infirmary.' This was a rich and fertile garden for Elizabeth's growth, and the chance of further advancement came with meeting influential doctors, patrons and supporters as her social skills widened even further. An introduction to genuine hypnotic techniques might have benefitted her as a medium, but the accounts of her séances lack any shading of such activity, unless the pacific behaviour of her live animal apports is considered. Perhaps Mr Fradelle taught her the 'magnetic eye' – the fixed stare. Flamboyance seems to have gone with the speciality and Elizabeth was there to absorb it. The culture was extraordinary – wild and optimistic, but dedicated altruism was not, really, her penchant. It should be noticed that as a working, trained, therapeutic mesmerist, she would have been entitled to a professional fee, which might have kept her when she parted from Nicholl. Frank Podmore, puzzling about her status and the cost of the apported flowers, not knowing about the sculptor in the background, summarised these matters quite neatly:

> Mrs Guppy, even during the few months in which,
> as Miss Nicholl, she practised as a professional mes-
> merist, can scarcely have found her main incentive

in the hope of gain. On the assumption of fraud, the mere cost of the flowers lavished on her sitters must have swallowed up any probable profit from her increased clientele. And even such a motive would have ceased with her marriage.[5]

Hypnosis has sometimes been advanced as the explanation for baffling mediumistic effects – particularly DD Home's most uncanny manifestations – but scarcely anyone now believes that 'mass hypnosis' of a number of sitters did the trick. Alfred Russel Wallace was an indignant denier of the mesmerism theory:

> The assistants at the séances of Mr Home or Mrs Guppy are not in this state ... They do not lose all memory of immediately preceding events; they criticise; they examine; they take notes; they suggest tests – none of which things the mesmerised patient ever does ... The mesmeriser has the power of acting on certain sensitive individuals ... and all experience shows that those who are thus sensitive to any one operator are but a small proportion of any body of people ... The visitors to Mr Home or Mrs Guppy all see whatever occurs of a physical nature.

Mr Benjamin Coleman interviewed Elizabeth informally at a séance in April, 1867, with her escorting 'father' in attendance. The venue was 24, Arundel Gardens, Bayswater, the home of Mr John Tawse and his family, and it was there that Elizabeth coolly bamboozled the earnest spiritualist enquirer:

> Miss Nicholl, it appears from her own statement to me, knows absolutely nothing of spiritualism. She has never read a book upon the subject; she is unacquainted with the Davenport controversy, and did not even know that there is such a distinguished unraveller of psychological mysteries as Mr Edmund

[5] Quoted by Nandor Fodor, *Encyclopaedia of Psychic Science*, p.155)

Yates, the 'Flaneur' of the 'Star', nor indeed was she aware of the host of other clever fellows who can imitate her 'tricks', and satisfy the credulous multitude that she is a 'clever impostor', that she 'biologises her audience,' and makes them believe they see flowers when no flowers in fact are there. Happily, however, Miss Nicholl does not intend to trust herself to the tender mercies of such persons; she is determined not to make a profession of spiritualism, nor to give a public exhibition of her powers; she will avoid sitting with promiscuous parties, and until she has more experience, and is able to overcome the nervous agitation from which she suffers, I have advised her to give up these sittings altogether. She has, it is said, great magnetic power, and to this branch of the subject she has wisely decided to devote her time.

To qualify herself, she is giving a few months' service to the Mesmeric Infirmary, under the tuition of Mr Fradelle, and when she has obtained the necessary knowledge of treating disease, she will make mesmerism her profession. I have no doubt, from her robust constitution and genial disposition, she will be very successful as a magnetic healer, and that she will find a large field of usefulness for the exercise of such powers as she may possess in this way.[6]

The following September, Elizabeth was still persevering at the infirmary. She was the medium at a well-attended and eventful séance at the home of Cornelius Pearson, an artist then of some renown. Three spirits conveyed the message that they were present and would do all they could to provide proof of their power, but, unfortunately, the medium's physical condition was unfavourable, as she was much fatigued by a long day's work at her professional duties as a mesmerist. Her two major enterprises breathe ambition, determination and physical and mental

[6] *Spiritual Magazine*, May 1st, 1867.

strength. The assembling of apports, harvested flowers – large hollyhocks, bindweed (very easy to compress) and so on – packed into their hidden receptacles, panniers or pockets, was in itself a considerable task.

In spite of her expressed plans for the future, the lure of the séances won. The single glory appealed to her more than the healing team. Anyway, she was on the brink of other favourable and life-changing events. Meanwhile, her fame was growing, she was an exciting new medium much in demand and she bore the seal of approval of Alfred Russel Wallace.

The time came when Elizabeth felt obliged on occasions to submit to being searched. This was in intellectual circles, where 'scientific investigation' was a priority. She could always refuse, on some delicate pretext, but risked losing a smidgeon of her sitters' blind faith. Same-sex searching was implicitly the only practice in those days and in the case of a private medium, consent was, naturally, a prerequisite. That is not to say that a professional medium was open to search without consent. Since 'Miss Nicholl' was proferred to her sitters as coming from the same class, delving into her layers of clothing must have been an embarrassment for all concerned.

She encountered an unusually suspicious host, when, on April 29th, 1867, she went to 8 Essex Villas, Kensington. Samuel Carter Hall (1800-99) FSA, man of letters, editor of the *Art Review*, was a strong spiritualist, a believer in DD Home, and, in 1874, chairman of the British National Association of Spiritualists. He wrote a letter to the *Spiritual Magazine* to report that:

> A large number (exceeding twenty) of natural flowers, cowslips, heartsease, and violets chiefly, were suddenly thrown upon the table round which we were seated; among them being two somewhat large branches of apple blossom. They were fresh as if just gathered, as were also the cowslips – a flower that easily droops. Miss Nicholl had come to us from her residence at Hampton Wick. I can no more account

for their entrance into my room than I can for other phenomena of spiritualism – the doors and windows were closed. Although there is a pear tree blossoming in an adjacent garden, I know of no apple tree near at hand.

But my object in writing you is this:- It has been asserted that on such occasions Miss Nicholl takes flowers with her – that in short she is a cheat. I did not give ear to such report; but I felt, as I always feel, that every medium should be sternly tested, for impostors are no doubt plenty enough. At my suggestion, therefore, Mrs Hall and her friend, Mrs Senior, immediately on Miss Nicholl's arrival, took her into Mrs Hall's dressing room, and with the instant approval of Miss Nicholl, examined minutely every portion of her dress. They found no leaves or flowers: nothing that could in the slightest degree insinuate deception. That a willingness to dream is foreign to her nature may be only an opinion.[7] It is my opinion, however: but it was utterly beyond her power to have concealed the flowers that were scattered about our table. I have seen phenomena more wonderful; but none that I have been able to test more conclusively, so as to obtain conviction that there was neither delusion nor fraud.

She had won him round, as she generally did: 'One of the branches of apple blossom is on my table as I write; the other was taken by an eminent physician who was present.' No differently from her other admirers, he proudly bore the apports away for display, just as they all did, framing them, mounting them, photographing them, or cramming them into bell jars.

A stout, tall woman was well constructed to accommodate places of concealment in her clothing or about her body. Layers of perhaps three petticoats – red, white, or striped – were worn in the 1860s, and it was noticed that Mrs Guppy sported volumi-

[7] Perhaps he means that he detects a lack of spirituality, a hard edge.

nous petticoats. In 1872, six of the articles might be worn. Crinolines, bunched voluminously around the table were recognised as affording scope for 'crinoline mystification', but, 'by 1866, many were discarding crinolines for flounced muslin petticoats; or using a crinoline which would fold inwards when the wearer was seated.'

Hidden pockets in the skirts and petticoats are undoubtedly the clue to many mysteries, and detachable pockets, similar to those used by poachers, in the shape of a bag with a side slit, suspended from the waist, no doubt had their place: women travellers abroad found them invaluable, right up to the close of the century. Drawers of silk or flannel were fashionable, and scarlet flannel knickerbockers, confined just below the knee by elastic would have been useful repositories. There were no 'bust bodices' until 1889. Corsets were worn, and they had possibilities.

The bustle appeared in 1868 and was of vast dimensions by 1871. Sometimes a smaller 'pannier' was chosen. Especially if it were adapted, it could have provided a cage for living apports. Elizabeth already presented a massive silhouette, and might not have wished to enhance her conspicuous bulk, but, on the other hand, she was a realist, and her appearance was not her prime concern. Outdoor clothing, shawls, cloaks and muffs were brought into cold séance rooms during the winter.

The credulous were easily satisfied. At the previously mentioned séance at Arundel Gardens, Bayswater, Benjamin Coleman 'jocularly' (as he put it) suggested that Miss Nicholl might have brought the apported flowers in her pocket. They included, incidentally, a bright damask rose with a profusion of green leaves, the petals secured by a fine wire artistically entwined around them, as if a skilled florist had arranged it, to prevent the leaves from falling, and two azaleas. Miss Tawse was eager to refute that idea, because she had seen the medium, during the afternoon, playing with her children and they had filled her pocket with their toys. Good-naturedly, Miss Nicholl immediately turned her pocket out on the table, and there was not the slightest trace of flower or leaf, 'as there must have been from the fragile azaleas, the leaves of which fell off as we handled them.' Therefore, according to wise Benjamin Coleman, 'It is satisfactory to be enabled to say that the flowers were not concealed in the only place they could have been.'

This particular séance was not entirely typical, in that Elizabeth betrayed 'agitation', which was, from our perspective, a ploy to get her own way. She seems to have prepared only the shower of apports and then to have exhausted her box of tricks. In order to postpone the climax of flowers, she set up some delaying tactics: 'We sat round a table in the drawing-room, and at once obtained the usual rapping sounds; we were told by the invisibles that we should have a remarkable manifestation if we would exclude all light. To this Miss Nicholl strongly objected, and we lost most of the evening in endeavouring to obtain the necessary conditions, short of total darkness.' Later, after the main event and some minor manifestations not worth recording, it was said, 'we should doubtless have had some other extraordinary exhibition of spirit power had the medium been able to command herself; she was, however, so extremely agitated, and so earnestly begged that the light should not be put out again, that we deemed it best to break up the sitting.' The real Mrs Guppy never lost control.

Early in her psychic career, two spiritualists were drawn, separately, to the exciting new medium and became an important and enriching part of her life. Mrs Catherine Berry and Miss Georgiana Houghton were both mild amateur mediums, but the difference between them and Elizabeth Nicholl was that everything they did, everything they believed in, came from a sincere heart, while everything that Elizabeth enacted was false. She was the dominant figure at the séances which they arranged, and they had subsidiary rôles. They were older women of the middle class and she was strong and youthful beside them. Without manly support, one a widow, the other a spinster, they lived comfortably in London, not friendless, and employing resident servants. Spiritualism was the cornerstone of their lives. They knew each other, but they were not close friends. Mrs Berry had considerably more money than the genteel spinster, but Elizabeth was not after their cash. Their warm homes provided plush theatres for her star performances and she enjoyed the wines and jellies and the company of convivial people who imagined that they had so much in common with her. She flourished and grew majestic at their tables, her chair a throne. Each of the two hostesses latched on to her in a possessive way. Miss Houghton, especially, was of an emotional nature, prone to crushes, and she always believed in Elizabeth. Mrs Berry, who was more austere, had moments of doubt. Later, her comparatively innocuous world of séances with Elizabeth became more curdled when wily young male professional mediums out for all they could get entered the mix. Miss Houghton kept her doors closed to them.

From our point of view, it is fortunate that both Mrs Berry and Miss Houghton published their chronicles of the séances in substantial books which have survived for posterity. They also sent near-contemporaneous accounts of the events to the spiritualist periodicals, spreading the word about Mrs Guppy's miracles. Mrs Berry's own consuming interest began in 1864, when she had just returned from taking the cure at Vichy. She did not know what a medium was, and had never heard of table-turning so she was cynical when a friend, Miss Roe, insisted on bearing her home to meet a poor clairvoyant, who was accompanied by her own magnetiser. The session went badly: Mrs Berry had no pity when the woman's face became distorted as if in great agony, and was convinced that she was an impostor. She could be tough and unyielding and would not reconsider when told that, after she had left, the clairvoyant had been so ill that she had been sent home scarcely conscious, heavily entranced, in a cab.

Even so, she was intrigued when Miss Roe, taking her hand, announced that, from her touch, she was surely a medium herself, 'and I should not wonder if you became queen of the tribe.' It is no surprise that their next assignation was in Mrs Marshall's small back room in Bloomsbury. The two Mrs Marshalls and young Emanuel looked hard at Mrs Berry, but soon the magic began, the raps came, gentle at first, and, in less than twenty minutes, the sceptic became a believer. From then on, 'Life to me without [spiritualism] would be a dark and dreary shadow. Spiritualism is the beacon that lights me on. From that time I made it a rule to attend a séance at Mrs Marshall's once a week. I cannot tell you how I looked forward to those days; and I ever look back upon them as some of the brightest I have passed.'

She took her friends with her, and no doubt the Marshalls were grateful for the interest of their new, and solid, benefactress. Tables rushed with great force from the far end of the room and sticks and umbrellas emerged from their corners. The sitters heard the banjo twang, the guitar ping, and the piano sound its notes – and all in daylight or gaslight. Soon, Mrs Berry discovered that she herself had special powers, to magnetise, develop, and heal. She learnt to hypnotise so powerfully that, it was said, she could make several people fall to the ground with a mere wave of her hand. Her cosseted, routine existence became alive with drama and purpose. She turned her hand to 'spirit drawings' and, through her example, Emanuel also took it up. Their products were totally dissimilar, although Mrs Berry believed that if all such drawings were collected together, a giant chain of meaning would be discerned. Trance, or automatic art, was considered to be spirit directed, on the same principle as automatic writing.

Mrs Berry thought that her pictures would, by any ordinary observer, 'be pronounced as chaotic, but a more minute survey of them reveals a wonderful design in construction and purpose whatever it may be. On several occasions, when I enquired the meaning of them my spirit-guides told me that they were illustrative of the origin of species.' (*My Experiences in Spiritualism*, p.167) Elizabeth had no interest in this variation of spiritualism, although, in the company that she kept, she could not have been ignorant of the bare bones of Darwinism. Psychic art was a hobby for those with leisure, and that she certainly lacked. If it were true that Nicholl had instructed her in various art forms, she might have had the capacity for drawing and the use of paints, but, obviously, her childhood education had not been the same as that enjoyed by the middle-class women with whom she now associated. Her mystery depended upon her apparent connection with the dead.

There was a non-professional medium of Glasgow, David Duguid (1832-1907), who brought spirit art into his séances, even though they were already rich with event and manifestation. It began in 1866, when he felt his arm shake, and a cold current ran down his spine. At first he produced rough sketches, and his spirit influence felt hampered by Duguid's having had no artistic training, so he took lessons at an art school, and began to produce minutely painted little cards when the lights were put out. It all ended in disaster, when he was 73 years old, but that is not the point.

Mrs Berry was introduced to 'Miss Nicholl' in 1866, and fruitful séances took place at both their homes. The sculptor's studio was a fine setting, and Nicholl himself was often in attendance. Overheated, no doubt, by the intensity of the happenings, swarms of butterflies and sprays of intoxicating perfumes, Mrs Berry, under doctor's orders, took to her bed, with a special attendant at her beck and call. Elizabeth paid her a home visit which lasted for several days and can only have further inflamed the patient. Something happened that had a tinge of Conan Doyle's speckled band. Mrs Berry screamed when she felt a faint presence fall on her, seeming to come from the canopy of the bed or the ceiling. She found her pillow and part of her coverings strewn with white camellias, while all along Miss Nicholl had been sitting like a statue with her hands crossed over her massive bosom.

Harm and violence could occur at a séance; Elizabeth had a wild streak which was normally under control. Alfred Russel Wallace himself was the victim at one of her sittings, when the spirits were playing a guitar which had been placed on the table for them. In the darkness, there was a palpable hit when a severe blow was inflicted on his temple, and blood flowed. 'It was my own fault entirely,' said Wallace, 'I broke the conditions – the orders were to join hands; and I was very curious to know what sort of hand was playing the guitar, and that was the cause of the blow.'

Miss Georgiana Houghton, who was holding séances with Elizabeth in parallel with Mrs Berry was a kind and sociable person, whose photograph shows a plain and homely countenance. Born exotically in the City of Palms, Grand Canary, in about 1825, in London she lived with her mother at 20 Delamere Crescent, Westbourne Square, Paddington. Her mother died in 1868, and was another spirit to summon back; she had had many bereavements. Miss Houghton was a survivor, and remained uplifted and optimistic, even when she was impoverished by the expenses of putting on an exhibition of her spirit paintings at a gallery in New Bond Street. Her heavy loss amounted to £303. It wiped out much of her capital, a legacy from Aunt Helen Harman Butler which had provided the income on which she had been living.

One of the many visitors to her exhibition was of the Darwin school of evolution but, unlike Mrs Berry, she had a strong resistance to the theories, not accepting his proofs of how the utter nature of animals might be changed into something else. After he had gone, she was 'bothered' but not in any way convinced, troubled by how the 'specious arguments' might be met. She appealed to her guides for counsel: 'Receive your illustration from your own loved work. Look at the rainbow! Where are the links in creation so close as the tints in its arching bow? Who may say where one shades off into another? Yet the blue remains blue; the red, red; and the yellow, yellow: the several creations are distinct, however closely they may be allied, or however harmoniously they may be blended.'

Miss Houghton felt that she became a medium in 1859. That was before Elizabeth's beginnings, and, of course, as usual, Mrs Mary Marshall, who did not care what good or bad consequences flowed from her ministerings, as long as she survived, was her first inspiration. Throughout all the strange experiences which followed, Miss Houghton's piety was unquestionable, and she became a strong Christian Spiritualist (v. post). She perceived in Miss Nicholl, the new medium, a vital element that was absent – she had not properly embraced the religious element of spiritualism. Now, Elizabeth had no inclination or aptitude for mystical reverie or trance utterances on the nature of the spirit world. She lacked the education for classical or theological allusion, poetic effusion or impressive abstraction: these accomplished performances were beyond her, and she knew it. Miss Houghton admonished Elizabeth that she had not yet (in the summer of 1867) realised the full sacredness of her mission, and she ought to open all her séances with prayer. Elizabeth was happy to do so, where the setting was appropriate.

The new religion of spiritualism, which she was obliged to master if she were to thrive at the hearths of the educated middle-classes whom she cultivated, was very different from orthodoxy, although it was possible to carry both systems. As ever, adjustment counteracted gloom and confusion. The spiritualist doctrines were startlingly different. There was no resurrection of the body. Christ was a Great Teacher, who descended to set an example. God was a more remote figure than had been imagined before. Angels there were.

Alfred Russel Wallace recited the spiritualist credo in approving terms in *Miracles and Modern Spiritualism* (p.108). The spirit survives after death in an ethereal body 'gifted with new powers, but mentally and morally the same individual as when clothed in flesh.' There is no translation to Heaven or Hell. The spirit is set on a course of apparently endless progression starting from the level of moral and intellectual development to which he has raised himself in his terrestrial existence. There is no punishment, nor reward. 'There are no evil spirits, but the spirits of bad men, and even the worst are surely if slowly progressing. Life in the higher spheres has beauties and pleasures of which we have no conception.' The spirits know no more of God than we do. Prayer may often be answered, though not directly by the Deity.

Wallace's change of heart was most remarkable: 'Up to the time when I first became acquainted with the facts of spiritualism, I was a confirmed philosophical sceptic ... I was so thorough and confirmed a materialist that I could not at that time find a place in my mind for the conception of spiritual existence, or for any other agencies in the universe than matter and force. Facts, however, are stubborn things.' (*ibid*, p.vi) Wallace came to believe that man had a soul – that is, the spirit – which had been placed into man by God in a separate evolutionary process.

As we have seen, Elizabeth White from Hull was a deciding link in Wallace's conversion to spiritualism. Whatever religious instruction she had received in her childhood, she was now swimming in a millstream of new ideas and adapting with all the strength of her native cunning. It is likely that she did not believe in religious spiritualism and quietly adhered to her own traditional beliefs. In spite of their difference in intellect, Wallace influenced her less than she influenced him.

3

Netting Mr Guppy

SAMUEL GUPPY'S NAME WAS BEGINNING to crop up at the séances. A favoured sitter, and member of the inner circle, he had been a convert to spiritualism since 1862, by his own account. That was four years before Elizabeth sprang up, fully armed with flowers and fruit in 1866. We know that she had made her home with William Grinsell Nicholl since at least 1861. There is no evidence that the sculptor had had any interest in spiritualism before he took to escorting his 'daughter' to the séances, but there is a very strong possibility that he provided the link to Mr Guppy.

In 1864, Samuel Guppy was resident in west London at 45 Great Marlborough Street, a good address. Sharing his billiard room was a sculptor. Is this a pointless coincidence, or was this Nicholl himself? He might indeed have required a secondary studio in town, given the weight of his commitments. To support this proposition, there is proof that he was listed at number 45 in 1869, five years later. (v. Boyle's Court Guide, 1869). Admittedly, that address might have attracted another noted sculptor in 1864. Earlier, in 1855, Raffaelle Monti (1818-81), the Italian, famous for his 'Veiled Vestal' was listed there, and also at 10 Princes Street, Hanover Square, when being examined at the Court of Bankruptcy. He might well have swum with Samuel Guppy's shoal of Anglo-Italian friends. By 1861, however, Monti had gone from Great Marlborough Street.

The source of the interesting possibility that it was Nicholl who introduced Guppy to Elizabeth lies in the Revd Charles Maurice Davies' *Mystic London*, published in 1875 (page 294):

One evening I accompanied the Davenports to Mr Guppy's residence in Great Marlborough Street.[8] After supper Ira, the eldest of the brothers, Mr Guppy, and myself, adjourned to a dark room, which Mr Guppy had had prepared for experimental purposes. To get to this room we had to pass through a room that served the combined purposes of a sculptor's studio and a billiard room. Emerging from this room we came into a yard, in one corner of which the dark cabinet in question was constructed. Taking our seats, we extinguished the light. Mr Guppy was at the time smoking a cigar. This was at once taken from his hand, and carried in the air, where it could be seen by the light given out by its combustion. Some whisky and water was standing on the table. This was handed to us to drink. When it came to my turn, I found there was but little left in the glass. This I pointed out. The glass was forth-with taken from my mouth, and replenished and brought back again.

Mr Guppy was jovial and hospitable, and, if Nicholl were the sculptor in residence at number 45, it is a reasonable guess that there was conversation, even billiards and Havanas, and that Elizabeth was a guest. No doubt Mr Guppy admired the fleshy young woman. In 1863, as we shall discover, the whole atmos-phere of the house changed, and spiritualist books appeared in Mr Guppy's library. If Nicholl, who could not marry Elizabeth, and Guppy who did, were acquainted, whether she was passed on, stolen away, or some natural progression took place, we shall never know, but there are no overt signs of discord between the parties.

Keen to establish a state of spiritualist virginity, Elizabeth denied all knowledge of the Davenport brothers, but if she had been welcomed at number 45 she should have known about the

[8] The raconteur is not the Rev Davies himself, but an unidentified speaker at the first Annual Conference of the British National Association of Spiritualists in Lawson's Rooms, Gower Street, in 1874.

cabinet in the yard and the important occasion of their (paid for) visit. Mr Guppy was obviously greatly impressed by the Davenports, who were skilled magicians and showmen. The *Illustrated London News* of June 30th, 1865, reported that, 'The Davenports have made an alliance with Mr Guppy, the author of the celebrated work, *Mary Jane* (*v. post*) ... Guppy has fitted up a château near Paris, and is going to convert the savants of Europe. Well, did not MM Mesmer and Cagliostro once try to do the same?' This is not intended as a benevolent comparison. Although there is much to be said for Dr Mesmer, Count Cagliostro (1743-95) was an outright charlatan, alchemist, necromancer, and inventor of an elixir of immortal youth.

Mrs Britten (*op.cit.*, p.74) was familiar with these events: 'In 1865 the work of experimental spiritualism was greatly aided by the introduction of the celebrated American mediums, the Davenport brothers, who were induced to visit Paris at the instance of Mr Samuel Guppy, a wealthy English gentleman, devoted to the study of spiritualism and its phenomena. The French Court was receptive to spiritualism, and the Emperor, as reported to the London *Spiritual Magazine* by Mr Benjamin Coleman upon information received from someone who was present at the occasion, was so impressed that he provided a fine dinner and paid a munificent fee to the Davenports.' Nothing more was heard about the château of séances, but perhaps the knowledge has been lost. If Mr Guppy did found a folly in the clouds, that could explain why he was eventually not so wealthy as people thought, but it is more likely that his infatuation with Elizabeth and all her activity took precedence.

Samuel Guppy made the whole story of his spiritualist background and matrimonial history more complicated by publishing, in 1863, an anonymous tome, ludicrously entitled *Mary Jane*. This is the strangest chimaera of a book that can be imagined. The first, longer section is composed of reflections and recollections, all with scientific bias, but then it blends unexpectedly into a shorter section, ostensibly autobiographical, concerning his induction into spiritualism, through the psychic activity of his wife, and his theories thereon.

The truth is, however, that in 1863 he had no wife. He was a widower. In 1855, his first wife, Georgina *née* Prothero, whom he had married in 1838, had died in Malta. He was to marry Elizabeth White in 1867. There was no second, interim wife. The most extensive, widespread searches have failed to reveal such a person, and all the record instruments agree that Samuel Guppy had only two wives. An invented wife might have been the reason for the anonymous publication, rather than bashfulness about coming out as a spiritualist.

Subsequent commentators have not understood that there is a difficulty, because they have not known that Georgina had been long dead before *Mary Jane* appeared. Mrs Britten (*op.cit.*, p.160) writing in 1884, took it that:

> Previous to the decease of his first wife, Mr Guppy's attention had been drawn towards a succession of extraordinary disturbances occurring in his own house, and which continued for many months, in the form of rappings, movements of furniture, direct writings ... After the death of his first wife, Mr Guppy being introduced to Miss Nicholl, found in that lady's mediumship, a very striking counterpart of his invisible friend Mary Jane's performances. The interest thus excited, not only ended in Mr Guppy's complete conversion to spiritualism, but also in the transformation of Miss Nicholl into the wife of the wealthy scientist, in which position, as a non-professional medium, Mrs Guppy was enabled to exert a widespread influence both in England and many of the Continental cities.

Nandor Fodor was completely confused, with an entry in his *Encyclopaedia of Psychic Science* under the heading, 'Guppy, Mrs Samuel I, medium for psychical phenomena, apports, automatic drawings and psychic lights. Accounts of her phenomena are given in *Mary Jane* ... ' The next heading is 'Guppy, Mrs Samuel II' and it covers representative séances of Elizabeth Guppy. For good measure, he then states that 'After Samuel Guppy's death his widow married for the third time ... '

Frank Podmore, of whom better might have been expected, was unaware of the problem, saying in his *Mediums of the Nineteenth Century* (*op cit.*, Vol. II, pp.65, 171) that, 'Another interesting private medium in the early years was the first wife of Mr Samuel Guppy, the author of *Mary Jane*. In this lady's presence raps were heard; a guitar was played under the table ... ' Calling Mr Guppy 'Not a professed metaphysician, but merely a garrulous and entertaining old gentleman,' Podmore remarks, drily, that 'he had the singular good fortune to marry in succession two remarkable physical mediums.'

Mary Jane reads convincingly enough as the exploits of a real wife-figure, set against a domestic background and has always been taken seriously as non-fiction even if the truth of the psychic happenings be doubted. One journalist thought it was fiction, but he had not actually seen it: 'A book will shortly be published, under the absurd title of *Mary Jane*. Any reader seeing such a book announced would naturally conclude that it was a domestic novel or some pretty tale, relating the trials and temptations of some servant girl, of course virtue being triumphant at last. But no; it is no such thing. It is to be a spiritualistic novel ... ' There may be some malice in the classification.

Perhaps the psychic content of the book is an invention, a composite, welded from a medley of Mr Guppy's experiences with mediums. He might have thought that the device of a wife with psychic powers would be more persuasive. It was all done for the glory of spiritualism, not for self-aggrandizement. If, however, he was involved in some kind of relationship with just one woman who was deceiving him about her powers, that could have been the reason for anonymity, and the motive for glory of the cause remains the same. If he were actually living in sin with a gold-digging harpy, a false medium, his family, and society, would have disapproved. Respectable spiritualists of the type of Miss Georgiana Houghton and Mrs Berry would not have had anything to do with the ménage.

An important clue to indicate that Miss Houghton approved

of Mary Jane and its publication lies in the inscription on the title page of the copy of the book in the Harvard College Library: 'The Author begs Miss Houghton's acceptance of a work which he wishes was more free from error. Sam Guppy. Jany 4th, 1863' (should be 1864).

There is a fanciful alternative explanation, but it is perilous, not susceptible of proof. If, as has been proposed, Nicholl was the sculptor sharing Guppy's billiard room in 1864, and Elizabeth and Mr Guppy had already met before the publication of Mary Jane in 1863, could Elizabeth herself have been the medium who was convincing him? The manifestations lack the full splendour of her apports in 1866-7 and later, but they are not incompatible with her talents and some of her sidelines. They were routine psychic activities at that time. If that were the case, then, when she was 'discovered' by Fanny Sims and Wallace in 1866, she was engaged in a monstrous pretence and a blatant display of acting.

Could there have been an element of wishful thinking that Elizabeth was already his wife and sharing the matrimonial bed so cosily described in Mary Jane? Did she perform in the séance zone in the yard, or had that been erected specifically for the use of the important Davenports? Was Samuel Guppy's bedroom also a stage?

A clinching detail might be that the inscription to Miss Houghton anxiously sought reassurance that he had got it right – i.e. that the psychic happenings were realistic and accurate in her expert opinion. If a real wife had been responsible for the events, he would have been happy to transcribe them as he perceived them.

To turn to the text of the book, in its original, intended form, it was a collection, scarcely a sequence, of personal essays on the issues of the day, with his thoughts and very decided opinions on life, manners, politics, philosophy, the history of the human races, slavery, and religions. Above all, it was expressly the fruit of a materialistic mind. Science was king, especially chemistry, which he had studied. It is diverse, entertaining, genial, infused with heavy wit, humane and likeable. Today it would be thought dry. It is not the product of a great mind. He is discursive, and already shows a fatal failure to keep to the point which is to worsen with age. It is difficult to guess if he would have been popular at dinners, or found too opinionated and boring. He tells us, without giving a reason, that he did not have an Oxbridge education, unlike his brother and brother-in-law. It is typical of his bluff humour that he laments that deficiency because 'a boy educated at Oxford or Cambridge would be certain to carry cricketing and rowing to any part of the world he might go.' People were only too happy to say that he was eccentric, but that was probably after the publication of *Mary Jane*. Wallace was not called that. A man of the world, a Freemason, a character, Samuel Guppy seethes with information, comparisons and anecdotes.

As his version of the format goes, the original book was ready for print at the end of 1862, but then he was introduced to spiritualism and formulated his own unique explanation, which, all written up as a lengthy coda to the main text, delayed publication until 1863. This sequence of events should not be relied upon, or only in part, since there is a fundamental dubiety about the reality of the 'wife'. It is odd that he so valued the psychic content that he entitled the entire volume after his theory. The whole was embellished by specially commissioned lithographs in pastel colours of spirit drawings of flowers which are not of the beauty and interest that Guppy ascribes to them. All of his worldly wisdom is eclipsed by the spiritualist foliage which smothers it.

Mary Jane is fairly rich in autobiographical material, but far from saturated with it. Of course, he would be interested in phrenology, popular in mid-century, and he went to De Ville's in the Strand to be 'phrenologized'. The results do seem to fit him rather well, and he thought so, too. His qualities were:

1 Obstinate – may be led, but won't be driven.
2 Passionate, but soon over.
3 Not sly.
4 Very restless.
5 Not cruel.

6 Fond of ladies.
7 Cheerful.
8 Not over-religious
9 Fond of music, but bad timeist.
10 Clever at picking up a language.
11 A good judge of a straight line.
12 Fond of travelling.
13 Can draw plans, but not landscapes.
14 Imaginative.
15 No miser.
16 Rather fond of children.
17 Conscientiousness rather large.
18 Self-esteem rather large.
19 Tolerable mathematician.
20 Remembers what he sees.
21 The power of tracing effects to causes.
22 Hope rather large.
23 Constructiveness rather large.

Samuel Guppy's expansive world is markedly different from Elizabeth's 'cabin'd, cribb'd, confin'd' existence, so far. Intending to pass the season at Wiesbaden and return to London for the winter (as he informed a friend, Thos. –, Esq., in a letter written from the International Exhibition, July 1st, 1862, included in *Mary Jane*, p.59), 'In the midst of riding and walking and enjoying myself, a monster caught me suddenly and imprisoned me for three weeks.

> No one likes to acknowledge the first attack of the gout. It is either a chill, or rheumatism, or a sprain: for although gout is a highly respectable complaint, when only talked over with a pleasant physician who makes things comfortable, still, if one reads carefully over a few medical works, it seems like an iron ship attacking a wooden one, and if you don't get rid of your opponent you will be sunk. One man I heard of, as soon as he felt premonitory symptoms, took to

walking inveterately till he walked it off. My friend [Dr Barter, of St Ann's Well, Cork], considers the human body as a sponge, of which the pores have got choked, and so by pouring water in at the mouth, and driving it out of the pores of the skin in his Turkish baths, he cures all complaints of obstruction. I cured myself by drinking nothing but lemonade, in such quantities, and so strong as to surprise a medical man who once dined with me. However, enough of the gout, from which I hope never again to have a visit.

The leaves were falling, and chilly blasts sweeping the avenue of Wisbaden, before my persecutor allowed me to leave my room, and instead of returning to England, I got away south as fast as I could: stopped at Marseilles, where just then the war with Austria was in agitation, saw the army embark and then the Emperor; and then having become acquainted during my stay in Algeria with several French officers, I determined to follow the army leisurely, and go to Venice ...

We may note that there is no mention or presence of a wife in these lonely wanderings. He has been 'all over the world, except the poles, and the centres of Africa and Australia.' All his later life, he harked back to his Bohemian rhapsody: in the mountains of that country, he 'used to spend a month in midwinter, after the earth had put on its ermine of snow. When I arrived, I knew what I had to do. From the old grandfather and mother, to the fine youths and blooming girls of the family down to the baby in arms, if there was one, everyone had to be kissed. As for the girls, they said to themselves, "He is come to take us out sledging by day, and to waltz with us at night ... "

'Then began our life; in vain the uncle said, "You had better make your wills before you get into a sledge with him," they cared nothing about being rolled over on the snow, only got up, shook themselves, laughed, and jumped into the sledge again; and then at night, at the balls, there is a custom in Bohemia, you are expected to waltz at least once, with every young lady you know, and if you forget her, some kind friend will come up and whisper, "What is the matter, you have not danced this evening with Röchin." As to being tired, there is no such thing; the rule is, when you have waltzed yourself into such a fever that a drink of cold water would kill you, you must drink pure water and go on. I ought to pay a tribute of recollection to you, Agnes, then nineteen, tall, with jet black hair, elastic as a piece of whalebone; when you waltzed, all stopped to admire you.'

Could this Dark Lady, incidentally, wrongly interpreted or remembered, be at the root of the 'Agnes Nicholl' myth?

Samuel Guppy held decided views about the ideal constitution of a medium, asking a series of questions, while being careful, because 'mediums are very easily put out of temper': 'Have you a good taste in dress? And in jewellery? Are you proficient in making all sorts of ladies' knick-nacks? Can you ride five-and-twenty miles over hill and dale, and find your way back alone? Have you good eyes? Do you excel in archery? Are you a good pistol-shot? Are you excessively nervous; but with a resolution which carries you through in spite of it? Are you jealous, and can't help it?' This sporty paragon from a privileged background is nothing like Elizabeth. It could bear a resemblance to his departed wife, poor Georgina, but, equally, could be a frothy fabrication. No genteel woman of Georgina's class would have employed deliberate trickery and acquired apparata in order to enthrall her hapless husband.

Mary Jane was one book that Elizabeth had to know and admire if she were to marry Samuel Guppy, visit the Continent, and dine with nobility. She had to study his initiation into spiritualism, and, of course, Mrs Mary Marshall was the stewardess at the door, although his first impressions were far from positive. In 1862, Mr Guppy relates, wrapped in his cloak of anonymity, his old friend, W, whom he had known intimately for many years, with a long interval, while he himself was abroad, vehemently insisted on taking him to a séance. W, too, had always been a complete materialist, but now he was deeply dyed in spiritualism, and Guppy told him bluntly that the best thing he could do was to go to some highly respectable lunatic asylum and state his belief – which would entitle him to immediate admission.

Nevertheless, when W came up to London to see the second great International Exhibition, held in South Kensington, they arranged to visit W's 'very good honest mediums', found by Guppy to be 'two uneducated women in Bloomsbury', who were only too obviously Mrs Marshall and her niece. The elder, on enquiry, said that her powers were a gift from childhood. The séance was a failure. Uncle William was invoked, but the alphabet spelled out 'unkel'. He told Mr Guppy to fear God and lead a holy life, but Guppy took exception to the platitude. Nor was he mollified when one of his brothers announced himself, also spelling his own name wrongly, in spite of his Oxford education, because he was still a denizen of this world. A lady present received the message: 'You shall have power to believe yourself and convince your husband.' Finally Guppy announced that he would not spend another half-crown on such nonsense.

'Some days after,' the narrative continues, 'W and I, and B were at the Exhibition, and the "ruling spirit", like a cork, came uppermost, and he asked if I had any objection to have the media at my house. "None in the world," said I; "but I have a great objection to pay them half-a-guinea for coming, besides their cab hire".'

W paid, and the séance began at seven o'clock. Again, it was an abject failure, and Guppy thought it worth mentioning that 'when the media arrived, and were asked as usual to walk upstairs, they would not allow any one to follow behind them: and as it is rather indecorous for the lady of a house to walk up and let her guests follow her, it gave rise to some polite pressing, which was of no avail; they would not put any one in a position to see their shoes; so that whether the rapping machinery was there, is uncertain; but B once tapped the leg of the table so exactly with his boot, that the elder medium said it was a spirit.'

W became incensed, in discussion afterwards, and the treadmill for fraud came up as a remedy, but, by some five months later, in March, 1863, Guppy relates, he himself has undergone a change of heart, read all the important spiritualist books – '2894' pages' – and it has all come about through the agency of his wife. She is newly introduced through the novelette-ish device of saying that the recipient of the message from the spirits, the unnamed 'lady present', was in fact his wife – 'Now, this lady was my wife.' A bombshell, indeed!

What had happened was that Mr W had visited, just after the exhibition had closed, and, still not cured, had suggested some private table-turning. Mr Guppy abstained, but the round table was fully occupied. 'Some young ladies were home from school, and visitors present also.' In this way, and elsewhere, Mr Guppy builds up a domestic background. He certainly had no daughters or granddaughters of his own at school. Anyway, the next day, when he returned from the city, his wife told him that the table turned for her. She had been experimenting, alone, at a small, japanned table. Gradually, Guppy was won over, invented tests, and the strange events multiplied.

Then, 'One day, a lady called who had given much attention to spiritualism; and, on our relating our experiments to her, she said, "Mrs – is an undeveloped medium".' Is this not exactly the scenario, the same words, that attended Mrs Guppy's development in 1866? The expert showed them how to use an alphabet, and lo, the table had a voice! This was the turning point. 'I found myself now in presence of intellect; in fact, of an intellectual being; for, as I was satisfied that the phenomenon depended on the emission of certain elements, and that phenomenon ceases the instant the hands were withdrawn from the table, it was clear that the intellect was a quality or property of those elements.'

The matter had, he felt, to be investigated from a chemical point of view, and the new 'Being' had to be christened. He had no proof that it was the soul of a departed person, but, even so, 'An intelligent being, to be talked to, must have a name, and the house was full of children from school, and country servants.' 'Mary Jane' struck him as an approachable, convenable name. 'You may be sure that, on finding a third party so unexpectedly domiciled with us, we asked it every possible question, and we received replies, the sense and accuracy of which pleased and startled us, as clearly proving a distinct and partially superhuman intelligence.'

There will be no assertion in these pages that Mr Guppy was insane. His idea was extreme, to be sure, but he can be seen to be struggling to apply his science as other men of superior intelligence were engaged in the same battle. The idea of 'Odyllic vapours' emanating from human individuals is not original; he was carried away by the currently popular theories of Baron Reichenbach, but he was very easily carried away, being a persevering, thinking person, yet somehow lacking a vital discretion. His curiosity was boundless, but he was led astray by his desire for connection.

Guppy now begins to introduce material which – he does not realise – emphasises his gullibility, as in: 'If my wife lay on the sofa, the responsive rap would come apparently from behind the sofa; and even in bed, the conversation was carried on by Mary Jane, either by raps over our heads, or apparently on a chest of drawers close by the bed. One night, after we were in bed, I was talking with Mary Jane, and I perceived that my wife was getting sleepy, and it entered my mind to test whether the emanations continued during sleep, so I continued the conversation. By degrees, the responses became slower and fainter, and by the time I was convinced that my wife was fast asleep, they ceased altogether.' Does he not seem to be evoking a genuine bedroom scene?

'Matters were in this state,' he goes on, 'when we changed our residence, and some very talented, highly talented lady friends having taken a great interest in these phenomena, and being also mediums, though not of the power of my wife, we agreed to hold regular séances, excluding all other visitors.' The newly-informed circle, he says, obtained extraordinary results, which are, in fact, part of the common repertoire of the day: slate-writing (the wife covering her hand with her black silk apron as Mary Jane guided her); a guitar held under the table by the wife playing a good tune. 'Now,' Mr Guppy says innocently, 'I happened to sit so at the round table that by bending my body slightly to the left, I could see the guitar; whereas, while sitting upright, I could not.

Imagine now the fastest waltz being played on the violin, [by a visiting music-teacher] and accompanied by the guitar; when I bent my body quietly round till I saw the strings, the guitar ceased playing instantly. I recovered my upright position; the guitar resumed the accompaniment. I repeated this several times.'

There was an 'uncomfortable family day. One servant going away, who, if she was sent out, stayed twice as long as needful, and it was not worthwhile to find fault with her. A new servant come, with whom it would have been unreasonable to find fault; the dinner behind time; and a valued medical friend, who only stayed to dine, as he was told it would be ready at five, and he had patients very ill waiting for him; the cook out of temper – I have my reasons for mentioning these things – W was come for two days. After dinner, a lady friend looked in; we sat to the table; Mary Jane gave ill-defined answers; the lady went home leaving my wife and W.

'W seemed discontented; I was put out at some little occurrences.' That night, the table was violent, tilting and stamping and frightening the wife. W was in his element and wanted the table to go right up to the ceiling. They took their hands away and all of a sudden the table rushed up to the wife, and a chair, which was standing alone, three feet from her, skimmed at her, 'just as a leaf moves on a turnpike road by the wind.'

'Now for a puzzle,' Mr Guppy says, 'I have gone up to go to bed with my wife; at the bedroom door we have separated; I went into my dressing-room behind the bedroom, but with a door communicating with the bedroom – a door of the very slightest deal, in front of which, in the bedroom, is a chest of drawers; and, after I had closed the door of my dressing-room, I have heard excessively loud raps, such as I suppose could be heard all over the house. Going immediately into the bedroom, fearing my wife was frightened, I found her beginning to undress. "Did you rap?" "No." "There were very loud raps indeed on the door." "I have heard nothing." The same thing occurred to my wife, who asked me if I rapped. At last I said, "If ever you want me before I return from my dressing-room, rap and speak, that I may know".'

With all respect to Mr Guppy, the real puzzle is the identity of this woman, in this remembered or invented scene. He sees the geography of the room clearly, but the syntax is uneasy.

Mr Guppy was fascinated by phosphorus, and was convinced that an excess of the element in the body is the key to insanity. Mediums made use of the element in order to produce luminosity, although there was a telltale smell. The wife-figure exhibited to Guppy a phosphoric light playing about her fingertips, like moving glow-worms in the darkness, with a strong odour of phosphorus. This event was the climax of the psychic disturbances in the Guppy household. 'Mrs S—', as he calls her, since that period, 'has had a very severe illness and inflammation of the lungs, from imprudently staying in a damp garden, and was consequently under very strict medical treatment; and during that time the phosphorescent appearances on her fingers ceased entirely; and once, in sitting down to the table, (which the doctor prohibited) it would scarcely move.'

Perhaps the severe illness was a memory of Georgina's decline and death, or a neat conclusion of the detailed psychic episode. In case anyone should wonder if she were involved in spiritualism before that death in 1855, it is not inconceivable that she had encountered it in the 1850s. After the American 'invasion' when Mrs Hayden (who took payment) came to England in 1852, table-turning was all the rage. Podmore (op.cit., Vol.2 pp.7-8) says that 'An epidemic of table-turning had broken out on the Continent in the autumn of 1852, and spread, though tardily, to this country in the early months of 1853 ... table-turning was within the reach of all, and seems to have been practised as assiduously by all classes of society in Bath, Manchester, or Edinburgh, as in London itself.' DD Home did not arrive until the spring of 1855. Samuel and Georgina could even have visited America where spiritualism was well established. Mrs Marshall did not set up until 1858. Only notionally, then, Georgina could have indulged in amateur table-turning, but Mr Guppy would have had to cobble on to these memories his later, racier experiences at the tables of professional mediums, thus creating a second hybrid, like his book itself.

Samuel Guppy's ideas did not catch on, but his sincerity was recognised and he was not mocked in spiritualist circles. His authorship of *Mary Jane* was an open secret from early on. He could not be blamed for caution: the stigma against conversion to spiritualism was severe. Newton Crosland, in his autobiography, *Rambles Round My Life*, (1898) influenced by his wife, 'devoted more than twelve months to the study of spiritualism, and finally decided to give a lecture on the subject at the Deptford Mechanics' Institution on the 27th of February, 1856. That public display sealed my fate. I was seriously prejudiced by this publicity. I felt that a great truth wanted an advocate, and I brought out a little book on the subject entitled *Light in the Valley*, illustrated with copies of spiritual drawings by Miss Anna Mary Howitt and others, which was received with derision by the press, and finally it was sacrificed and sold off at a ruinous loss.'

When Crosland appealed to the spirits to solve a legal matter in dispute, his position in society declined disastrously: 'Clouds, social and commercial now gathered about us. Old friends pitied and deserted us. Some people would not ride in the same railway carriage with me. Some would not pass close to our house; they crossed over to the other side. Others would not engage servants that left our employment. My partner and clerks left me in a body. My foreign agencies were withdrawn, and at one fell swoop I lost £600 per annum. Of course this sort of thing had to be lived down, and lived down it was. I was not going to allow myself to be beaten by a mob of ignorant foes, however distinguished.'

Mary Jane appeared in the mainstream press, at the author's expense, through the auspices of William Howitt (1792-1879) a cultured, interesting man of letters, a leading spiritualist, who had travelled in Australia, done a spot of panning for gold, and had already published a spiritualistic novel of his own, namely, *Tallangetta, the Squatter's Home* (1857). His strong beliefs obviously did not damage him, because in 1865 he received a pension of £140 on the civil list. It was reported, (*Louth and North Lincolnshire Advertiser*, August 1st, 1863) under the heading, MARY JANE COMING!, that, Mr William Howitt, in a long letter to a London newspaper defending himself from some attacks in the *Quarterly Review* respecting his views on spiritualism, concludes his letter by the following:

> And now, sir, I come to a most extraordinary fact. A gentleman of high scientific and chemical knowledge living at this moment in London, a professed and out-and-out materialist; a man who does not believe in any soul or spirit; that he has got any soul or spirit himself; who believes only in matter and its properties, has sat down and practically searched into the alleged phenomena, and has just printed, though not yet published, a book under the odd title of *Mary Jane*, in which he announces that every one of the so-called spiritual phenomena is real: that he and his wife have obtained them all, and more than all ... I shall go no further into detail [having provided an amplitude of detail of the psychic happenings], because the book is already printed and must soon see the light. I have seen it ...

William Howitt was also devoted to chemistry, and *Mary Jane* would have been immediately appealing to him for that reason, although he was of higher intellectual fibre than Samuel Guppy, writing eloquently about his brand of spiritualism, which 'Has taught us not to fear death, which is but a momentary passage to life; that God is disciplining the human race for an eventual and universal restoration, that He is beginning to teach laws of matter hitherto unnoticed by the acutest men of gases and crucibles; and that above all, spiritualism teaches us the authenticity of the Scriptures now so violently attacked ... Finally, it teaches us to live in all purity of thought and deed, knowing that not only the ever-open eye of God is constantly upon us, but those of an innumerable company of angels and devils, to whom we are as well and as openly known as our own consciences.' [9]

Mr Guppy's reaction to a long feature on *Mary Jane* in the *Spiritual Magazine* must have been ambivalent. The attention was

[9] *Spiritual Magazine*, of which Howitt was chief contributor, 1865, p.162)

flattering, the quotations from the narrative and the theoretical content were most extensive, but the ultimate critical verdict was not enthusiastic. In the August issue of 1863, the polite comment was that, 'His ideas are both novel and bold, and they are put forward in the general spirit of a philosopher and man of science ... We have had the pleasure of making the personal acquaintance of the author, and we find that the phenomena are not only continuing, but that they are increasing in intensity.' It would have been quite natural for any 'wife-figure' to be mentioned as a part of any new and continuing manifestations, but she is absent from any consideration.

The second part of the notice in the following September issue of the magazine is more stringent in tone: 'It was then that "Mary Jane" was born and shortly afterwards she was christened, and invested with all and more than all the attributes of the rest of her Majesty's subjects, excepting visibility, and a certificate from the superintending registrar of the district. The author is not at all taken aback, but shews himself quite equal to the situation; though some readers perhaps may think him rather hasty in converting particular facts into general propositions, and that his logic is a little slipshod.'

Continuing the discussion, the 'very bold hypotheses' of the emanating vapours 'if it does not merely amuse, is likely to startle men of science even more than the spiritual theory itself ... The fact is that our author confounds conditions with causes. Certain conditions are found necessary to certain effects, *therefore*, he reasons, they are the efficient cause of them. This is just such a mistake as it would be to attribute a telegram to the wires instead of to the operator at the end of them ... The subject has its physical side, and also its spiritual side; and neither should be ignored. The author of *Mary Jane* approaches the inquiry from its physical side, and we are glad to hail him as a fellow-labourer in this field.'

Finally, the *coup-de-grâce*: 'We have only one other observation. To build up an hypothesis on a small body of experiences, however extraordinary they may be, is simply to invert the pyramid, to rest it on the apex instead of the base. A much wider range of observation and investigation is needed to justify our author in building a philosophical theory of the spiritual phenomena.'

Mary Jane had not proved a great success, but Samuel Guppy was not the man to be discouraged, and spent the rest of his life in the spiritualist sphere, bolstered by his real, second wife, Elizabeth. The Odyllic vapours played no part in her séances and it does appear that he gradually abandoned his hypothesis. All in all, although he had lived an exciting life, and pondered long and hard about what he had seen and learnt, he had not achieved so much as other members of the illustrious Guppy family. These men and women were ambitious, pioneering, innovative and creative, of colonial type. Samuel's background was in commerce and he had a good, practical knowledge of engineering.

Because of the Guppys' impact on society, satisfactory information is still available on their careers, and, additionally, there is a rich seam of material in a most unexpected source – the autobiographical work, *Child of the Tropics*, by Yseult Bridges (1888-1971) the author of admired studies of classic Victorian crimes. Samuel Guppy was her great-uncle, and she was born Yseult Guppy. Her exotic and rather beautiful book, published in 1980, has significant data on close relatives and also bears a good family tree, which can be used in conjunction with later researches.

By what seems now a remarkable link over time, she actually met Elizabeth when she was a child, visiting England and meeting Guppy relatives. Her comment is careful, and loyal: 'I found Elizabeth, as her family knew her, a most warm and kindly person.' She is familiar with *Mary Jane*, but she, too, is confused by the sequence of events, thinking that Samuel Guppy's first wife, Georgina Prothero, was 'strongly psychic'. Then, 'A rich man, he retired at the age of forty-five', and turned to investigating spiritualism, expressing the matters in *Mary Jane*. Afterwards, his doubts were extinguished when he met 'the remarkable medium, Agnes Nichol [sic], who eventually became his second wife.' It is disappointing that Yseult Bridges clearly did not know that Georgina had died too early to be the 'wife' in *Mary Jane*, but it is confirmatory that she knew of only two wives. She would surely have known if Great Uncle Samuel were thrice married. If she had amplified her statement that Georgina was strongly psychic, that would have been more than useful, but it looks as if she is merely relying on *Mary Jane* and making the usual mistake.

According to Mrs Bridges, the Guppy line can be traced back to the 13th century, to Nicholas de Gupehegh of Tetworth, Dorset. In the 17th to 18th centuries, the Guppy family were at Farway House, Farway-in-Chardstock, western Dorset, 'near the lost village of Guppy, still marked on the map but now uninhabited'. Then, on the discovery of calamine, important in the manufacture of copper, on some family property, Samuel Guppy (1), that is, 'our' Mr Guppy's father, moved to Athos Court, Bristol, and set up as copper merchant, iron-founder and West India merchant. He lived from 1755 to 1830. In 1795, at St Stephen's, Bristol, he married a comely woman of distinction, Sarah Maria Beach (1770 or 1772-1852) who came from Wincanton. She was, most unusually, a clever inventor in a man's world. Her 19th-century patents included a copper-sheathing nail to limit the growth of barnacles on ships' timbers, and a bed with built-in exercise apparatus. In 1811, she proposed improvements for a suspension bridge which predated the works of both Thomas Telford and Brunel.

Samuel (1) and Sarah Guppy spawned half-a-dozen children. 'Our' Mr Guppy (Samuel 2), the eldest child, was born in Bristol on November 25th, 1795. He and his next brother, Thomas, owned the Quakers' Friars Sugar Refinery and vinegar manufacturers, in Merchant Street from 1826 to 1840 and Samuel was wont to describe himself as a sugar manufacturer, or sometimes as a merchant. He knew a great deal about steam engines and his writing employs frequent metaphors drawn from steam and rail. He spent much time in India, as well as Italy.

Thomas Richard Guppy (1797-1882) was a highly successful marine engineer. Isambard Brunel was his more flamboyant partner, and, in 1830, they founded the Great Western Railway Company, followed, in 1835, by the Great Western Steamship Company, building the SS *Great Western* and the SS *Great Britain* – transatlantic steamships. Like his mother, Thomas was an inventor and innovator. He suffered from tuberculosis, and eventually the symptoms became so grave that he left England for Italy, where he lived and died, on June 28th, 1882, at the Villa Guppy, outside Naples. The climate obviously suited him, because, with renewed energy, he founded there a large ship-building and engineering firm. Messrs Guppy and Patterson also employed several hundred men in an extensive iron foundry. *The Times*, in his obituary, said that he was probably the oldest member of the English colony in Naples, and the *Roma* extolled him: 'We Neopolitans regarded him as a fellow-citizen, for he had spent nearly half his life among us, improving our metallurgical industry, which he may be said to have introduced here.'

The *Bristol Mercury* (July 8th, 1882) proudly marked his death on June 28th, and remembered his 'intelligent face, his readiness of purpose and his active and energetic demeanour.' They took pride in the fact that he had invented a new type of lifeboat, duly patented, and that just before his death he had been selected by the Italian Government to design and construct a torpedo boat. He had far outstripped his brother, Samuel, from their days at the sugar factory. His private life, however, was not so happy: he did marry – Henrietta Collins Jennings of Congresbury, but her life span was short, only from 1810 to 1845. He lived for many years with his mother at Richmond Hill, Clifton, Bristol, according to a plaque put up at the house.

Robert Guppy (1808-94) was the third son of Samuel and Sarah. A graduate of Pembroke College, Oxford, he was called to the Bar (Middle Temple), practised in England, but became enchanted by Trinidad and moved there in 1839, settling in San Fernando, where he continued as a lawyer. In 1834, he had married Amelia Parkinson (1808-86) of Kinnersley Castle, Herefordshire, who was a considerable artist and one of the select band of Victorian women explorers.

Amelia was undoubtedly a true eccentric, but not, of course, a blood relative of Samuel Guppy (2). It was thought that she felt stifled and frustrated by her life in Trinidad, far from cultured circles, and her unsettled state of mind when she reached the age of 63 contributed to her decision to explore the upper reaches of the cascading Orinoco River in South America, a desperately dangerous expedition, alone, apparently, without masculine support. In Trinidad they began to call her 'mad Mrs Guppy'. For a whole year she was incommunicado. Her son, Francis, set off to find her, but their canoes, paddling in opposite directions, passed each other in the night. She reached home safely, if haunted-looking, but Francis died of a jungle fever. Yseult Bridges tells this story with dramatic effect.

Robert and Amelia's eldest son, Lechmere (1836-1916) was Yseult Bridges' father, and 'our' Mr Guppy's cousin. He was a respected palaeontologist and naturalist, a brilliant, gentle, amiable scholar. He it was who discovered the little, black Guppy fish – named in his honour *Girardinus Guppy* by Dr Albert Günther at the British Museum – which swims and darts in a myriad of aquariums. He, too, had fallen under the spell of Trinidad, and settled on the island when he married a well-born, mannered, French girl, Alice Rostant (1853-1917). It was a love-match, and their large family spread the Guppy name across North America and other parts of the world.

The three brothers, Samuel, Thomas and Robert Guppy, had three sisters. The eldest, Sarah Maria Ann, born in 1801, married Joseph Rawlings, a barrister. Their first daughter, also named Sarah Maria (1824-1924), married Frederick Gibbon. Yseult Bridges, as a child, visited 'Aunt' Maria Gibbon at her home in West Kensington: 'She was small with aquiline features, exquisite manners and a lively sense of humour. She did intricate and delicate needlework, and presented me with a set of small dolls dressed in the fashion of a mid-nineteenth century household.'

The other two Guppy sisters, Mary Elizabeth, born in 1806, and Grace, born in 1809, remained spinsters, and died young. Robert was their prop and stay and saw to their needs. Their wills have survived. They were resident abroad and wanted to settle their affairs at an early age; perhaps they were valetudinarian. Certain family tensions are apparent, and Samuel was clearly not their favourite brother. He was often abroad, but so were Thomas and Robert.

Deep in the anonymous text of *Mary Jane* (p.202) there are

some blunt references to Samuel's sisters: 'I may mention that in our family there are two spinster ladies (not old) who have caused great dissentions [*sic*] by introducing their opinions and advice upon the younger married ladies and youths of the family – hinting that the brothers, husbands, fathers and uncles were not in the true road to salvation, and so creating much discomfort and heart-burning. If these ladies had fulfilled their own true mission on earth, and tutored their own babies just as they pleased, much discomfort would have been avoided. There ought to be some half-way house to heaven, and when ladies get too good they ought to be sent there.'

Mary Elizabeth's will was executed on May 14th, 1839, and she died in Florence in 1841, aged about 40. She left hundreds of pounds to her nieces and to her beloved friend, Sarah Elizabeth Maude. Her jewellery was to be divided between her sisters-in-law, and one of her paintings was to be given to her mother, Sarah Coote, as a proof that she had not forgotten her filial regard for her. The remainder of her paintings were to be divided between her brothers, Thomas and Samuel, and also whatever sum of money, not exceeding one thousand pounds, there might be of hers at interest on the Sugar House (i.e. the Friars' Sugar Refinery). The remainder of her property, real and personal, she devised, together with such of her books and foreign curiosities as he should choose, to her dear brother, Robert Guppy, whom she appointed executor, in conjunction with her brother, Thomas.

The captious reference to her mother, the inventive Sarah Maria (*née* Beach) is perfectly explicable. Samuel Guppy (1) died in 1830 at the age of about 75, when she was about 60 years old, and she then married a much younger man, Charles Eyre Coote (1799-1853). Yseult Bridges supplies the information that Coote turned out to be a compulsive gambler, 'which eventually reduced them both to semi-dependence.' This was Samuel Guppy's mother, and he, and all the family, had to stand by as the disaster ran its course. Sarah Maria died in 1852, and Charles Eyre Coote followed her the very next year.

Miss Grace Guppy, the youngest of all the siblings, born in

1809, similarly left a will, executed in Paris on April 15th, 1858, which reflected the family dynamics. Two-thirds of her property went to her dear sister, Mary Elizabeth, and the remaining third part to her dear brother, Robert: both were named as executors. She declared that her sole reason for not leaving any bequests to her older brothers (Samuel and Thomas) whom she tenderly loved, was that she considered that they were not in need of it. Grace died in Paris when about 47 years old. Both of the sisters so traduced in *Mary Jane*, therefore, were dead, although represented as alive. That is, unless some, at least, of the first section of *Mary Jane* had actually been written previously ...

'Our' Mr Samuel Guppy took his first wife from the same mercantile and engineering class as his own. His brother, Robert, was the connection, acting in his legal capacity for Philip Prothero, of Bristol, whose family had owned estates in Trinidad soon after the island was captured by the British in 1797. Philip's daughter, Georgina, was Elizabeth White's predecessor. The wedding took place at St Andrew's, Clifton, on October 10th, 1838. It would seem to have been a very suitable marriage. However, some apparently deeply felt and acutely observed passages in the chapter of *Mary Jane* that is entitled 'Man and Woman' (p.144) may hint that the union was fiery. Acting as it were in an advisory capacity to a male friend, Mr Guppy calls up an imaginary wife:

> Truly she is a Garden of Eden.
> But in that garden may be the seeds of a plant worse than the Upas tree; quicker of growth than the bean of Jack the Giant-killer, nipping all her virtues worse than the potato disease, or the vine öidium.
> That plant is Jealousy.
> When that springs up, the virtues and graces fly like affrighted ghosts before an avenging fate.
> A casual innocent remark is enough.
> The knife and fork are laid down at dinner – nor bit nor drop again pass those lips. That small black cloud betokens a tempest. I have seen a tornado level

large trees, and strip the leaves off the yielding willow; I have seen the sails blown into pieces the size of towels, each detaching piece going off with the report of a gun.

You have attempted to explain; explain indeed – try to put fire out with oil – No! not that – try to put fire out with gunpowder, and you will see something like trying to explain.

Now begins a scene to which Shakespeare is tame.

The face assumes a Medusa look; around the eyes varying shades of yellow, with edges of greenish hue appear, and seem to move under the skin. I have seen a billiard table ruined, doors burst open, valuable papers torn, the servants pale and trembling, and the furniture of the room resembling the state of the earth the day before the Creation.

I thought the pier-glass and buhl clock would follow, but there was a pause.

You ask, Maria [enlarging his audience] if I have really seen all this; Oh yes! and this picture is as mild as England's sun compared with Africa's burning zone: for woman's feelings are convertible: she may be all love, so intense that she cannot bear the beloved to be out of her sight; then all jealousy, and woe betide the object of it!

Carried away by these feelings, like steam when it bursts a boiler, she becomes reckless, and her own life or that of any one else counts for nothing. Take the easiest arm-chair and a footstool, and light a cigar, and be quiet as in the finest scene in an opera, and don't think for a moment of using force, unless you see that something serious is going to happen.

At last there is a pause – be quiet – the voice falters, be quiet as death – the storm is breaking – a few minutes more you will hear sobs, then tears and sobs – then protestations of such love that life without you would not be for an instant endurable – and then –

you may go to bed. A woman is never so intensely affectionate as when she has been doing some mischief.

Such bravura words, evoking a life lived intensely, deny the image of 'poor old Mr Guppy' as he was viewed when Elizabeth, by association, introduced him briefly into the public eye.

The birth of children to Georgina and Samuel brought sadness into the marriage. Four obscure pregnancies are traceable, the first three sons fading from records. Laura May was born in Tuscany, at Leghorn, and baptized on June 4th, 1840. Albert Edward was born at Clifton, Gloucestershire, on January 27th, 1842, and was still alive in 1851, staying with a Prothero uncle and family in Clifton. Maria, baptized on January 22nd, 1843, was buried on January 26th, of that year, at Camberwell, south London.

The fourth child, who did survive, and of whom much must have been expected, was Samuel Henry Guppy. There is a considerable amount of information about him, although the family would, clearly, have preferred it to be hushed up. Samuel (3) became insane. Born late in 1843, at first he did well, becoming a civil engineer, but he was a lonely figure, deprived of his mother at the age of twelve, when she died abroad, and he never married. There is a bleak view of him in 1871, at the age of 27, boarding with a master plasterer, William Gorman, and his family, at 28 Bower Lane, Maidstone, Kent. On May 4th, 1866, *The Times* recorded Mr SH Guppy as a passenger on the sailing Indiaman *Hotspur*, arriving at Portsmouth from Calcutta.

In 1880, he was incarcerated, put away, and lost his place in the world. He had become dangerous, suddenly perhaps, but not necessarily so. For no good reason, in Spital Road, Windsor, he sprang at a harmless pedestrian, who had only recently recovered from a long and serious illness, and kicked him and struck him violently on the chest. His victim was Captain Bulkeley, a Berkshire magistrate and a director of the Great Western Railway. An assault on a Justice of the Peace was a serious and notable matter. Mr Norris, surgeon to the Royal Windsor

Infirmary examined Samuel after he had been apprehended and found him to be not of sound mind. Chief Superintendent Hayes, of the Windsor Borough Police, later told the magistrates that his enquiries had revealed that both parents were dead and that his relatives held a good position in society.

On October 28th he was produced in court to be formally certified as insane and was removed forthwith to the county lunatic asylum, namely, Littlemore, Oxfordshire, which had been opened in 1846. There he languished, a person of no importance, with his 'occupation unknown' until he died on August 28th, 1883, aged 41. The cause of death was certified by FN Pilkington, Resident Medical Officer, as phthisis (tuberculosis) and heart disease. It is surprising, considering the social and financial standing of the Guppy and Prothero families, that he had not been transferred to a carefully chosen private asylum, where he would certainly have been more comfortable.

Georgina Guppy died aged only 44, in July, 1855. The *Malta Family History* recorded her death: 'the wife of Samuel Guppy of Ballykhal, Calcutta, buried July 28th, 1855.' The *Bristol Mercury* of August 4th, 1855, also confirms this untimely death, noting that her father, Philip Prothero, was deceased.

Bereaved, Mr Guppy was unsettled. In 1858 (April) he was at Balmoral House, Gipsy Hill, Norwood, south-east London, appearing on a list of subscribers, headed by the queen, endorsing the work of an American 'horse-tamer', named JS Rarey. Even vicious horses were improved, without whip or spur, violence or drugs.

This, then was the background, the proud and distinctive family, into which Samuel Guppy proposed to introduce his different and graceless intended, but, *amor vincit omnia* and he had been without a wife for more than a decade. Anyway, spiritualism was the alloy which united man and wife.

4

The Medium Abroad

THE MARRIAGE OF SAMUEL GUPPY, widower, and Elizabeth White, spinster, took place quietly on December 10th, 1867. The chosen church was St Luke's, Chelsea, where Charles Dickens had married Catherine Hogarth in 1836. The entries show Mr Guppy as 'gentleman', residing at 278 Kings Road, Chelsea. Elizabeth recorded her real father, Charles Taylor White, also as a 'gentleman', and her residence was 45 Great Marlborough Street – Samuel Guppy's actual home, indeed. The curate – JE Norwood – presided. The witnesses were not family members, merely Thomas J Hawthorne and Charlotte Fossett. Regardless of the legal exactitude for purposes of the certificate, Elizabeth was incorrigible, and the following announcement was placed in the *Pall Mall Gazette* of the same day, December 10th: 'Guppy-Nicholl – At St Luke's Chelsea, Mr S Guppy, to Elizabeth, granddaughter of Mr WG Nicholl.'

Samuel was just 72, and Elizabeth was nearly 30. It was not untoward for a widower to marry a considerably younger woman in the expectation of more children. A difference in class was much more likely to cause malicious gossip. Samuel Guppy did not care. He had caught a voluptuous mermaid, who appealed to him, and she had mystic powers, which fascinated him. Her siren coils had brought in a new protector, with money, who was a buffer against a world which she knew to be cruel, and he would leave her well provided for. The sculptor could offer no prospects, and now her social status had risen triumphantly. Anyway, she was rapidly gaining celebrity in her own sphere. Mr Guppy's credentials would validate her very nicely as he carried the torch of belief in her powers which, previously, Alfred Russel Wallace had held aloft.

There is no hint or evidence that the marriage was anything but happy. Elizabeth loved children, and managed – it cannot have been comfortable for her – to present her husband with two babies, Thomas, born in Italy in 1870, and Samuel, born in England in 1872. Elizabeth and Samuel appeared to others to make up a compatible and companionable partnership. Wallace once successfully introduced them to a friend of his, St John Mivart, and was 'somewhat surprised at Mivart's appreciation of the Guppys, because of the great contrast between them; he [Mivart] extremely refined in speech and manners, and some-what fastidious in his acquaintances; they both rather brusque and utterly unconventional; yet he evidently recognised in them a straightforwardness of character, kindness of heart, love and truth, and earnestness of purpose, which are vastly more impor-tant than any amount of superficial polish.' (My Life, p.300)

What must most strike us now is the disparity in the educa-tion and culture of the Guppys. Wallace's lumpen pair, joined together in perfect harmony, like some rustic statuette, does not feel right, and, anyway, he was not the best judge of social differ-ences. Mr Guppy could mix with anyone, and Elizabeth stood at his side, hugging her secrets. Their conversation cannot have been entirely of spiritualism, however obsessed Samuel was by this time, and however anxious she was to maintain the illusion. He himself, before Elizabeth's reign, had expressed strong views on the wife considered as a sociable and agreeable companion. If not stimulated in her mind by, at the very least, a challenging ser-mon every Sunday, she would be poor company. 'It's not her fault, poor woman; what can she talk with you about? and women must talk, and you don't want to hear about the house-keeping.' He had no desire to cramp an intellectual woman into a mere housekeeper, 'just as Chinese women cramp their feet into wooden shoes.'

It is very clear that for so long as Elizabeth could command a séance, she was never going to be a mere housekeeper again. The Guppys certainly did not form one of the husband and wife teams that put on joint séances. She was the expert: he was the admiring beholder, never an acolyte, and in the privileged position of being allowed to embrace the untouchable medium. No one suspected him of unseemly involvement, and his distance from his wife's effects in its way enhanced her reputation. If he had even merely assisted her in an entirely overt manner, she would have been less convincing. Husband and wife each occupied separate globes of existence, he sizzling with fervent ideas about the nature of spiritualism, she seething with notions and deceit, both floating in an ether of connubiality.

It was an unusual set-up. Mr Guppy, worshipful of his Sibyl, increasingly isolated himself from clubbable friends and lived for the thrill of the darkened séances. Elizabeth was content. She had come out of obscurity and she wore a badge of being different and special. The vexed question is for how long Samuel believed in her, stayed innocent and gullible. The rehearsals, concealed stock of props and *machina*, contact with shady conspirators, and, as ambition grew, her abstractedness, should all have raised doubts and sent him back to his chemistry books. He was not in his dotage, as enemies of spiritualism liked to suggest. Besides, people *do* keep great secrets from their spouses: bigamists, serial killers, do so.

Elizabeth's séances continued shortly after the wedding, just as they had taken place up to the brink of the ceremony. Early in 1868, Mr and Mrs Guppy, as they now were, left for the Continent, where Samuel felt comfortable and had many contacts. He wanted to show off his own medium in all her glory, and she was his bride. He was doubly proprietorial. He had not exactly married his cook – a famous social gaffe – but there must have been little embarrassments and they would not be so obvious abroad. Elizabeth, as far as is known, had not travelled before, and, to judge by *Mary Jane*, if the money held out, Samuel gave her the best time of her life. He speaks of jewellery, augmented as it becomes unfashionable, and dresses: 'I have known a whole wardrobe of beautiful silk dresses which had been shut up during a three months' trip to Baden-Baden, taken by a kind of endemic, which ran through every one of them. I ventured to ask in a medico-philosophic tone of voice, "What was the matter with them?" "They won't meet, not one of them!"

Then again, you will learn all about ladies' horses and saddles, opera boxes, and travelling trunks.'

Spiritualism was in full flower in Europe and enjoyed the patronage of the aristocracy and royal courts, in a way that did not exist in England. Elizabeth's poise and confidence as she embarked on a triumphal tour are frankly astonishing. Tidings were sent back from abroad, so that she was not forgotten. Spectacular sittings at Naples, Florence and Paris were recorded. In Naples, the venue was a palace, owned by the Duchess d'Arpino. One evening, the Princess L'Aquila and the Countess Castellana were present. Doubts were expressed that Mrs Guppy might have apports concealed about her person. Mr Guppy had stayed away, and could not support her. A troublesome Parisian, Madame Val d'Or had suspected that Mr Guppy was a hench-man, but Elizabeth had confounded her. This time, she insisted on undressing, and donning a dressing gown belonging to the duchess, over which they considerately threw a shawl, to keep her warm. Then they took her to a new room, and the flowers came.

There was a well-known occasion in Florence, at the home of Thomas Adolphus Trollope and his second wife, Frances Eleanor (Ternan). Trollope (1810-92), an author, was the elder brother of the more famous Anthony. He had settled in Florence and was very friendly with visiting writers of importance: Dickens, Browning, George Eliot, Owen Meredith and many others. Therefore, if Mrs Guppy could impress the Trollopes, her reputation could spread in the right circles. It did help that Thomas Trollope was already a devotee of DD Home, but Browning, famously, called him 'Mr Sludge, the Medium.' On December 29th, 1869, Trollope wrote from the Villino Trollope to the London Dialectical Society: 'With regard to the sittings with Mrs Guppy, I can only say that the greatest watchfulness on the part of those taking part in them failed to detect any trace of imposture. The physical phenomena which took place (in the dark), such as the sudden falling on the table of a large quantity of jonquils, which filled the whole room with their odour, were extraordinary, and, on any common theory of physics, unac-countable. The room in which this took place had been careful-

75

ly examined by me, and Mrs Guppy's person had been carefully searched by my wife.'

Mr Guppy himself staunchly contributed his versions: 'On lighting the candle the whole of Mrs Guppy's and Mr Trollope's hands and arms were covered with jonquil flowers. The smell was quite overpowering. The doors had been locked, the windows fastened. Had a bunch of jonquils been in the room before the séance it would have been detected by the smell.'

The Princess Marguerite was present at séances at Naples, the *Spiritualist* reported reverentially, and one evening she asked for some specimens of the toxic prickly Italian cactus. Soon, a score of these unfriendly plants appeared on the table and were removed with tongs, because you did not want them to penetrate the skin. Mrs Guppy was known to have presented stinging nettles to séances. On another occasion, the spirits brought white flowers with a repulsive smell. One female sitter vomited, but the medium was made of sterner stuff. The mass of offensive flowers was thrown on to the fire, in front of all the 'nobles'. Live starfishes were brought; the sea was not much more than a hundred yards from the house.

Longfellow, the American poet, called upon Mrs Guppy at Naples. He told her that he had sat at many séances, but had never witnessed anything satisfactory. He had never recovered from the trauma of losing his second wife, Frances Elizabeth Appleton, who had burnt to death on July 9th, 1861. Mrs Guppy gave him some comfort when she agreed to a sitting, and, while he held her hands, several orange-boughs were brought by unseen agency.

At a séance under the aegis of the Spiritual Society of Florence, the spirits brought a heap of multi-coloured sugar plums. When the lights were put out again, there was a rattling noise, and the candle revealed the sugar plums all assorted as to colour. This display was intended to demonstrate that the spirits could distinguish colours, as had been questioned.

In the same place, at a different time, the room had been made very warm at the request of Mr Guppy, who had complained that they were all shivering on the previous occasion.

The major apport, this time, was a large lump of beautiful ice, about one-foot long, and one-and-a-half inches thick – a slice. It arrived in the darkness with an awful crash, as if a chandelier had fallen. This happened more than an hour after the beginning of the séance, and it was only then that the ice began to melt. The British Ambassador, Sir Arthur Paget, put on a séance at which they held Mrs Guppy's hands and asked for a noise. There was a loud concussion on the wall, like a gun.

When Mr and Mrs Guppy returned to London in September, 1870, her fame was not at all tarnished. The biographical feature of 1870 in the *Spiritualist*, with fabrications (*v. ante, passim*) served as an announcement that Mrs Guppy was back in town and fully operative in the most ladylike way. There had been an element of sharp risk, abroad. One light struck too soon, and she would have been exposed and ridiculous in grand company. At first they lived at 131 Holloway Road, North London, but by 1871 they were settled at 12 Highbury Hill Park, with the census wrongly showing Samuel's age as 60.

The household had expanded considerably: they had brought back a baby, Thomas Guppy, who was now one-and-a-half-years old, and an Italian nursemaid, Giustena Via, aged 18, and born in Venice. Another servant, Elizabeth Neyland, given as a 22-year-old Londoner, was actually 29. She was to better herself as Mrs Guppy coached her to become a medium, an assistant at last. Once, so noted in 1861, she had been a 'general porter'. Allowing servants to sit in at séances was not unknown, but this was going much further and, one would have thought, tended to erode Elizabeth's lofty image. It was a modest matrimonial home in North London, not the abode of a very rich man. By contrast, widowed Mrs Catherine Berry, the spiritualist, living at 242 Oxford Street in 1871 was employing a housekeeper and four domestic servants. This time, Elizabeth Neyland did not come from the docklands. Her father, Thomas, from Sussex, was a gardener for his lifetime, living at three consecutive addresses in Palmer Street, Islington, over a period of 30 years. He married Harriet, and Elizabeth was the sixth of nine children. In 1878, she was to marry a gardener from Middlesex, Edwin Southern, and Charles, Rosa and Edwin were born. Her spell as a medium had not raised her in society.

Very soon, the flow of séances was resumed. Mr Guppy began to take more of a back seat as he aged into his seventies, not always putting in an appearance, content with his books, his billiards, his cigars, and his wife's jumbo meals. Mrs Berry and Miss Houghton welcomed the travellers in delighted anticipation of fresh wonders. They had not, previously, relied on Elizabeth as their only medium, and during her fruitful absence they had made do with less congenial, sometimes male, psychics, where mutual warmth and sentimental regard were lacking. Mrs Marshall had been invited to supper – a feast of chicken, tongue, beef, jelly and wine. Payment had often been expected, but Mrs Thomas Everitt (1825-1915) of Pentonville, later Hendon, the wife of a prosperous tailor, came into the private category. Her séances were said to have begun in 1855, but she did not become well known until 1867. In that year, at a séance with 'Miss Nicholl' she was thrown into her first trance. With a more solid social background than Elizabeth, she had not had to struggle in the same way for recognition.

The two women knew each other well, and Mrs Guppy would have quite expected Mrs Berry and Miss Houghton to entertain her while she herself was in absentia. She became sought-after and her husband was close beside her: in 1873 he was appointed President *pro tem* of the British National Association of Spiritualists. Her special talent was the production of microscopic handwriting at remarkable speed, and she used classical quotation from known books. She was also an exponent of the 'direct voice' heard through a speaking tube made from paper or cardboard. Her control was 'John Watt'. Direct voices and controls were not Mrs Guppy's expertise. If other mediums were present she left this sort of thing to them. She herself was rarely 'entranced' and it was not in her nature to claim that she was operating under the influence of a specific, named control. Nor did she represent herself as in need of protection and guidance by spirits. That is not to say that she did not know everything that was going on in the spiritualist world. Mediums such as

Herne and Williams (*v. post*) were fervent, improvising actors, reproducing accents of all kinds – Indian, Hebrew, Welsh, Queen's English – and ready for exchanges of wit. Mrs Guppy had probably not entirely eliminated the incriminating Hull accent. In trance, she spoke in muted tones as herself, which was perfectly acceptable, and delivered tame and careful platitudes of the type which Mr Guppy had so disliked when emanating from Mrs Marshall!

Elizabeth found that an obnoxious young professional – Frank Herne – was well installed at London séances, but she quickly came to terms with him. Now entering on a period of intense activity, where she was not always a single practitioner, and restricted by her own limitations, she was able to achieve maximum diversity by combining her skills with others. She was risking so much, especially betrayal. Gleefully, the conspirators choreographed in advance their pool of effects, sometimes improvising daringly at the scene, sometimes drawing on their shared special knowledge of sitters' family histories and bereavements. False and sincere sat elbow to elbow, and then doctors and clergy scurried home and wrote up their notes. In a small circle of six, three might be false. Credulous believers were overpowered by the united forces assembled to deceive them. Today, we may find it strange that a private, if dissembling, medium was happy to cavort with unashamed, paid, fraudulent persons, thus colluding with them, accomplice to their fraud. 'Fraudulent medium', as now sometimes applied to Mrs Guppy and similar psychics may not even be the correct term for someone practising strictly on her own, knowing that her effects are not genuine but careful not to solicit material gain. The séance room, in this case, is to be regarded as a private theatre, the medium an amateur performer, receiving only psychological gain, with the sitters making a free choice to witness the phenomena.

Mrs Berry became closely involved with Frank Herne. In 1870, she was 'impressed' by her spirits to undertake a public work in connection with spiritualism, and she decided to preside over Herne's séances at James Burns' Spiritual Institution, 15

Southampton Row, for a six-month period. She was successful at investing gravitas, and she was regarded at the proceedings as a medium in her own right. Of course, she took no share of the admittance fee of one florin. Many spirit voices were heard, and not everyone present appreciated the contributions attributed to 'Bluff Harry' – that is, King Henry VIII.

When Mrs Guppy was first recorded on her return, reinstated in the familiar surroundings of Mrs Berry's small séance room, with its handsome cottage piano, both Mary Marshall and Frank Herne were present, and her typical flower apports were not a part of the proceedings. It was rather as if she were watching points, as a concertina floated, Herne's waistcoat was found draped around her own ample torso, a bird warbled and flapped, and three spirit voices conversed on this and that, but no doubt she used her strength to help to lift the piano to the ceiling. The truth is that Mrs Guppy's massive centrepieces and stately visual glamour of the old days were beginning to become more fragmented in the eternal search for novelty.

Sometimes, then, there would be a mixed scenario: Herne was thrown into a trance, raised from his chair and carried over the circle, while on the table lay flowers arranged into chaplets and garlands. Herne was already practising the levitation which was to be an important feature of the circle. On May 19th, 1871, in a rudimentary rehearsal for Mrs Guppy's famous flight a month later, he let it be known that he had been walking along the street, in mid-morning, and had had a strange, sick sensation, and lost consciousness. After some minutes, he found himself in the Guppys' house, two miles away. Mr Guppy was roped in as a hapless witness. He explained to Benjamin Coleman, who was investigating the event:

> My dear Sir, I was on Friday morning on the basement floor. Mrs Guppy was in the breakfast room adjoining, with the door open and had spoken to me. Suddenly she screamed, and said that something had tumbled down. I at once entered the room, and there was Mr Herne on the settee, looking dazed like

a person half-awake. When he got the use of his fac-
ulties, he said he did not know how he had come,
that he was going somewhere else, and in the street
felt himself giddy, and knew no more. Our back-
door was padlocked, our street door was shut as
usual, and the windows were all closed. No servant
let him in. It certainly is not an ordinary mode of
making a morning call, although there are plenty of
precedents in sacred and profane histories of this
sort of locomotion.[10]

On receipt of his letter, Benjamin Coleman hastened at once to
Highbury to make further enquiries, and found that, 'The break-
fast room is below the level of the road, and the only window of
the room, looking out on a grass plot in front of the house, is for
safety, screwed down and never opened. Mrs Guppy, I was
informed, was standing with her face to the window looking
down at her needlework upon the table, talking at the same time
to Mr Guppy, who was washing out some chemical glasses in the
adjoining room, six or eight yards distant, when she was greatly
alarmed by seeing what appeared to be a dark bundle fall on the
settee which is under the window. Her screams brought Mr
Guppy instantly to her side, and he seeing Mr Herne, addressed
him in strong language, demanding to know what he wanted,
and why he was there?'

Mrs Guppy began to introduce 'Miss Neyland' into the proceedings, her erstwhile servant more now of a companion, a rein-
forcement, and, as it turned out, a passable actress in her own
right when circumstances demanded it. She was warmly received.

On an occasion when Mrs Berry particularly wanted to
impress some guests, at a séance also attended by her schoolgirl
niece, Emma, who stayed with her from time to time, the combi-
nation of Mrs Guppy, Miss Neyland and Frank Herne brought
about a chaotic and somewhat contentious formal event. Mrs
Berry was carefully explaining to the two strangers present that
the spirits would probably bring fruit and flowers, when

[10] Letter to the *Spiritualist*, May 22nd, 1871.

Elizabeth experienced one of her explosions of facetious and inappropriate jocularity: 'I've been to the Zoological Gardens, and if they would bring the elephant from there, that would be a manifestation indeed.' Miss Neyland backed her up, nervously, perhaps: 'Or that fox: I should so like that handsome fox.'

Mrs Berry was getting rattled. 'Nonsense!' she said. 'Don't ask for anything extravagant – fruit and flowers are best to have brought.' As darkness calmed the atmosphere, there was alarm when the hostess, Mrs Guppy, and Miss Neyland all screamed and called for a light. A match was struck, and there was a white cat crawling over Mrs Berry's shoulder, like a furry caterpillar, and a little white Maltese terrier was standing on the table, looking around in some confusion – as well it might. Mrs Guppy said at once that they were her pets, and that she had left them safely at home. They were put in an adjoining room, and the cross little white dog yelped all evening. The noise must have added to the tension. A small spat ensued, ominous of trouble to come. Tactlessly, Mrs Guppy and Herne had a small enterprise of their own to pursue. She, when the spirit voice of 'John King' came forth, held Herne's hands and, with his permission, put her fingers against his lips. Now, she said, she was in a position to state on oath that Mr Herne himself was not the speaker.

Mrs Berry, a bystander at this independent charade, at her own séance, put on at her own expense, in front of her own visitors, took exception to the test. She felt that she had the right to feel offended 'at a suspicion of being a party to deceit' which had been implied. Defending herself, and her colleague, Mrs Guppy put it that she had asked Mr Herne to agree to the test in order to satisfy a certain distinguished spiritualist. After this embarrassing scene, 'John King' poured oil upon the waters of dispute, and persuaded Mrs Berry that her position had been in no way compromised. 'John King' was a constant motif of the 19th-century séances. His first appearance was with the Davenport brothers in 1850. He was represented as having been Henry Owen Morgan, the buccaneer who was knighted by Charles II, and appointed Governor of Jamaica. In England, Mrs Marshall was the first to claim his influence. 'Katie King' manifested at the

Davenport séances as 'John King's daughter,' speaking in a shrill, direct voice, and she moved on to materialise famously as a white wraith at Florence Cook's séances at Hackney in the 1870s.

Elizabeth's séances, often joint, with Herne, entered a phase of puerile 'transportation' of banal objects, such as a roll of lace, a heavy galvanic battery, apparently anything to hand, and often portable from house to house. Three ducks, prepared for cook-ing were brought into the circle at the Guppys' house. No one, ever, laughed. All three, Mrs Guppy, Miss Neyland, and Frank Herne floated in the air: Mrs Guppy tried to prevent Herne's ascent, but was drawn up with him, both in their chairs. Rather unfortunately, at this moment, the door was opened, and Herne fell to the ground, injuring his shoulder. Mrs Guppy alighted, with a loud crash on the table, where, on production of a light, she was discovered, comfortably seated, although alarmed.

A newcomer, Charles Williams, another professional medi-um, joined Mrs Berry's circle in late February to early March, 1871. Previously unknown to Mrs Berry, he was already a friend of Frank Herne, and 'the boys' as they soon came to be called, developed a close association, living and working as psychics at 61 Lambs Conduit Street, Bloomsbury. Both Herne and Williams were strikingly young: Herne was 21 in 1871, and Williams was 22.

Frank, properly Francis Gideon, Herne, came from a nautical background. He was born in Portsmouth in 1850. His father, David, born in London in 1819, was a warrant officer in 1851, and ten years later, he was a gunner with the Royal Navy. He and his wife, Ann, who came from Portsea, Hampshire, had seven children, of whom Frank was the second in line. The eldest son, David, was ship's steward's boy on HMS *Desperate* by the time he was 16, but Frank chose to break the family tradition, and made for London, where he gave his first séances in January, 1869.

Charles Edward Williams confided his life story to Henry E Russell, who published an article in the *Medium and Daybreak* of July 17th, 1874, entitled 'Mr Williams and his Mediumship'. As usual, the early psychic signs are picturesque and dramatic:

A strong desire for a seafaring life, evinced in boy-hood, was for years most strenuously opposed by his mother. Finding, perhaps, that the desire was so per-tinaciously entertained that he would never settle down to any regular employment onshore, Mrs Williams at length consented to his making a trial trip abroad. Accordingly, in the month of August, 1868, he was appointed midshipman on board a large East Indiaman, and made two voyages from London to Calcutta. On the last of these voyages, either on the outward or homeward passage, about 1869, occurred the first manifestations of any note, such as raps, and movements of objects. On one of these occasions referred to he was standing near the capstan, on which were placed some tin pannikins and other things, from which a group of sailors were refreshing themselves, when suddenly, to the amaze-ment of Mr Williams as well as the seamen, the whole of these articles were lifted up by unseen agency and floated overboard. Of course in such a position of affairs the presence of such an uncanny person on board was looked upon with grave suspi-cion by the superstitious minds of his shipmates, and his no doubt unenviable feelings tended greatly to wean his inclinations from pursuing further a sea-faring life ...

In some way, not suffering from shyness, Herne and Williams made themselves known to DD Home, who, in the spring of 1871, was attending formal test séances instigated by William Crookes. On April 11th, on one of the earliest of these occa-sions, at the home of Serjeant Cox in Russell Square, Bloomsbury, all three, Herne the Hunter, William the sailor, and Home in his glory rose and hovered in the air. The two strong and agile young men were worthy pupils. Home had reviv-ified the saintly feat of elongation of the body and he taught Herne how to do it, in an alarming extension of his already leptomorphic six-feet-two inches. 'The boys,' from their utterances, had both received a passable education. Mediumship was an urgent imperative. It paid the rent at Lambs Conduit Street, and they applied themselves with dash and flair. Again, Elizabeth assimilated and adapted, thoroughly embroiled with them, and she became 'Lizzie'.

Mrs Berry arranged a special, small séance, in honour of young Emma, who was leaving for school in Germany and wanted to have a last sitting to give her courage. Mr Guppy turned up for this special event and a quartet of persons were present: Mr and Mrs Guppy and Mrs Berry and Emma. When the voice of 'Katie King' came through, only Mrs Guppy could have been responsible for it. Mr Guppy had to make what he would of the high, shrill tone. She announced that she would make a wreath of purity and goodness for Emma Berry, and the girl and Mrs Berry were revealed crowned with wreaths. 'Katie then made a most flattering speech, very classical and very pretty,' Mrs Berry reported, but there was a shrewdness in her, because she added, 'Either she (Katie) is better versed in mythology than we gave her credit for, or she must have had a spirit dictating it to her.' Apparently, as Katie was speaking of Helen and Paris, two apples were placed in Mrs Berry's hands. The whole séance, with perfumes and lights delivered at designed moments, showed signs of very careful preparation. The wreaths, one chaste and beautiful, the other gorgeous with colour, were photographed and copies were presented to Mrs Guppy. The editor of the *Medium* wrote up what happened next:

> The spirits at once desired her to take a four-wheeled cab, place into it the photographs, a box of paints, a wet sponge, and a piece of red flannel to pin up against the windows to keep the light out. She was to enter the cab, and in that manner to be driven four times round Regent's Park. The coachman got tired, and at the end of three rounds he declined to drive her farther. On getting out, Mrs Guppy found the photographs were beautifully coloured, one of them

being still wet and scarcely finished. At the bottom of them both was rudely sketched, "Painted by Katie."

The approbation of Mrs Berry was still important to Mrs Guppy, and she set aside a spirit room dedicated to Mrs Berry at the house in Highbury. An inaugural séance was held there. Unusually, silence was maintained, and the awed atmosphere was all the more effective. A spirit form, possibly Miss Neyland, became visible by a peculiar light (probably phosphoric) and was seen to be inspecting some of Mrs Berry's spirit drawings. It was Mrs Berry's apotheosis: a wreath of flowers was placed on her head, another on her wrist, and a bunch of flowers in the left hand, with a branch in her right hand. As she sat there like a queen with her coronal she waved the branch and two people toppled to the ground in a trance.

She held a séance with Herne and Williams at her own house. As 'the boys' left, Mrs Berry and a friend stepped out on to the balcony in the moonlight and saw them walking away, arm-in-arm. 'John King' later instructed Mrs Berry, at a circle, to order a cabinet to be made for 'the boys' and then there would be some extraordinary manifestations. Mrs Berry could well afford the expense, and the private place was fitted up, à la Davenport. A recess was fitted with a wicket which could be padlocked. There were two apertures, covered with small curtains of dark cloth, through which the mediums' clothing, and then some arms and hands could emerge, to the sound of spirit voices and superlative singing. Mrs Guppy let 'the boys' get on with this new venture without her active participation, and, anyway, their cabinet was cramped, only just wide enough for them to sit on a narrow seat at the back. Nevertheless, a year later, she did construct her own modest cabinet – a common wooden cupboard fastened over a corner, with several window openings cut out. On a trial, attended by the Countess de Medina Pomar, moonlight from two uncovered windows provided some visibility. The faces of Mrs Guppy and another medium, probably Miss Neyland, were thrust through a lower opening and at the same time a small face, not life-size, appeared at an upper opening. It was as white as alabaster. Another similar one popped out, and they nodded in answer to questions. The performance was not very well received, and was compared to a Punch and Judy show.

In case of adverse comment, Mrs Berry replaced the wooden wicker gate with an impressive iron, Bastille gate, reaching from ceiling to floor, secured by a strong patent lock, with one key only, kept by Mrs Berry at all times. The spirits were heard complaining about the obstruction, and, after a long wait, some hands did eventually protrude.

There had been signs of friction between Mrs Guppy and Mrs Berry: Elizabeth was expansive, humorous, earthy, while Mrs Berry was serious, not amused, and not a 'push-over' although ultimately remaining convinced. None, however, could have anticipated a total rift in their relationship. It was Elizabeth Guppy's fault, and she must have regretted it deeply. It was a fatal miscalculation and she had not taken into account Mrs Berry's sense of dignity. There was a large and distinguished gathering at Highbury, with the Countess de Medina Pomar, and her son, the Duke de Medina Pomar.

Mr Benjamin Coleman was there, keeping a strict eye on the proceedings. In Mrs Berry's bitter words: 'In about ten minutes, after having had a few of the ordinary manifestations, we were favoured (?) with an *extraordinary* exhibition of spirit power. A shower of feathers began to fall upon us, and continued falling till they lay on the table to the depth of several inches! It was just as though a feather bed had been emptied upon us. I felt extremely annoyed at this, and requested to be allowed to leave, when Mrs Guppy, being in one of hilarious moods, called out to the spirits to bring some tar, so that I might be "tarred" as well as "feathered." Thereupon, I rushed out of the room, followed by Mr Coleman. When we got into the hall, we found ourselves so covered with feathers, that it took a servant more than an hour to make us fit to be got out of doors. In consequence of this séance, Mrs Guppy and I became estranged for some years.'

Mr Guppy desperately attempted to heal the breach, assuring Mrs Berry that he did not have a feather bed in the house. She was obviously suspicious, as well as upset. Her host 'was surprised that I should have shown any temper, thinking himself that it was a capital joke, but I could not accept it in such a light, for my dress and bonnet were entirely spoiled. The dress being of black silk trimmed with crape, the feathers clinging to it, made me look more like a magpie than anything else, and I was in such a state that no lady would like to return home in. At the same time, [Mrs Berry adds hastily, clinging to her fundamental beliefs] it was a wonderful manifestation, although not one to my liking, and I would much have preferred a shower of flowers, which my spirit friends generally give me.'

Then there was trouble with 'the boys'. They had made it very clear that they resented the fortress 'cage', as they called it. On the last day of January, 1872, they demolished it. 'Locks, bolts, and bars were rent asunder, and the gates were smashed to atoms.' Supernormal power seemed to have been employed in what was interpreted as the spirits' attack on the two mediums. Mrs Berry was furious, again, and very nearly abandoned all idea of holding séances at home. Instead, she set up a new room and the cage was no more. Herne and Williams remained in favour with both Mrs Berry and Mrs Guppy even after the two women had gone their separate ways.

'The boys' carried on with quite violent behaviour: a seven-foot-high folded screen was thrown noisily across the table, and 'one of the mediums was rather inclined to be boisterous, which is always unfortunate, as the spirits will partake of the medium's conditions.' A vicious note had crept in, and Mrs Berry was being taken advantage of. Not feeling very well, she decamped for a rest at Margate, and, for the time being there were no more gourmet suppers or fees. Back in London, she moved to Connaught Square, and reflected. On March 28th, 1873, she wrote a letter to the editor of the *Medium* which was of importance to spiritualists, coming as it did from a person of high regard in the movement. It was a stinging reprimand, but ultimately a majestic apologia for spiritualism:

Dear Sir,

You are aware that I never have been thoroughly satisfied with the manifestation called 'spirit faces'. I
have sat at many of these séances, but always had a
doubt upon my mind as to their genuineness. I am
now satisfied that some are not genuine, and I would
advise all who go to witness these manifestations to
take my experience, and put mediums through a far
stricter test than they are at present subjected to. It is
no use searching the cabinet or room where they are
to sit; the beard, masks, and draperies are not there,
they go in with the medium. My advice is, search
them, and instead of using cord to tie them with use
cotton. Fastened with cotton, they cannot move
without its breaking, but with cord, never mind how
many knots may be made, they can and do extricate
themselves. Again, I would advise that the instant a
spirit-face is seen at the aperture and disappears, the
cabinet, or door of the room, should be thrown
open. If, then, the medium be still sitting in the
place where he should, you will have the happiness
of knowing that you have witnessed a genuine spirit-
manifestation ...

I do not intend it to be understood that I believe
all the 'spirit-face' manifestations are deceptions. I
should indeed be sorry were I to think this, for I
fancy I have seen a dear friend return and show himself; but this is the only occasion on which I have
seen any likeness ... I must say that I do not throw all
the blame upon the mediums. A demand comes
from every quarter for spirit-faces, and nothing but
spirit-faces will satisfy. The demand has been greater
than the supply, and this has induced the deception
– for we must not forget that mediums are like ourselves, mortals, and open to the same temptations,
but with this difference, that they are less under self-

control. Spirits can at all times have access to them, and take possession of them; and who can tell whether the deception that is now being carried on is not the work of some lying spirit called forth by a mighty power, the result of which we know not of at present, but may know hereafter.

Although Frank Herne continued to be Mrs Berry's medium, giving complete satisfaction with a new, doleful control, named 'Peter', Charles Williams was conspicuously absent from her reported séances. In the autumn of 1874, she moved away from the hothouse centre of English spiritualism to Brighton. Georgiana Houghton had been just as eager to welcome 'dear Mrs Guppy' back to her séances at 20 Delamere Crescent as Mrs Berry had been, and accepted Miss Neyland without question, observing that her 'mediumship in several phases was rapidly developing.' Whether or not the private sitters used to slip a modest gratuity into the palm of the sorcerer's apprentice it is difficult to say. Mr Benjamin Coleman would have been able to tell us. The matter was a social minefield. Everyone knew that Miss Neyland was employed by Mrs Guppy and her servant status was inescapable. Mrs Guppy, who was generous, turned her out in fine quality dark clothing for the séances, of that we can be sure. Awkwardly, if she were viewed as an extension of lady-like Mrs Guppy, payment could have caused offence.

Mrs Guppy had been training and rehearsing her assistant to exhibit a new phenomenon well tailored for Miss Houghton and her mystical nature. She was to be a clairvoyant and a clairaudient. In the darkness she would claim to see and hear all manner of ghostly visitants. The style was exclamatory: 'Oh! there is an angel – it is Gabriel!' she would cry out as Mrs Guppy sat discreetly mute. Then a soft, quivering sound would come, like angel wings, and illuminated letters [she said] shimmered brightly. Miss Houghton's Mamma appeared, and her brother, Clarence, and her nephew, Charlie, who was drowned in the great *Carnatic* disaster on the Red Sea, and a fair young girl, Môtee, who played on a harp and sang a seemly hymn. It was foolproof, virtually, with no window for error or discovery. Miss Houghton's friends and relatives were not going to strike a sudden light.

The appetite for séances was insatiable, and, with the important added influence of Mrs Tebb, they became complicated, coloured with religious symbolism, numerology, interpretation of dreams, and elaborate repetitive themes radiating out from Miss Houghton's personal losses. She did not appreciate rough, coarse spirit behaviour, even a little mild throwing of cushions, and Mrs Guppy, usually an astute 'psychologist', except, notably, when she was feathering Mrs Berry, did her best to cater for her refined tastes.

Miss Houghton's home circle was made up of a small number of regular sitters, mostly women, and typically there would be a few of her intimates, and two or three false mediums. If it is obvious that they were assisting Mrs Guppy, then that is a good rule of thumb by which to identify them. Miss Houghton trusted them all. Herne and Williams were not admitted – she had an instinctive distaste for them – and she did not, anyway, have the funds to disburse professional fees. Mrs Mary Elizabeth Tebb (1836-1914) is a special case, worthy of interest. Although her contemporaries in the spiritualist world, and in other spheres, knew exactly who she and her husband were, and their achievements and social position, today, relying on Miss Houghton's memoirs, it would not be difficult to feel doubtful about her status as an amateur medium. When we see her in the thick of the séances, mesmerising and being mesmerised, sliding in and out of trance, prophesying freely, with visions of the departed and the living, we can, surely, be forgiven for feeling suspicious of her sincerity, because she seems, on the face of it, to be a part of the false forms produced by Mrs Guppy and Miss Neyland. For example: Mrs Tebb announced, 'I feel as if an effort were being made to raise me, but you must not speak to me, nor touch me.'

Miss Houghton relates, 'she spoke occasionally, and her voice sounded up, and Mrs Guppy said that she had seen her feet above the level of the table. Then the spirits immediately rapped in the affirmative.'

Mrs Tebb was very suggestible, and tipped over into her trances like a poised spring-balance. What probably happened was that Mrs Guppy and Miss Neyland did lift her up, inert in her trance, or try to do so. Her voice could have sounded high up, if, like Miss Houghton, you believed that she was being raised. It was Mrs Guppy who chipped in with what she said she had seen, and she, or her accomplice, did the rapping.

Mrs Tebb and Miss Houghton were close friends and kindred spirits, entirely sincere in their Christian and spiritualist beliefs. They spent many private hours together, with mutual mesmerism, and, often, Mrs Tebb was in an induced trance state, uttering a remarkable, but not unique, flow of mystical and prophetic rhetoric. She described the fields and mansions of the afterworld, and Miss Houghton wrote it all down. Grasping the situation, Mrs Guppy cleverly embraced and utilised Mrs Tebb, not allowing her to be turned into a rival.

The truth is that Mrs Tebb had an unimpeachable background for her beliefs and practices. She was brought up and educated in a setting where spiritualism was one of the expressed ideal tenets. She was born Mary Elizabeth Scott and lived in Adin Ballou's utopian community at Hopedale, Massachusetts, where the principal aims and interests were temperance, abolitionism, woman's rights, education, and spiritualism. Adin Ballou founded a factory town in the setting of a religion-based commune, and called the whole enterprise 'Practical Christianity.' The members lived in their own separate homes: this was not Free Love.

William Tebb (1830-1917), born in Manchester, England, moved to America in 1852 as an emissary of the Vegetarian Society, and was influenced by Ballou, making frequent trips to Hopedale, where he met, and in 1856, married Mary Elizabeth Scott. They had four children: Florence, William, Christina and Beatrice. In the 1860s, the family moved to England, to escape a malarial outbreak in America. Tebb became a director of a company that manufactured chemicals, and built up a vast fortune. Probate was granted in 1917 in the sum of £158,798, which is now worth around £5 million in today's terms, and he had already spent generously on charitable causes. He was a well-known philanthropist, and Mrs Tebb, too, was recognised for good works of a more private nature. William was anti-slavery, pro-animal rights, anti-vaccination, co-founder of the Royal Normal College for the Blind, and a campaigner against premature burial. He had some interest in spiritualism, and attended séances, without undue fervour.

There is an excellent photograph of Mrs Tebb: she is the previously not greatly noticed figure on the left of the image of Miss Houghton and Mrs Guppy in Miss Houghton's *Chronicles* (see picture 13, page 206). Her comparative youth, character and vitality shine forth. If we did not know better, she looks, from her position and pose as if she were part of the plot to deceive Miss Houghton, but we now know that you would not, ever, offer her a fee for psychic services, nor would you suspect her motives.

On November 25th, 1870, so soon after their return from Italy, Mrs Guppy gave a large, psychic birthday party for her husband. Eighteen guests, including Miss Houghton, attended the séance at the new house, and, sad to tell, Samuel did not enjoy the occasion at all. Someone brought up the topic of his old friends, the Davenport brothers, and the spirits proposed that he should have his hands tied behind him to his chair, in imitation of Davenport wizardry. Unfortunately, he took very strong exception to the proceedings, and his protests rang out embarrassingly as his waistcoat was unbuttoned and his pockets emptied. He pleaded for the candle to be lit, and from his point of view the party – in his honour – was a failure. Mrs Guppy munched the apported fruit. The table rocked like a ship at sea, with the mediums – Mrs Guppy and her apprentice – still returning to the *Carnatic* tragedy. Samuel said that they were quite welcome to break his table, and they did so, reducing it to a wreck. Was Mr Guppy going along with his wife's party for him, or was he exasperated?

Hospitality flowed at Mrs Guppy's birthday party séance on January 22nd, 1871. Miss Houghton was one of the three-dozen guests. Mr Guppy was in good form: when Miss Neyland announced in the darkness that a pigeon of hers had just returned, he said that it would be a desirable thing if they (the sitters) could all be converted into doves. The *pièce de résistance* of the gala evening, calculated to affect the largest possible number of people present, was precisely the same event that was to alienate Mrs Berry later than year – a snowstorm of downy feathers. The difference was that anyone was welcome to go up to a bedroom afterwards, where an empty feather bed cover was openly on display. Miss Houghton's temperament was markedly sweeter than Mrs Berry's, and she bore no resentment:

> At first it created much laughter and amusement, but fancy the state of mens' woollen coats, to which the small particles so clingingly adhered: – then the hair! The velvet dresses! Oh! Dear, it *was* a fluffy manifestation, and one not easily to be forgotten ... The *guests* were somewhat smothered, but the labour afterwards entailed upon the hosts and their assistants in clearing the house was something tremendous, and it was long before all vestiges of the birthday fete were absolutely removed.

Miss Houghton did not share Mrs Guppy's jolly and all-embracing welcome of outsiders at her own séances, where, of course, there was no supportive husband. Her view was that 'the sittings in this house have been exceptional, – not at all intended as evidences for the sceptical, but for the purpose of reaching the highest phenomena they could, which can never be attained amidst conflicting atmospheres: therefore under no circumstances could a complete sceptic or a so-called enquirer have been admitted, although the favour has often been solicited, and might perhaps have been difficult to refuse.' That is why her séances, so harmonious, lacked the edge of danger, but they were respected, well-known, and influential.

After the room had been 'harmonised' by a preliminary social visit, Mr and Mrs Everitt were invited into the circle, and the evening dramas, although always genteel, an assembly of friends, became a little more adventurous and crowded, with 'John

Watt', in desembodied voice, joining the company. The spirits lacked the power to raise Charlie's turquoise pin, deep down with him in the *Carnatic*, but Charlie – Miss Neyland saw him there – brought a mother-of-pearl shell from the Red Sea, all salty and wet. Miss Houghton was beside herself, in a state of exultation as the séances flowed on, and that was when, in 1871, she made an unfortunate decision and impoverished herself in the cause of spiritualism. Mrs Guppy was not to blame, nor Mrs Tebb; they merely provided encouragement, and were not the instigators.

The history of the affair was that people admired her surreal spirit paintings, abstract watercolours which she thought were automatically executed under the influence of her spirit guides, and represented spiritual truths. An artist, 'Mr L' advised her that they were good enough to be exhibited, and, in good faith, he introduced her to Mr McNair, the Secretary of the Society of Artists who held the Dudley Gallery, Egyptian Hall, Piccadilly. He made arrangements for a four-month exhibition of 155 pictures at the New British Gallery at 39 Old Bond Street. One might wonder if the choice of venue was ideal, because the one found most suitable as to size and situation first needed expensive repairs as Miss Houghton's responsibility. What no one apparently realised, and she was not going to tell them herself, was that she was of slender means, living comfortably enough in a state of equilibrium, while relying on the security of a received legacy from her Aunt Helen, of which £300 remained. The ancillary costs of the project – £300 – were horrendous, and the short point is that she lost the lot. Against all expectations, she failed to find a buyer for any of her pictures, except for one sold at the private viewing beforehand.

Pathos lies in the fact that she sent a copy of the catalogue on extra-fine pink paper, bound in white calf and gold, as the etiquette required, to Her Majesty the Queen, but received not even an acknowledgement. Although the central premise of the exhibition was generally unacceptable, it did receive favourable attention in some non-specialist quarters. The *News of the World*, for example, was very fair:

At the first glance the pictures seem only masses of lines and colours – extraordinary mazes, but without a defined plan; the brilliancy and harmony of the tints, however, engage attention, and the idea presents itself to the imagination of a canvas of Turner's, over which troops of fairies have been meandering, dropping jewels as they went.

Miss Houghton, the lady executant, is a clever and tasteful artist; and furthermore, a sincere believer in what she says. We do not recognise in her extraordinary achievements more than what an accomplished and patient artist, with thoughts bent in a particular direction, could produce; but her conviction claims respect, and although we have met with nothing to induce us to believe in the spirit theory, we readily acknowledge the thorough conscientiousness of Miss Houghton's belief.

Alas! Georgiana was afterwards so grievously financially embarrassed that she resorted to pledging her jewellery. Her attitude was rueful, but accepting. She was not tempted to burn her pictures as, she mentions in a separate context, happened to young Emanuel Marshall in a dark moment. Mrs Berry, whose solvency was far superior, was in no way discouraged by Miss Houghton's misadventure. In 1874, she put on a grand exhibition of 500 spirit pictures, in Brighton. While her chaotic, curdled paintings tended, it was thought, to show the origin of species, Miss Houghton's were more on the lines of sacred symbolism, with fruit and flower emblems.

The duping of Miss Houghton by Mrs Guppy was not attended by malice. She was a good and kind woman, and an affectionate regard for her suffused her circle. The wonders gave her pleasure and the mediums found their own pleasure in the séances and, no doubt, a sense of power as they played upon the emotions of the believers. Sometimes there was, perhaps, hilarity in the planning. The coat of many colours was a successful farce. Mrs Guppy executed the first stage of it by depositing upon the table in the darkness a mound of what Miss Houghton herself came to realise were tailors' samples of variegated pieces of cloth, weighing one-and-a-half pounds.

The message came, *via* the alphabet, from Miss Houghton's Mamma: 'My dear daughter, you must wear a coat of many colours.' Preston, the cook, who was a good needlewoman, volunteered to make up the coat in the shape of a sleeveless Javanese garment, called a Kabaya. Isabella Houghton, Georgiana's sister-in-law, who had one, sent a pattern. Mrs Tebb, thrown into trance utterance, interpreted the symbolism:

> Only a chosen few can ever wear the garment you will wear, only the best beloved: good deeds, and ill deeds as well, form substantial and, – in the sense that spirits understand, – *material* substances, which can be fashioned by loving hands to promote the comfort of the spirit. The spiritual garment will be lined with crimson, to denote the warm human love which you shed around you, and which will return to you ... This garment is worn over a white lawn robe
> ...

And so on. Mrs Guppy's ruse had stimulated a complicated vision, expressed in a fountain of words. Mrs Tebb herself went out and bought a piece of beautiful crimson merino for the lining, and Preston sewed it in. Worn over a white muslin body, the coat of many colours solemnly adorned Miss Georgiana Houghton at her home séances.

5

The Flight of the Enchantress

WHILE MISS HOUGHTON HAD BEEN preoccupied with her exhibition, Mrs Guppy, all unknown to her, had been planning the most ambitious feat of her career. It is quite modern to our eyes, because it is an illusion. She needed the help of Herne and Williams, and they provided the stage for the event at 61 Lambs Conduit Street. The date was June 23rd, 1871, and it was a Saturday evening. Two loci had been prepared, and that was why Miss Neyland, who would normally have accompanied her mistress was left at home, in the rôle of providing corroboration. Timing – synchronisation – was of the essence.

A dark séance was in progress, with eight sitters, one woman and seven men. Whether or not they had been warned to expect something out of the ordinary never emerged, nor whether they had been specially invited, but a few there present were experiencing a séance for the first time in their lives, and paying for the privilege – the total, smothering darkness, darting star lights, and the floating music box fluting out sacred music.

They had ascended to the first floor (there were two floors above) where there was a double drawing-room, communicating by large folding doors, and were ushered into the smaller back-room, (12ft by 10ft-4in) which was usually kept darkened for séances on demand. The folding doors were then locked. The sole window was completely covered. The room was bare, and cramped, due to the size of the oval table, with its chairs, which seated ten, so sitting was virtually shoulder-to-shoulder. A small cupboard was shown open, with miscellaneous objects on the shelves, which could have been props, with a use, or merely intended to disarm. In all probability the cupboard itself had a very decided use, or there would have been no point in having it there.

These premises were Herne and Williams' workplace, adapted accordingly. Secret access was the most important aspect. It was known that even the most skilled self-appointed investigators could miss panels drilled out of wainscotting, door panels, cupboards, and so on. In this case, a little adroitness with keys, doors and lighting may have been all that was required. The oval table, which nearly filled the room, allowed limited space behind the sitters. Strategically, Herne and Williams manned the opposite ends of the table. The folding doors lay at the back of one side of the table. There was also a no doubt crucial extra door, its exact location not divulged, which led out to a passage. The theory was that, if opened, natural light would come in, because it was high summer, and the proceedings began before 8 pm. This door, too, was now locked.

Once the atmosphere had been established, with the Lord's Prayer, the voices of 'John King' and 'Katie King' began to be heard. 'Katie' was asked if she would bring something. 'Yes, yes,' was the reply. Then a person, thought at the time to be one of the visitors, but obviously one of the mediums, said, 'jokingly', 'I wish she would bring Mrs Guppy.' Another voice said, 'Good gracious! I hope not. She is one of the biggest women in London.' Then 'Katie' cried, 'I will, I will.' John's rough voice shouted, 'You can't do it, Katie.' They were all laughing by then: the idea was ridiculous.

'John King's' voice rang out in the darkness, 'Keep still, can't you?' Someone said, 'Good God! There is something on my head!' and there was a heavy bump on the table. Mr Edwards, of Kilburn, put out his hand, and said, 'There is a dress, here.' A wax match was struck and there indeed was Mrs Elizabeth Guppy standing on the table, in the middle, with all the sitters still in their original places. 'John King' shouted, 'Well, you are clever, Katie.'

The towering apparition stunned the assembled company. They checked the time; it was ten minutes past eight. They began to worry about Mrs Guppy. She seemed to be in a trance, and managed to stay motionless, although one account says that she was trembling all over. They were afraid to rouse her and cause her harm. The achievement of keeping still and not wobbling on the table was considerable, because one hand, holding a pen, was over her eyes, and the other clutched an account book. In order not to upset her, the light was put in the other room, and the door was closed for an instant. 'John King' said, 'She'll be all right, presently.'

After about four minutes, the statue moved, and streamed with tears like Niobe, very agitated. They asked her what had happened, and she told her story. The last thing that she remembered was sitting by the fire at home with Miss Neyland, entering household accounts in her book. It was noted that the ink in her pen was wet when she materialised, and the last word in the columns (later said to be 'onions') was incomplete and wet and smeared. Now she complained bitterly that she was not properly dressed in visiting costume, and was barefoot, because she had taken her shoes off by the kitchen fire. When, she said, she woke up in a dark place and heard voices all around her, her first thought was that she was dead. Then it flashed upon her that she had been transported to a séance. She was very relieved when she recognised one of the voices, but she had no shoes or bonnet to go home in. It was jokingly rumoured that Mrs Guppy was *en déshabillé*, and, years later, in 1918, Dr Abraham Wallace wrote, in *Light*, that she 'was arrayed in a loose morning gown, with a pair of bedroom slippers on, and in a more or less *décolleté* condition.'

After her recovery, a brief séance was held, and Mrs Guppy's boots were brought in the dark, and a bonnet, and some clothing. A bunch of keys fell into her lap, and a pair of Frank Herne's slippers dropped from above, grazing the head of Mr Henry Morris, a respectable merchant from Manchester – all of this in the light.

Naturally, the doors were found to be locked and it was observed that one of them (which?) could not be opened (anyway) during the séance, since the back of the chair occupied by one of the sitters was hard against it. They noted that at the time of the 'thud', Herne was talking, while his hands were held on either side. His voice will have been a distraction from any unwanted ancillary noise made by Mrs Guppy's entry into the room. The thump was clearly intentional.

As Mr Mason wrote in the *Echo*, a newspaper which printed his account without derision, 'The possibility of her being concealed in the room is as absurd as the idea of her acting in collusion with the media.' Quite so – in regard to the first proposition, but, obviously, having prepared her costume outside, she had entered by normal, mortal means. Trick locks on the doors would have sufficed, or Herne and Williams could have had their own apprentice working outside. The skill – and it was a considerable skill – was to enter silently in the pitch blackness which was her enemy as well as her friend, step up on to the table and hold her pose, like a sculptor's model! This was not an appropriate setting for a great spring up, and it is suggested that a medium, probably Williams, vacated his chair for the final ascent.

It is no wonder that Elizabeth was quivering all over with 'nerves' and physical effort, but then she had been clambering on to tables since the days when she had been astounding Alfred Russel Wallace. 'Nictalopes' were said to be rare people, who could see in the dark in psychic settings, but no such claim is put for Mrs Guppy.

Convinced that history had been made, but, even so, priding themselves on their investigative thoroughness, the group deputed four of their members to proceed to Highbury to take statements from any occupants of the Guppys' house. Mrs Guppy, who had obviously anticipated this move, 'strongly approved of the suggestion', and the party of four, with Mrs Guppy, packed into a couple of cabs, which were driven, on request, nose-to-tail. It was a pantomime, and also a parody of a Sherlock Holmes adventure.

It was Miss Neyland, of course, who opened the door to the deputation. She had been waiting in anticipation, and she had to get the story right. They all trooped into the back parlour and interrogated her. She spoke out boldly: she had been downstairs with a newspaper, while Mrs Guppy entered her accounts. They were sitting on either side of the fire, and the door was closed. They were talking, and when she looked up from her newspaper, Mrs Guppy had vanished. There was a kind of haze under the ceiling. She searched the downstairs rooms, and went to Mr Guppy, who, characteristically, was playing billiards with Mr Hudson, a photographer who lived in the neighbourhood and had been helping Mr Guppy with some amateur photography. Hudson, as we shall see, was no ordinary practitioner, but a shady character in need of extra fees. He was also a very nice man.

Samuel Guppy showed no concern about the disappearance of his wife – in a puff of smoke, as it were – and, distancing himself, delivered one of the dry quips which had increasingly become his response to strange happenings. 'No doubt,' he said, 'the spirits have carried her off, but they will be sure to take care of her.' Anyone is free to guess that he had been coached, or that nonchalance might equal disbelief. There could be a touch of sarcasm. Unworried, Guppy, and Neyland had sat down to supper, and shortly afterwards, the lonely husband had gone off to his bed. Their passive response to a crisis cannot be explained in ordinary terms.

The investigators asked about the exact time when Mrs Guppy was missed. Miss Neyland thought that it might have been about 9 o'clock, whereupon Mrs Guppy told them that the clock downstairs was half-an-hour fast, and so it was when the whole party examined the scene of the disappearance. Mrs Guppy's shoes were on the carpet in front of the fire, by her chair. A partly charred body would have completed the picture of a spontaneous human combustion.

Later, Mr Guppy told the investigators that his wife had come to him and his guest once or twice in the course of the evening, suggesting that they should have supper, but they declined, as it was too early. So, Mrs Guppy had had to make her departure for Lambs Conduit Street without sustenance. In the aftermath, she was 'weak and ill' for several days. It was only a year or so since she had given birth to Tommy, and she had pushed herself to the limit.

For the moment, she was queen of the séances, and the publicity may have exceeded her expectations. It was not all good, naturally, but she was well up to that. She did not do it again. Faked levitation on that scale was a big effort, and it was better to rest on her laurels. *The Times* was to be very hard on her. On June 24th, 1886, following the death of DD Home, the newspaper attacked her in terms of her class. Holding little respect for mediums, and remarking that spiritualist adherents, with few exceptions, were to be found in inferior social positions after the civil trial of Lyon v Home, the tirade continued: 'The famous Mrs Guppy who was brought through the air from a small house in one of the suburbs to a house in Lambs Conduit Street, carrying with her the still wet pen with which she had been entering her household accounts when the spirits carried her away, and attired in a negligent [sic] costume adapted to the character of her occupation, was the sort of person from whom the believers of the next few years were recruited, and was probably a fair specimen of the class to which spiritualists were at last driven to appeal.' The journalist would not have dared to write like that if Mr Samuel Guppy had still been alive, and, indeed, it is possible that he had not bothered to check if Mrs Guppy were still alive – as she was.

After her 'floatation', Mrs Guppy was undamaged in the world of spiritualism. On the contrary, as the *Spiritualist* reported on October 15th, 1871, 'It is no easy thing to get a séance with Mrs Guppy, as so many wish to see her manifestations, and the members of her circles are usually very high-class people.' Mr Guppy, always Elizabeth's champion, simmered grimly, especially when her 'corpulence' was used against her by the general press as if it were a moral fault, or a symbol of guilt. He made a move, but it caused further derision. Writing to the *Daily Telegraph* (September 19th, 1871) he announced:

> Dear Sir, I will bet my wife's diamonds against the Crown jewellery (to make it a national affair) that she shall, after so strict a examination as to satisfy a jury of matrons, go either into the inmost recesses of

the Bank of England, or into the deepest dungeon of the Tower, and, the doors being locked and guarded, there shall be brought to her something she did not take in with her. It may be the elephant, or a lion, or tiger, or dog, or cat, from the Zoological Gardens, if the committee allow it, or it may at first be only flowers or fruits, but *something she did not take in with her.* Something that will prove, as surely as engineers send a ball through an iron plate, leaving a hole where it passed, that spirit power can as surely convey a living organism, plant or animal, through iron doors and stone walls, leaving no marks of its passage.

The characterful rhetoric is undimmed. There is love and proud regard. He has been the donor. She did not come to him with diamonds. He seeks to establish his wife's social position by reference to his own wealth. But the Crown Jewels were sacred to the outraged public, and what they did not perceive was that this 'bet' was a monstrous joke, one of Mr Guppy's extravagant *jeux*, written with tongue-in-cheek. The *Telegraph* had an inkling:

It is hardly unfair to suspect that Mr Guppy was aware how safe a challenge he was making. Nobody, not even the Sovereign herself, has authority to dispose of the Crown jewels, or to pledge them in a wager – the Queen holds and uses them as virtually tenant for life. But surely Mr Guppy might offer a moderate bet. There are gentlemen who would be willing to win Mrs Guppy's diamonds if staked against something equivalent, or even more than equivalent; and a distinct victory of such a kind ought to be satisfactory to spiritualists if they wish their theories proved. It is generally supposed that they shrink from hard, cold, and scientific tests; dreading the fate of the unhappy gentleman who had to pay £500 because he would make a wager that the world was flat. Indeed, if Mr Guppy does reject our humble suggestion, we shall believe, despite his faith in the spirits, that he is a very sensible man in thus preferring his wife's diamonds to any doubtful demonstration of her spiritual powers.

How dry is that last remark?

A fair example of the indignant school, taking it all too seriously, is to be found in the *Era* of September 24th, 1871:

Fair play is said to be a jewel, but jewels in the case of Mr Samuel Guppy do not necessarily imply fair play. But who is this gentleman with the Dickensian appellation? Mr Samuel Guppy is altogether an extraordinary specimen of humanity. To begin with. He flatters himself that he lays a fair wager when he stakes his wife's diamonds against the Crown jewellery (to 'make it a national affair,' says the off-hand Guppy) that Mrs Samuel Guppy shall be examined by a jury of matrons ... There is something irritatingly absurd in all this. To attempt to make anyone believe that Mr Guppy had diamonds equal in value to the Crown jewels is tolerably cool to begin with, while the brag of pretending to 'make it a national affair' by staking diamonds of which no one has heard against jewels which the nation cannot touch, is sufficiently contemptible. The religion of spiritualism and the study of a most perplexing and difficult question are not advanced by mountebank wagers. The mysterious and awful difficulty of the spirit world, about which we know possibly as much as we ever shall, or are intended to know, remains just where it was, in spite of Davenport cabinets, Fry lectures, rope tricks, dark séances, and the elephantine gambols of Mr Guppy. Spiritualists, and by spiritualists we mean earnest, upright men, ought to be ashamed of the assistants who make the world stink in the nostrils of all who have clear brains and are not candidates for Hanwell [Asylum].

With invective of this severity offered to him, Mr Guppy, with his experience of India, should have heeded the bad omen which came to his house. As he told the editor of the *Spiritualist* on Wednesday, September 13th, 1871:

Sir, Three weeks ago a lady made me a present of a tame hawk, a kestrel. It had one wing clipped, and had a small chain to one leg – could fly a little. On Saturday last, I, wife, child, and nurse went on a visit to Mr S, Central Hill, Upper Norwood. We went by the 12.50 train. We left at home Mrs Parker, a relative, and Rosa, the servant. I requested Mrs Parker to feed my hawk, which had its perch on a photographic head-rest in my room, but was not fastened to it, as it was tame, and would let itself be handled.

That evening, at about 9.30 pm, at a séance at Mr S's, the company began proposing that each should ask the spirits for something. Mr Coleman said, 'I wish Mrs Guppy's hawk to be brought.' In a minute the hawk, dead, without its chain, was brought. The spirit said that the hawk had fled away at 9 o'clock and that a cat had killed it. On Sunday morning, at Mr S's, my wife was dressing; I was not up; something dropped on the bed; it was the hawk's chain. On Sunday afternoon, at 5, we returned home per train. I said to Mrs Guppy, 'Don't let us say anything about the hawk, but hear what they have to tell.' As soon as we entered our house, Mrs Parker said, 'Oh, Mr Guppy, we are in such trouble about the hawk. I went to feed it and it flew out of the window. I went into the garden and saw a black cat and flung a trowel at it.' Mrs Parker afterwards stated 'It was when the cuckoo-clock struck nine.'

Elizabeth Guppy must have been the first person to take a dead kestrel in her bag on the train to Upper Norwood. She was in good form, having been away to Ostend for a holiday, accompanied by little Tommy and the nurse.

Mr Guppy was mulling over the repercussions of his 'bet' and on October 15th, 1871, the *Spiritualist*, where he was very much *persona grata*, printed a long letter, a three-cigar effusion, from him at 2 Birchfield Road, Birchfields, Birmingham, where he was staying with a friend of scientific bent. Anyone who had taken the bet seriously could now see it is an 'elephantine gambol' with an elephant as the star turn. His habitual sense of the absurd was in full flow. It was a fantasy that was meant to disarm, making light of his unintended lese-majesty. Those spiritualists who had not read *Mary Jane* must have been bewildered by the flights of satire and the incorrigible digressions. Even Bohemian Agnes pops up again.

Standing first is a formal letter marked, 'To the Editor of the Daily Telegraph' and saying:

> Sir, I have received your editorial communication of the 19th inst., and observe that you have booked my bet, and hold me to it, and threaten me with the fate of the gentleman who wagered that the earth was flat, if I back out of it; or avail myself of the subterfuge that the crown jewels cannot be pledged in a wager.
>
> Very well; in all friendliness I say, 'Lay on Macduff.' I am willing to commute the value of the Crown Jewels at a very moderate sum – say three thousand pounds; a very trifle to you – and I would make a further bet that my wife would spend it all in a morning's shopping, of course I mean in absolute necessaries for herself and little Tommy.

Following this preamble, there is a draft of a ridiculous 'indenture' witnessing the lodging of the sum of £3000 against the Guppy diamonds, with three umpires – His Grace the

Archbishop of Canterbury, The Right Hon WE Gladstone, and
Mr John Bright.

The communication continues with a mis-named 'Postscript':

> I am in clover with a friend here; he begs me to bring
> you down with me next time; you'll see a letter from
> him shortly. Mine are not worth putting on the same
> file. You should see his studio – ultimate atoms bot-
> tled and labelled. Oxy-hydro-magnesia photographic
> apparatus, for magnifying and printing atoms.
> Branch of spirit post-office; invisible letters deliver
> and read themselves. Machine for weighing wishes.
> Mr Crookes has one also ... Mr Crookes says he
> weighed several ladies' wishes and found them very
> variable – pity he did not state particulars; however,
> I can supply some. My wife, at Naples, in a delicate
> condition had lots of wishes, corals, cameos, dia-
> monds, and once a young fox, which accounts for lit-
> tle Tommy being so sly. No, ma'am, she did not eat
> him; she put him in the orange garden and petted
> him. The way I managed was this – without letting
> my wife have the slightest idea that I was trying
> philosophical experiments on her, whenever she
> began wishing I gave her a full purse; then, by noting
> down the deficiency in pounds (and fractions) when
> she returned it to me I got accurate observations,
> and filled the purse (without her knowing it) ready
> for the next wish.
>
> I have compressed my letter, in order that its length
> may not be an obstacle to your giving it to an expec-
> tant public. The postscript you may find room for, or
> not, as you please. You see, this is a world-wide event;
> it will go through Europe, America, Australia, like
> an electric shock. The umpires are well chosen –
> men of the first calibre – they will not refuse to act
> ... Mr Bright has deserved well of his country; he is
> now angling; he might willingly exchange angling for

fish for angling for information from the spirit world. You will really have no trouble in the matter except signing the cheque. My wife will be the worst off; she will have to do without her diamonds while they are at the bankers.

I was frightened last night. Coming home late, in my friend's close carriage, from a visit some distance in the country – the night just such as a highwayman would choose – my friend began in a hollow sepulchral tone, not in his usual cheery voice: 'The "Telegraph" will hold you to your bet – you cannot get out of it.' Poor I, who only sought to shield my ill-used wife, to get in the claws of that hydraheaded monster the press. It took an honest glass of brandy and water hot to restore my nerves; I never was so *impressed* before but once, and that was when I was made a freemason. I tell it you short. In an unguarded moment – the ladies will understand me – I think I had taken too much champagne – I consented to allow myself to be proposed. I got a paper that I was accepted, and fixing the day. – I felt rather nervous, but like this bet could not back out. The eventful day came. I saw the author of my embarrassment in the morning; he was cheerful. As he was going away I falteringly said – 'Have you any hints to give me as to this evening?' 'No, no,' said he, 'nothing particular, only, you had better put on clean linen.' What my feelings were as I was conducted up that long passage, to rooms where neither screams nor groans could be heard outside, I leave your sensitive readers to imagine. I drop the curtain on that night.

By-the-bye, there is a great deal of nonsense in the "Daily News" of September 15th, signed "Walter Thornbury"; and among other platitudes he designates my wife as a 'fat lady denominated Guppy.' I hold the editor responsible; he ought not to take in such trash and put it in his shop window; however,

if he will write me a note and say he blushes for the
article, I will forgive him. I have a bet as to whether
an editor can blush. Besides, my wife is not fat; it is
all good solid flesh, with very little bone. I think I
ought to know. And if she *were* fat, I have not
offered her for sale, and therefore newspaper editors
and correspondents should keep their cattle-show
language for suitable occasions.

Referring to the grand Lambs Conduit Street séance, Mr Guppy
sticks to his guns over his reaction to his wife's disappearance:
the deputation sent to the house had found 'That, sad to say, Mr
Guppy so far relied on the spirit message so received, that he ate
a hearty supper and went to bed (and so I should again if I was
sleepy, without even insuring in the Accidents Company, for I
am satisfied that the most powerful monarch, and the most sav-
age tiger, are just as a tame rabbit in presence of that power).' His
trusting belief in spirit power has not lessened since the days of
Mary Jane: 'My opinion of familiar spirits is that people should
keep them at home and let them be useful in the family – not
parade them in public. One Sunday morning my wife came to
me and said the baker's boy did not come, and we had not a bit
of bread in the house. "Send for some." "The shops are all shut;
I don't know what to do." In two seconds a loaf of bread was
placed on the table. "Was that you, Katie?" "Yes".'
   The 'Postscript' is resumed on September 25th, and he is full
of assurances that he will not back out of the wager. This thought
sends him into a flight of reminiscence which is delightful for us
to read but was scarcely germane to the context:

> I never backed but once in my life – tell you how. I
> was just able to be trusted with a gig on a plain turn-
> pike road, when my father was obliged to let me take
> his through London city. The gig was quite new,
> dark green, patent springs and axles; my father had
> seen the patentee about them, and our black horse
> 'General' could carry sixteen stone safely across

country. I am intimate with horses; I paid Rarey [*v. ante*] ten guineas. Let me see a man's favourite cob, hack, and hunter, and I know the man.

I spent a winter in the Bohemian mountains. Any horse they could not manage they brought to me. Once I bought a mare of the Duke's forester; she had been two years in the forest because nobody could manage her. She was dun, wall-eyed, with three white legs. The cavalry riding master said he would not trust one of his men on her. She looked mischief. She had a peculiar habit of walking about on her hind legs, and rubbing your legs against the wheels of any wagon passing.

Fine times I had on those mountains. A covey of sledges would start for a ball fifteen miles off with the bells jingling. The bright moon on the snow-laden firs made it a fairy scene. Headlong down the mountain, now across the frozen brook, and up the hill. Look back. Five sledges have capsized in the brook; the spirits carried us safely over. In many a morning drive I have capsized a sledge load of Bohemian girls in the deep snow, but they only shook their feathers and jumped in again. But the saying in that country was - *who rides with Guppy should make his will first.* And then the ball; the Bohemian girls pouted if I forgot to ask an acquaintance to waltz, and the ball was not complete unless tall, slim Agnes, the banker's daughter, with black eyes and raven locks, and 'the young man of the name of Guppy' were there. Happy days; how stupid London seems. I shall go back there some day, and leave the sulphurous underground railway, and the overworked ministers, and the dilatory House of Commons to muddle along as well as they can ...

I forgot my father's horse and gig. He told me to be very careful in driving through the streets. I got into a jam, backed, and the pole of a gentleman's carriage

came crashing through the back panel. My father
was very angry. 'Don't back.' I philosophised, 'But if
you can't help it?' 'Then don't put yourself in a position where you can't help it.' This advice I give to
gentlemen thinking of proposing to ladies, and if
they follow it, there will not be so many actions for
breach of promise. After the bet is decided, as there
will be many people yet unconvinced and ready to
take odds, I shall be willing to bet the same thing
over again for trifles – say, a gross of champagne, a
case of Havanas, or a pony phaeton and pair for my
wife, and a Shetland for little Tommy.

This communication must be one of the strangest to have
appeared in the spiritualist columns. Inspired by his lyrical memories of his youth, Mr Guppy now moved into the whirling display of his pantomime. He imagines the advance publicity, remu-
nerative to the *Telegraph*.

Quotations of bet from London, Paris, New York,
Vienna – Emperor of China and Mikado of Japan
shake their heads and wonder what their Sister is
doing – King of Siam orders treble guards round his
White Elephant – Letters from Special
Correspondents – *Mrs Guppy Drove out in Highbury
Hill Park, attended by her Italian Nurse with Little
Tommy.* Description of Italian nurse, age nineteen,
brunette, – can't speak a word of English – strong
suspicions that she is an accomplice – looks inno-
cent – all the more dangerous – chemical composi-
tion of woman C+H+Ph. – Very combustible –
Serious Accidents from getting too near them in a
Ballroom.
   Visit of the Editor to Highbury Hill Park –
Brilliant Escort of Subs and Special Correspondents
– Legions of Printers' Devils in Attendance – Subs
and Special accommodated with a case of

Champagne and box of Havanas in North Saloon. Katie takes Printers' Devils into the séance room and treats them to hot ginger-bread nuts and burning snapdragon, which were brought in her usual way through the walls, the door being locked ...

Day of Trial Comes – Great Excitement – 'Telegraph' not to be had for love or money – all bespoke – Procession of Mrs Guppy to the Bank – Reception by the Directors – Her entrance into the Bank Vaults – Sacks of Sovereigns – Piles of Ingots of Gold – Bales of Bank Notes. *She is shut in – Wild betting* rather in favour of the Diamonds – LIGHT!!! – IT IS THE ELEPHANT – He is munching some carrots – How did he get there? – Some suggest by a secret branch of the Underground Railroad, privately made by the Directors to carry away Bullion in case the Prussians should come – Railway officials examined – Several Dogs and a few Cats passed on the line, but no Elephant – Might have come by a Goods Train – Couldn't fly, having no wings – Objected that Mr Home flew out of one window and in at another – How long did he take coming? Referred to the Royal Society – Royal Society says that unless the time of departure from the Zoological was accurately noted by a chronometer they cannot take notice of the event, and would not take notice of the sun unless he kept Greenwich time – Keeper says he don't know; threw him a basket of carrots and bolted the door – How long does it take an Elephant to eat a mouthful of carrots? – Objections: he might have stopped at a Greengrocer's on the road – Further objections – 'What is time?' 'Time is a succession of events' – Objected, that a Toad in a Rock for 500 years has no events – Toad an exception – if *you* drink six glasses of Brandy-and-water while I am fast asleep you have six events and I have none – Some people say, 'I have plenty of time,' others 'I have no time at all.' Has one person more time than another?

Mrs Guppy's return to Highbury Hill Park – Elephant cannot be got out – being hungry, *eats Bank Notes*. Deputation of Bank Directors to Mrs Guppy requesting her to hold a séance at the Zoological Gardens, and have the Elephant carried back the way he came – She graciously accedes to their request. Heavy betting on that event – Light!!! – The Elephant is brought back; *he has a package of Bank Notes in his trunk* – Directors of Bank summon Elephant before the magistrates, with Mrs Guppy and Katie as accomplices – Eminent Counsel employed on both sides – Damages laid at £200,000; £50,000 of notes eaten, £150,000 carried away. Counsel for Elephant admit that he ate, but deny that he carried away the first £50,000, and ask leave to bring evidence. Leave granted – Evidence brought in a wheelbarrow ...

Case remanded – Parties allowed to give bail – Zoological give bail for the Elephant – Mrs Guppy and Katie refuse to give bail – Magistrate orders them to be locked up – Counsel suggests that the only place to lock Mrs Guppy up in is her husband's arms, as no other prison would hold her – Magistrate orders Police to take up Katie – Police officers get their ears boxed by unseen hands – Raps all over the court – Magistrate's wig pulled off – Shower of Lobsters, Eels, red Herrings, and Periwinkles, mixed with the contents of ten feather beds – The chairs and tables begin dancing a quadrille, and the Court breaks up in confusion ...

The echoes of *Alice in Wonderland* (1865) are obvious. Whether or not Mr Guppy's surprised readers found his rather childish gambols totally hilarious, it is difficult to estimate. It is uncomfortable to witness his making fun of the subject in which he believes so passionately. His peroration, unexpectedly, is a plea for true mediumship to be rewarded financially.

After these exciting events, Mr Guppy's interest in spiritualism seems to have been reinvigorated, and he took to holding séances on his own account when Elizabeth was unavailable. He trusted Herne and Williams, whom he had named in his recent tract as examples of sound mediums receiving inadequate remuneration for their services. It is apparent that he had accepted the idea of spirits and their recall, and vaporous Mary Jane had evaporated. One of his new theories was that most of the power for producing direct spirit voices was drawn from the spine of the medium (the *Spiritualist* December 1st, 1872). Mrs Guppy was pregnant again in 1872 and Samuel, the second son, was born in the autumn. On November 15th, the *Spiritualist* commented politely that she, having of course been unable to sit for manifestations for some time, had 'begun to hold séances once more, and her very powerful mediumship will, doubtless, before long reach its full strength again.' She obviously had not yet entirely recovered, because at one séance only a few raps came, and at another, improving, a large bunch of chrysanthemums and some raps, pleased the sitters.

Meanwhile, Mr Guppy, not unlike Sir Arthur Conan Doyle, had taken to championing the underdog. He was drawn to the criminal case of Maria Giles alias Tranter, having read in the *Daily Telegraph*, November 1st, that she had been sentenced to five years penal servitude by the Recorder for Newbury (Mr Dowdeswell) for obtaining a sum of money by false pretences. Two women, one from a wild district in North Hampshire, had lost some goods while returning from Reading market, and consulted the 'cunning woman of Newbury', as she was known locally, in an attempt to recover their property. She said that she could help them, and went through an 'absurd ceremony', producing a glass, and pretending to bring up in it an image of the thief. She said that she ruled the stars, and if the nights were fine she would get quicker results. They paid her a shilling each, on contingency. She had been convicted six or seven times previously for similar offences. The Recorder said that such practices as those which the prisoner had shown for many years past as her livelihood were a scandal to society.

Mr Guppy expostulated: 'At first it appeared to me an illusion. Again and again I read it. "Five years penal servitude!" An elderly woman, no doubt. I imagined a kind of Mrs Gamp, taken from her comfortable home at a period of life, perhaps, when failing health demands every comfort. I began to reflect on the principles of punishment ... Now this woman had told fortunes, or given advice, true or false, about recovery of stolen goods. A servant-maid, or a carriage-lady, goes to her, consults her, and pays a shilling or half-a-crown. She pretends to rule the stars. Well, the Pope pretends to infallibility. However, these parties are not injured in person, and if they preferred spending the shilling or half-a-crown with her, or in a playhouse, or in a gin-shop, what grounds for punishment exist? I determined I would go to Newbury and inquire.'

He asked Mr Serjeant Cox, the well-known and respected spiritualist, and a friend, to provide him with a certificate to vouch for his status as an investigator, because, as an outsider and not recognised in Newbury, he might otherwise have been unwelcome. He also asked his lawyer to provide him with an abstract of the laws on of witchcraft. *Mary Jane* is full of his scathing references to the persecution of so-called witches, and it was a subject that he felt very strongly about. Just at this time, however, while he was considering the matter, he fell very ill with inflammation of the lungs, which prevented him from leaving the house. Still unable to get Mrs Tranter out of his head, as he put it, he deputed his neighbour and friend, Mr Hudson, the fellow billiards player, and photographer, to proceed to Newbury by the 10.15 train, and make his report, like Dr Watson.

Frederick Hudson darted efficiently around Newbury and had no difficulty in finding people who would speak to Mrs Tranter's good character: Mr Mathews, the hairdresser, Mr and Mrs Statey, who kept the Dolphin Inn, and Mr Brown, the builder. They all said that she was a sober, hard-working woman, a midwife, who was willing to nurse any poor person. Mr Brown said that she told fortunes with two glasses – like globes – and that he thought that the callers who implicated her were actually detectives. Brown passed Mr Hudson on to Tranter, the husband, who worked for him. Apparently Maria, at 58, was not quite the aged crone of Mr Guppy's imagination, but he was correct as to avocation. She had a son, who was a policeman in London, and a daughter who was in an asylum. Maria asked for very little money, and, importantly, had not had means to employ counsel. It seemed that local people had been getting up a petition.

Convinced that Mrs Tranter had been unjustly convicted and sentenced, Mr Guppy continued: 'I have placed the case in the most unfavourable light. Seven times has this woman been convicted, otherwise a most exemplary woman. But again, I ask, supposing in every street in London there was a cunning woman who told fortunes and gave advice about stolen property, where is the injury to person or property warranting any punishment whatever? As to witchcraft, if witches and wizards are punishable, then all the committee of the Dialectical Society are punishable.' He followed up this rather unsettling point with a conclusion that shows all too clearly that he was not a man of the law: 'The first thing we have to find out is whether, in the opinion of highly-educated men, there was any ground for imprisoning this woman at all. If there were not, the law ought not to exist a single hour longer than would suffice to blot it out from the statute-book as a stain on the national character. And after that would come the consideration what damages should be awarded to Mrs Tranter.' The *Spiritualist* thoroughly endorsed Mr Guppy's excellent letter, which might perhaps, they thought, result in saving the life of an elderly woman, and, 'Will some member of Parliament take up Mr Guppy's case, and draw the attention of the House of Commons to the laws relating to witchcraft?'

One day in 1871, Mr Guppy went into Pulvermacher's and paid 50s for a 'galvanic belt' as a remedy for his old enemy, gout, wore it for three months, got better (as could have happened naturally) and left it off. Then, 'On Saturday, 18th January (1873), several friends called (I am a bachelor at present, wife at Crystal Palace), among them Williams, the medium. I asked him to stay,

as I wanted to try something. After various trials the spirit directed us to hold each an end of the chain in opposite hands ...
Instantly up went the little table a foot, as though it were a feather, and danced about in the air. Williams then had to go and give
a séance in Lambs Conduit Street. On Sunday, 19th, young JC
came, a powerful medium, but not fully developed, and in indif-
ferent health. I tried the galvanic belt with him, but though he
felt the effect it did not act as in the case with Williams – in fact
the spirit said, "Take it away".'

Until he lost interest, Mr Guppy and his friends obtained satisfactory results from the chain, with blue lights streaming along
it. They dipped it in vinegar'd water, and an electric shooting was
felt in the arm and hand showing that an electric shock – very
possibly conducive to health – was being transmitted. Still he was
trying to link science to spiritualism. The editor of the *Spiritualist*
(issue of February 1st, 1873), appending a jocular footnote, did
not appear to be impressed:

> The experiments should be repeated many times,
> and a galvanometer should be placed in circuit to
> indicate what is really taking place, in order to make
> sure that John King did not mischievously gave an
> unusually good 'hoist' to the table in the ordinary
> way. The pranks of John King and the very lively
> spirit D [who, according to Mr Guppy, 'if not under
> control, would soon make mincemeat of all the fur-
> niture of a room' and was always asking for darkness]
> have to be taken into consideration. Mr Guppy had
> better buy another chain, without much fear of his
> house being carried away; [as Mr D, the spirit, had
> threatened if a second chain were added to give extra
> force to the experiments] indeed, if it were carried
> away, and seen sailing over London with Mr Guppy
> smoking placidly on the verandah, while making a
> novel trip in this way to the south of France for the
> winter, the event would be a glorious one for spiritu-
> alism, and Mr Guppy might return to England the

greatest Aladdin of modern times. Let him get
another chain by all means, and defy 'the spirit D' to
do his worst.

While the Guppys' Highbury abode was regularly darkened for
séances, and, no doubt, the neighbours, never mentioned, wondered at the traffic of frequent callers, Miss Houghton's congenial séances at home, however, were not destined to go on forev-
er. She had been unsettled by the intense experience of her exhibition and its financial consequences, and a new passion – for
spirit photography – was taking her over. On April 20th 1872 she
told her faithful circle that this was their last sitting. There was
devastation. Mrs Tebb said that she had known it. Elizabeth,
who had already lost Mrs Berry's regard and support, was most
upset: Mrs Tebb went into a trance after supper, but Elizabeth
felt ill, (being pregnant as well as bereft) and quietly slipped away
home to the comfort of Samuel Guppy. Symbolically, Miss
Houghton took down the layers of curtain material which had
shut out every chink of light from the séance room and recycled
it for more mundane purposes. She went regularly to Highbury,
by public transport.

A new visitor was turning up at Highbury in 1873 – Mr
William Volckman – a polished man of wealth from trade, of
polite, investigatory type – and no mortal being there present
could have predicted his future significance in the fortunes of
Mrs Guppy. Both Elizabeth and Samuel took to him, and they
became friends. On October 16th, he asked for a sunflower, that
rayed emblem of warmth, optimism and adoration, and the spirits dug up a tall one roots and all from the Guppy garden. On
another, unpleasant occasion, a live eel was revealed wrapped
around Mrs Guppy's neck, and she screamed and screamed.
Another live eel was writhing on the table, with a live lobster.
Miss Houghton bore them off gleefully in a basket and ate them,
not all at once.

Elizabeth was very nearly caught one night. It was June 23rd
1874, and the manifestations had been going so well. A bla-
tantly suspicious circular hole, with a hinge, had been cut in

the table by prior direction of the spirits and objects were being upthrust successfully. Mr Volckman received a long, fresh cherry-tree branch. It was not the one that had been taken to his own chambers at a recent séance, the one that he had asked to be re-transported, but it would suffice. Mr Guppy had had enough, and he went upstairs to play billiards. Perhaps that was wise. Sceptical Mr H was still there in the darkness, and the spirits decided to inflict grossly painful pin-pricks on his skin. He complained that they were one-inch deep, and he could endure no more. Up he sprang: 'Oh! I have got him! A light, quickly!'

'Hold fast,' said Mrs Guppy, as cool as ocean ice. 'And do make haste with the light!' But the first match missed, and Mr H carried on struggling violently with the mischievous entity he had caught. By the time that the candle had been lit, he had fallen, vanquished, on the ottoman, panting and breathless. He declared that he had got his arms around someone who seemed as large as himself – and he was tall and stout – and that he had seen something by the faint light of the first match before it went out. Mrs Guppy said that she was vexed that he had not retained his grip of the spirit. Mr Volckman had had to leave early to catch his train and he had missed the drama, but he would have been very, very interested, and soon he was to become the most famous spirit catcher of them all. For some reason, 'Katie' desired that Mr H's name should not be written up for publication.

The year of 1873 was marred for Mrs Guppy by a distasteful incident which was avidly reported in the general press. It was not so much that she was in danger – she could take care of herself – as that the newspapers mocked her mercilessly. She was going to find herself in court a number of times – this was the first – always as plaintiff or complainant, and never, absolutely never, as accused under the Witchcraft Acts. In this case, at Bow Street Magistrates' Court, a rogue cabman, Edward Thomas Vialls, was charged on a summons with wilful misbehaviour towards Mrs Elizabeth Guppy. The magistrate was the well-known Frederick Flowers (1810-86).

Accompanied by a friend, probably Miss Neyland, Elizabeth had been intent on going home to her husband and infants after attending a 'campanological séance' – that is, a variation when, through specialist mediums, hand-bells were rung by spirits in the darkness. This occasion may well have been the grand affair, attended by 60 people, when a benefit was given at the Spiritual Institution, 15 Southampton Row, in aid of Mr Cogman's Spiritual Institution at Mile End. Mrs Guppy was recorded as presiding over a secondary séance in the front room, supported by Miss Houghton and others, while Mrs Berry, in the back room assisted with the bells.

A gallant gentleman from the séance had hired a cab for Mrs Guppy and her companion and had paid the legal fare in advance for the long trip to Highbury. Mrs Guppy noticed that the horse was very quiet. The load was heavy, and the driver was fuming. He had already been paid. They had only reached Gower Street, when he pulled up and announced that the horse was a kicker. Unless they wanted their brains kicked out, they should alight. Mrs Guppy refused, unless he called another cab and repaid the fare. Vialls swore at them, and denounced them as 'a couple of Regent Street women.' Would he have said this if he saw that Mrs Guppy was a real lady? He got down in a paddy and actually unharnessed the horse there and then in the street, claiming that the tack had broken. The horse stood still, bare and bewildered, but enjoying the rest. Then the driver denied that the fare had been paid. Mrs Guppy had scrambled out, and he advanced towards her, with menace. She opened her umbrella and he dashed it to the ground and broke it. There must have been by-standers, because the police were called.

Vialls was defiant in the dock and said that the ladies had used bad language to him, but the magistrate declared that he did not remember hearing such a bad case. He sentenced the defendant to one month's hard labour, and suspended his licence for two months, but, as his family starved, the damage had been done to Mrs Guppy as the newspapers revived her famous transport across the chimney-tops and enquired why the spirits had not come to her aid this time.

Round about this period, Elizabeth, all jolly, took another cab ride (nine in a cab, she said merrily, so presumably it was a four-wheeler) to the August 'Spiritualists' Picnic'. This way-out gathering took place at the People's Garden, at Willesden, a 50-acre plot reclaimed from the scrubbiest part of Wormwood Scrubs. There were donkey races, and one-and-ninepenny teas, with which the spititualists regaled themselves in the most material fashion – none more so, no doubt, than Mrs Guppy. The Revd CM Davies, in his *Mystic London* (*op. cit.*, p.284-9 and also p.108-115) is our roving reporter here and shamefully, he, too, asked if Elizabeth had been 'floated' from Highbury, but she took it in good part. 'All the medium-power of London seemed present,' entering into the spirit of the outing, 'and the only wonder was that we were not all floated bodily away.' There was croquet, and dancing on the largest platform in the world, and the Osborne Bellringers gave a concert but failed to show their fabled powers of levitation. Samuel Guppy seems to have stayed at home.

There was a sad feeling of the end of an era when Mrs Mary Marshall, senior, died on February 12th, 1875, at the age of 76. *Thus* (to adopt the eulogy published in the *Medium*) *the faithful servant of the spirit was buried by her brethren, and a wreath of immortelles was laid on her coffin.* An unlettered woman, poor, under-privileged, she had lit the fuse of mid-19th-century spiritualism in London and influenced the minds of a surprising number of the intelligentsia.

The 'poor old lady' had been confined to her bed, and virtually destitute, but Miss Houghton and Mrs Tebb kept on visiting, and raised a subscription, which, in the end, defrayed the funeral expenses. Her countenance in her coffin was quite placid. The dissenters' service was read as they buried her in Paddington Cemetery, and, later, a tree was planted on her grave (no. 4004). She lay in unconsecrated ground because of what it was thought she believed. 'With none of the advantages of education, fortune, or social position, she was a simple-minded religious woman, who, in the words of the Catechism, did her duty in that state of life into which it had pleased God to call her. Faithful in the exercise of her gifts, she encountered with great good-humour the obloquy, ridicule and abuse often heaped upon her by the unthinking, especially by flippant, conceited writers in the public journals.' That was the view of Thomas Shorter, joint editor of the *Spiritual Magazine*.

Miss Houghton thought it right to say that, 'She had one weakness, poor dear, and that was aggravated by a weak head, so that a small quantity of liquor of any kind would, I understand, overcome her, but in my own experience, I have never witnessed any symptom of it, only I know that the accusation had been made.'

An old friend of Mrs Marshall, known only as 'Ruth' conveyed her reminiscences to the *Medium*:

> Mrs Marshall's parents lived in the East End of London. Her father was connected with the merchant shipping, and brought much that way at that time highly interesting from foreign parts to his family. The mother, a careful, devoted creature, became much astonished and often bewildered with the conduct of her infant daughter Mary Anne.
>
> When at an age to talk this child often predicted her father's voyages, and often made astonishing declarations of events she said she saw, heard, or knew, when no one around her could understand the source from which all this was derived. Her sister also constantly saw spirit-forms, and spoke from spirit-control respecting various events. Mr Marshall was by trade a cooper, and lived in the city, near Thames Street. His house was a centre for conviviality. Many of our public journalists were frequently to be found there. Hospitality and most extraordinary information went hand-in-hand there, and no reserve or holding back was the practice. Whoever chanced to drop in was welcome; strangers went away informed; and those who were regular visitors always found a round table with creaturely supports, and all heartily welcomed.

This went on up to the year 1856, when Mr Marshall passed away after a few days' illness, during which I visited him, and also attended the funeral at Bethnal Green. He was with us in spirit. From that date Mrs Marshall's career has been well known, and able pens can testify to her labours in her mission. One feature of her when a girl, I should like to mention. Mrs Marshall was a very industrious and ingenious needlewoman. She supported herself in very early life at embroidery. Fashion then required muslin dresses to be worked with sprigs. She had spirit-guidance to many a tasty pattern, which sold well and secured to her West End employers, so that she was always famous among business people, being always active and never at a loss, never hiding the spirit-directions she received.

Poor Mrs Tebb was haunted by the decline and death of Mrs Marshall. In trance, she addressed Miss Houghton in the persona of the departed medium, complaining that she was not at all happy; she had imagined that she would go at once to a heavenly home, but she had found no dwelling-place, and was just a poor, wandering, homeless spirit. It was the drink, she confessed with shame. Nor could she find a resting-place on earth, for if she went back to her old rooms, the same atmosphere of drink was hanging about the place and made her feel worse.

Mrs Tebb saw her ghost on an omnibus taking her to visit Miss Houghton: when she looked again, she had vanished. Contrary to popular belief, the spiritualists in these circles were not always seeing ghosts, and this was quite an unusual story, but Mrs Tebb did seem to attract ghosts. She thought that her former house in Dalston had been haunted, and it was difficult to keep servants. There were noises of a pistol shot, and a weight being dragged, and they felt that they were being throttled. Mr Tebb experienced the phenomena with her, and they both heard rustling movements following them as they looked over a house in Oakley Square, Camden.

These were 'real' phantoms, unlike Elizabeth's fabricated beings in her faked childhood. The ghost that was wanted, the most desired phenomenon of the spiritualist movement, was the spirit materialised through the influence of the entranced medium, who provided a passage back to the world of the living. If the lost Persephone could emerge from the curtains of the cabinet that still held the form of the medium, and walk and talk appropriately, there was the certainty of survival. Touch and sound were not enough. The ideal spirit-made-flesh, clothed in ethereal drapery, had to be seen in glory, illuminated with a streaming, eerie light. The medium had to be established as a separate entity, bound with ropes or threads. The risk of impersonation by the escaped medium, or a second party, was only too obvious. The active, experimental mediums were all working at it – the Holy Grail – and the stakes were high.

Meanwhile, a whole new world of ghost possibilities was opening up. Old-fashioned, sheeted phantasms were to take their psychic entrances into the spaces around the sitters in posed photographs, their heads bowed, their faces not very distinct in their veiling. Spirit photography was coming.

6

A Cast of Extras

FREDERICK HUDSON, THE PHOTOGRAPHER, LIKED to tell people that his house at 177 Holloway Road was haunted when he took the lease in 1871. It had been standing empty for more than a year, and at first he and his family were troubled by strange noises, which only ceased when he had a glass-house – a studio – put up in the garden. Mr Hudson (1818-1900), Samuel Guppy's billiards partner, was quite a famous photographer, for a time, when he branched into the esoteric and exacting art of spirit photography, finding it, briefly, more rewarding than ordinary portraiture, but more wearing upon the constitution. We have an image of his worn, foxy face and also a first hand, if phrenological description: 'He seemed about fifty-six years of age (actually 74 in 1873), of a sanguine nervous temperament, much like a retired actor; he possessed a good frontal brain, but low in the executive organs; self-esteem, firmness, and the instinct of persistence being all defective – a man you would not take for a deceiver, yet one you might suppose would be easily led.'

This commentator, John Beattie, a solid, professional photographer of Bristol, who was open to spiritualism, has left a sketch of the operative studio where miracles were done: 'We then went out to a garden and into as common a glass-house as any I have been in for years. It had an A shaped roof, with light on both sides. The side and roof lights were curtained with what had once been white but were now yellow curtains. At one end was a background painted seemingly in oil colour, of the usual tint. This stood about two feet from the wall, leaving room for a person to sit or stand in a partially dark place behind it. At the other end the usual operating room, freely lighted with yellow light.'

The space at the back was nefariously useful.

Frederick Augustus Hudson was born in January, 1818, in London. His father, Charles Augustus Hudson, who married (secondly) at St George's, Bloomsbury, Margaret Martyn, was described variously as 'carver and guilder' and 'gentleman'. Frederick's wife was Esther Eliza Goodrum, born in London in 1822. They married in 1841, at St Margaret's, Westminster, and they had a family of seven children, no doubt a causal factor of their financial problems. At first, Frederick made little progress in his married life, working as a 'porter' and living at 21 Regent Street, but then he discovered photography, the scientific invention of 1838, which opened up a new trade ideal for persons of no particular qualifications, but equipped with intelligence and flair. Small studios sprang up all over the place, and the photographers tended to move on to new territory when they had exhausted the demand locally. Frederick had studios, in succession, at 4 Upper Holland Street, Kensington (1862-3), 6 Victoria Grove, Kensington (1864-7), 6 Verulam Terrace, The Grove, Hammersmith (1865-9), and also had an interest in Ventnor, Isle of Wight (1866-9); a partnership there was dissolved in 1874. It can be seen that he was an experienced practitioner.

The haunted Holloway house in 1871 was filled with the Hudson family. Visitors had the impression of a pack of children running in and out of the rooms. Rosabel (22), a pretty girl, was her father's right-hand assistant in both orthodox and supernatural photography, and very probably an occasional 'spirit' in the sinistral part of the practice. Margaret Lydia, the eldest child, (born 1842-3) acted as receptionist, and Emma Sarah (born 1849) was a photographic assistant. Charles was 17, and Frederick (the younger) was only five-years-old. Esther, their mother, looked after them all, on a shoestring.

At some stage in his career, Frederick Hudson made the risky and momentous decision to diversify his business and augment his much-needed income. He never seemed to have sufficient capital funds. Spirit photography had a bad history, but, even now, people of the most sceptical nature are intrigued by an unexpected shape or mist on a photograph – a pillar or cloud hovering on a staircase, a transparent 'face' that seems familiar. Hudson himself is credited with being the first practitioner in England to succeed in producing 'extras' commercially, that is, formally, repeatedly, not by happenstance. The spiritualists pronounced him to be a medium and he played up to the rôle, claiming to be spiritually directed by rappings. He actively encouraged mediums, both sincere and false to frequent his studio in order to facilitate the efforts of the thronging, waiting spirits to make entry into the images.

The haunted house became a nest of mediums, a favourite place of resort, some of them conniving, producing cooperative effects, and there was real and tangible profit for those who wanted it, all under the wand of the master craftsman, Frederick Hudson. He became a nervous wreck, tremulous, quaking, the antithesis of the confident, roistering mediums of professional type. Here came hurrying Mrs Guppy, Mrs Everitt, and Herne and Williams, all as potentiating mediums, the last two undoubtedly receiving their fees, their cut. Hudson charged one guinea for three photographs, taken with the understanding that extras were highly desirable, but might not materialise. Surely Mrs Guppy, known for her private status, known to have married well, would not have put her hand out for a spot of pin-money of her own?

The sessions were like an extension of the séances without the formal circle, with familiar, bustling presences. Here came Mrs Tebb, ardent, prone to trance, never questioning the truth of the proceedings, and her dear friend, Miss Houghton, very close to Mr Hudson, supporting him in his tribulations, and feverishly magnetising everything in sight – the photographic plates, the developing fluids, the very chairs the sitters sat upon, and even the spaces where the spirits might appear. Surprisingly, even uncomfortably, to relate, Georgiana Houghton, who was glad of the money, seeing no wrong, happily accepted a fee from some sitters by arrangement for her mediumistic services. She had no inkling that Hudson was faking his results and cheating his clients, but she did feel unease when he was challenged by others. She was very loyal to him, and he put up with her when, on occasions, she stood beside him and monitored his undeniably clever processes.

What amazes us now is that the sitters could be fooled by such ludicrous, clumsy shams, made-up props like Guy Fawkes dummies, with crude masks, and accomplices swathed in muslin which made them look ghostly, but also shrouded their faces. The spiritualists' view, in the words of Arthur Russel Wallace, was that 'the human form is more difficult to materialise than drapery. The conventional "white-sheeted ghost" was not, then, all fancy, but had a foundation in fact – a fact, too, of deep significance, dependent on the laws of a yet unknown chemistry.'

It was up to the sitters, often painfully bereaved, to make the leap of recognition, not always at the time, but later, upon reflection, not willing to relinquish the imagined shock of reunion. Emotions were heightened to the extreme. That was what happened to Wallace:

> On March 14th, 1874, I went to Hudson's, by appointment, for the first and only time, accompanied by Mrs Guppy, as medium. I expected that if I got any spirit picture it would be that of my eldest brother, in whose name messages had frequently been received through Mrs Guppy. Before going to Hudson's I sat with Mrs G., and had a communication by raps with the effect that my mother would appear on the plate if she could. I sat three times, always choosing my own position. Each time a second figure appeared on the negative with me ... I recognised none of these figures in the negative; but the moment I got the proofs, the first glance showed me that the third plate contained an unmistakable portrait of my mother, like her both in features and in expression; not such a likeness as a portrait taken during life, but a somewhat pensive, idealised likeness.

Still I did not see the likeness in the second picture till a few weeks back I looked at it with a magnifying glass, when I at once saw a remarkable special feature of my mother's natural face, an unusually projecting lower jaw and lip. This was most conspicuous some years ago, as latterly the mouth was somewhat contracted. A photograph taken 22 years ago shows this peculiarity very strongly, and corresponds well with the second picture, in which the mouth is partly open and the lower lip projects greatly. This figure had always given me the impression of a younger person than that in the third picture, and it is remarkable that they correspond respectively with the character of the face as seen in photographs taken at intervals of about twelve years; yet without the least resemblance to these photographs either in attitude or expression. Both figures carry a bunch of flowers exactly in the same way; and it is worthy of notice that, while I was sitting for the second picture, the medium said – 'I see someone, and it has flowers' – intimating that she saw the flowers distinctly, the figure only very faintly. Here, then, are two different faces representing the aspect of a deceased person's countenance at two periods of her life; yet both the figures are utterly unlike any photograph ever taken of her during her life. How these two figures, with these special peculiarities of a person totally unknown to Mr Hudson could appear on his plates, I should be glad to have explained. Even if he had by some means obtained possession of all the photographs ever taken of my mother, they would not have been of the slightest use to him in the manufacture of these pictures.

These reflections appear in Wallace's *Miracles of Modern Spiritualism* (1875, pp.190-1) and Georgiana Houghton shows the portrait of Mrs Wallace in her *Chronicles of the Photographs of Spiritual Beings* (1882, Plate VI, no. 49).

What Wallace never touches upon, while adopting the received view that Hudson was the first to succeed in England, is the possibility that Mrs Guppy herself was the pioneer in the field. When she 'resolved for several reasons of a private nature, to perfect herself in photography and painting,' no one mentioned that her choice was spirit photography. Yet, in 1875, in his *Mystic London* (pp 347-8) the Revd Charles Maurice Davies, who was a kind of reluctant, careful, séance-attending spiritualist, and also an excellent observer of all manner of esoterica, describes an experience which goes exactly to this point:

> A now celebrated medium, Mrs Guppy, née Miss Nicholl, was, in the days of her maidenhood, a practitioner of photography in Westbourne Grove; and, as far as I know, she might have been the means of opening up to the denizens of the Summer Land this new method of terrestrial operations. Ever on the *qui vive* for anything new in the occult line, I at once interviewed Miss Nicholl and sat for my portrait, expecting at the least to find the attendant spirit of my departed grandmamma or defunct maiden aunt standing sentinel over me, as I saw departed relations doing in many cartes de visite in the room. I confess there was a kind of made-up theatrical property look about the attendant spirits which gave one the idea that the superior intelligences must have dressed in a hurry when they sat or stood for their portraits. They looked, in fact, if it be not irreverent to say it, rather like so many bundles of pneumatical rags than respectable domestic ghosts. However, as long as I got the ghosts I did not care about the dress. *Tenue de soir point de rigeur*, I would have said, as they do outside in the cheap casinos in Paris, or 'Evening dress not required,' if one must descend to the vernacular.
>
> Well, I sat persistently and patiently through I am afraid to say how many operations, and the operator

described me as surrounded by spirits – I always am according to Mediums, but my spirits must be eminently unsociable ones, for they seldom give me a word, and on this occasion refused to be 'taken' ... There was indeed a blotch on one of the negatives, which I was assured was a spirit. I could not see things in that light.

Foiled on this particular occasion my anxiety was dormant, but never died out. I still longed for a denizen of the other world to put in an appearance, and kept on being photographed over and over again until I might have been the vainest man alive, on the bare hope that the artist might be a Medium *malgré lui* or undeveloped. I had heard there were such beings, but they never came in my way. I was really serious in this wish, because I felt if it could be granted, the possibility of deception being prevented, the objectivity of the phenomena would be guaranteed. At this time I was heretical enough to believe that some ghosts were due to underdone pork or untimely Welsh rare-bits, and that the raps assigned to their agency were assignable to the active toes of the Medium which might be anywhere and up to anything with the opportunities of a dark séance.

The Revd Davies' prevailing tone was whimsical and even facetious – he was a skilled journalist of his time – and should not be taken to indicate a slanting of the truth of his observations. What he said he saw, he saw. No evidence has been found in the literature that he was regarded as anything but a reliable witness. If we take a strongly analytical writer – Trevor H Hall, the author of *The Spiritualists: The Story of Florence Cook and William Crookes* – when he looks closely at Davies' attendance at the Cook séances, he has no adverse criticism of his comments.

The time frame for Miss Nicholl to be selling spirit photographs 'in the days of her maidenhood' extends from her tuition by Fanny Sims in 1864 to the end of 1867, when she married

Samuel Guppy. From other allusions in his *Mystic London*, it is clear that Davies' acquaintance with Mrs Guppy continued after his visit to her studio. That is, he knew her in her marital status, and he was so specific about her single status that it is difficult to see how he would have made a mistake about the time.

The locus of the commercial enterprise, with its many successes displayed upon the walls, is powerfully evidential. Westbourne Grove is the exact area where the Sims' lived and worked when Elizabeth went to them as a pupil. Indeed, the Sims family positively colonised the Grove with their various studios. Edward Sims, Thomas's brother, also a photographer, had studios at 4 Sussex Terrace, 59 Westbourne Grove, and 13 Westbourne Grove between 1857 and 1861.

William Grinsell Nicholl had already taught Elizabeth the basics of photography. The perfection that she sought in Westbourne Grove appears to have been of the deviant kind, and it stands her up as a *professional* psychic practitioner, offering her services unashamedly for payment. Even if Elizabeth made up and draped the 'extras' herself, and operated her camera without help, it is obvious that Thomas and Fanny Sims must have known what she was doing, in a shop nearby that could easily have been one of their own. Fanny's rôle in all this is fragile. Wallace is silent. But he was not against spirit photography, nor did his enthusiasm for it wane.

Is there a factor in all this that is the cause of Thomas Sims' decision to decamp with Fanny to Tunbridge Wells, Kent, in 1868? He knew about spiritualism, but abhorred it. Away from the London scene, they lived at 5 Calverly Park Villas, and then at 3 Prospect Road, and Edward Sims was already resident in the little spa town, with its chalybeate spring, staying there from 1864 to 1868. Thomas had re-invented himself, and was now a 'portrait and landscape painter.' Years later, by 1891, Thomas and Fanny were back in London at 70 Lillie Road, Fulham, and Thomas lived until 1910, when, on November 14th, he died in Tunbridge Wells at the age of eighty-three. He was a widower.

Surely someone must have taught Elizabeth, from scratch, how to doctor the photographs? The people who were doing it were doing it for money. This was no sphere for a genuine person, acting in a trance, or convinced that she was influenced by spirit direction, to tinker with the science. Miss Houghton had taught herself amateur photography as early as 1856, and, in 1864, acting in concert with a spiritualist named Mr Tiffin, thought that they had obtained indistinct faces, although 'his chemicals were out of order, and the result was a very bad something, neither a negative nor a positive.' Two years earlier, she had read in the *Spiritual Magazine* about William Mumler's production of his first spirit photograph (November 5th, 1862) and she had bought the packet of three copies offered by that magazine. Miss Nicholl might also have been a purchaser.

First of all, in England, in 1851, there had been Richard Boursnell (1832-1909) but his partner complained that he was spoiling the plates, so he desisted, and was not fêted by spiritualists until 40 years later. William H Mumler, of Boston, Mass., produced results in 1862, and prospered, but then was doubted. He moved to New York but in 1869 he was put on trial there for fraud. In fact, he was discharged for want of evidence, but in 1884 he died in poverty. Spirit photography was obviously not a career for the faint-hearted, with the risk of criminal proceedings, and best avoided. Frederick Hudson was to rue the day when he changed direction. Edouard Buguet was a well-known French practitioner, successful in London for a period, but he, too, came to a sticky end. He started in Paris in 1873, but in 1875 he was tried for fraud, imprisoned for one year, and fined 500 francs. He did confess, but later recanted. However, his props of the trade – dummies, shrouds, false beards, pictures of heads glued on to cards – had been found by the police and it came out that his studio assistants had been dressed up as spirits. It was a notorious scandal, but it did not stop others from having a go at the extravagant fraud. There was a craze for the special photographs amongst the spiritualists and even outside the belief, a sense that there might be something in it.

This was the background against which a jittery Frederick Hudson chose to throw his dice, for the sake of his family, and Mrs Guppy was right there with him, when she had time and opportunity. He found himself in the thorny position of conniving with Mrs Guppy and deceiving Mr Guppy – his great friend. The web at the studio became more and more tangled as the two camps mingled and interacted. He had to remember who was with him, and who was an innocent. Mr Guppy already had some knowledge of photography. He said in *Mary Jane* that he had an amateur interest, and that he generally took a small apparatus around with him: this made life even more difficult for Hudson.

As for Mrs Guppy, with all her previous photographic expertise, she was at pains to dissociate herself from the actual practice, not wielding the camera, not contributing to the preparation and treatment of the plates, unlike helpful Miss Houghton, but active only as a medium from time to time, and as a friendly presence. It is quite difficult to understand why she was there at all, except that there was an element in her of liking to have a finger in every spiritualist pie. She was also there because Mr Guppy, independently, was very keen to experiment. She was certainly being cautious to avoid scandal, or worse.

It was in 1872 that the psychic explosion really took off at the Hudson studio. Miss Houghton imparted the glad tidings to the editors of the *Christian Spiritualist* and the *Spiritual Magazine*:

> It may be rather early to announce the new fact while in its embryonic state, but being a fact, you will be glad to learn that a spirit photograph has really been obtained here in London, and I trust that all the detail may be interesting to you and your readers. I went on Thursday last, March 7th, to Mrs Guppy's, and in the course of the afternoon, Mr Guppy shewed me three photographs, and told me that the spirit who usually converses audibly with them had given particular instructions as to the needful arrangements to be made, which they had carried out at the photographic studio of Mr Hudson ... which is very near their own residence, and those photographs were the result of their first trial. Mrs Guppy was within a kind of extemporised dark cabi-

net, behind Mr Guppy, who, while sitting in readiness to be photographed (of course in the full light of day), felt a wreath of flowers gently placed upon his head, and so the portrait was taken, while a large veiled figure is seen standing behind him. I believe they were artificial flowers which Mr Hudson had in his room for the use of any sitter who might wish for such an ornament. In the other two photographs there are also gleaming white figures to be seen behind Mr Guppy, but not very defined in form.

The improvised wreath and the large veiled figure speak for themselves. The queasy situation is that Mr Guppy's *wife* darted forward stealthily and deposited the wreath, just out of his eye-range, as he sat perfectly still for the photograph, and then, quickly draped, stood massively behind him, while his good *friend*, observed these happenings and wielded the camera. Afterwards, artlessly, Mr Guppy told Miss Houghton about the events, and she broadcast them to the world at large. The company of spiritualists, reliant on the credibility of Mr and Mrs Guppy, and Miss Houghton, believed every word of it. We might suppose that his wife and his friend gave Mr Guppy what he wanted, but that was not their intention. Hudson's motives were venal, but Elizabeth's were more complex. We have to look at the continuum of her psychic career to see that she pursued any avenue to advance herself as a powerful medium. Miss Houghton was a goose. No wonder that Hudson easily became flustered.

Wallace thought of the Guppys as a moral entity. On viewing a doctored photograph, he insisted with embarrassing loyalty that, 'Either there was a living, intelligent, but invisible being present, or Mr and Mrs Guppy, the photographer, and some fourth person, planned a wicked imposture, and have maintained it ever since. Knowing Mr and Mrs Guppy as well as I do, I feel an absolute conviction that they are as incapable of an imposture of this kind as any earnest inquirer after truth in the department of natural science.' (*Miracles and Modern Spiritualism*, p.188)

On that inaugural March day of 1872, Mr Guppy, aflame with the new discovery, suggested hopefully that as it was such a fine afternoon, Elizabeth and Georgiana might as well go over to Hudson's and try again, experimenting with Miss Houghton as the sitter. Mrs Guppy was not feeling very well, and was afraid that the attempt would be useless, but, says Miss Houghton, 'my spirit friends urged it, so Mr Guppy and I started immediately to get everything ready, leaving Mrs Guppy to follow us, and she arrived at the very moment she was wanted. While Mr Hudson was in his dark room preparing the plate, she told me that after I had come away, she had had a message from the spirit to the effect that Mamma would try to manifest herself, and to place her hand on my shoulder. Of course as soon as Mr Hudson began to develop his negative, we questioned eagerly as to whether there was anything to be seen, and hearing that there was, went in to feast our own eyes as soon as we could be admitted without risk of damaging it by letting in the light, and behind me there is a veiled figure with the hand advanced almost to my shoulder.'

And so it happened, with the attendant veiled figure hovering approximately in the right place. This was an important happening because it was termed by Conan Doyle in *The History of Spiritualism* (1926) as 'the first spirit photograph in England of which we have objective evidence.' (Vol.2, pp.28-9) The course was set. Georgiana was happy again, with a new purpose in God's cause. She was told by her spirit counsellors that she was to visit the studio every week, to develop the new marvel. Hudson began to allow her copies of the spirit photographs obtained, on professional terms, and she sold them to many interested correspondents and was able to cover her expenses and the cost of her railway journeys back and forth to Holloway. She was a prolific diarist of the events for the spiritualist periodicals and the news spread widely. Even through deep snow, when Mr Guppy solicitously kept Elizabeth at home, she tramped her way to Hudson's from the station, encouraged by the inner voices of her spirits. Elizabeth was pregnant. 'Dear little Tommy,' aged two, was beginning to appear amongst the living in the photographs, perched on an occasional piece of furniture or on a sitter's lap, dressed in velvet, with his legs sticking out in front of him, like a doll. There were no scruples about bringing children to séances – regarded as quasi-religious ceremonies, anyway – although presumably not to really frightening sessions when voices screeched or boomed and thuds shook the blackened room. Sometimes children as young as five or so were credited with psychic powers.

Drawn soon to the studio by the current reports, Mrs Catherine Berry first ventured there on April 19th, 1872, and she took with her Mrs Mary Marshall as her own professional medium, paying her appropriately. She thought that their visit was not anticipated, and they did not give their names, but no doubt they were recognised, or news of their intended visit had come on the grapevine. Mrs Guppy was not present, of course, due to the breakdown in relations between the two strong-minded women. Hudson was cautious when confronted with a clever medium who was not in cahoots with him. Mrs Marshall sat first, posed by Mrs Berry. The first two plates were blank, i.e. with no extras. As she sat for the third attempt, she produced the spirit voice of 'John King'. He told her not to sit again at the studio, but to invite Mr Hudson to her own house, and then she would get a good photograph.

Mary Marshall had resorted to her own repertoire, and Hudson was startled. As Mrs Berry observed, 'this made Mr Hudson open his eyes and look as only a man can look when he hears a spirit voice for the first time.'

Then Mrs Berry posed herself, with Mrs Marshall sitting behind the screen as medium, gravitating, no doubt, towards the advantages of that position. Mrs Berry's first plate showed an apparition by her side, but she did not claim it as one of her own, merely noticing that 'the face was well developed, and particularly handsome, but the eyes were shut.' This was Hudson's neutral contribution, for the fee, and to maintain his growing reputation. He was not going to combine forces with Mrs Marshall, an experienced, wily medium. We may wonder if Mrs Guppy had already passed on to him all that she knew about spirit photography.

For her second visit to Hudson – and she did not hurry back – Mrs Berry took with her in the September of the same year her familiar young friend, Frank Herne. Anything could have happened; he was not the sort to be passive in an exciting environment. While she was waiting for her copies to be developed, she took a chair and sat in the garden. One of Hudson's children, 'a bright little fellow,' who must have been Frederick *fils*, age five, came and stood by her side. She showed him one of the copies and pointed to herself, asking him if he knew who it was. He identified her at once, and then he pointed to a spirit form by her, and said, 'That's a ghost.'

Frank Herne, who was standing about six feet away, said, 'Don't show him that, Mrs Berry; you'll frighten him.' Something happened next, in full daylight, at about 5 pm, in an autumnal garden, that, as Mrs Berry tells it, is downright uncanny, like one of DD Home's best set-pieces. 'Scarcely had he [Herne] spoken the words [above] when I saw a spirit appear at the side of him, and strike him on the shoulder. Mr Herne instantly turned to see where the blow came from, and was startled at seeing the spirit. They were face to face, and the spirit an exact likeness of Mr Herne – in fact, his double. In a few seconds it faded away, and was no more seen.'

This special treat had obviously been designed for Mrs Berry. Herne absolutely did not have a twin, although he did have a brother, David, who was five years younger, or John Thomas, six years older, or William, seven years older, or Thomas, nine years older. Most of them were sailors on the high seas. There was Charles aged 17, a member of the ingenious Hudson household, but one could not reliably assume that Herne could have persuaded Hudson to second him to impress Mrs Berry. If that *were* the case, then little Frederick might have been schooled for his part in the drama. Mrs Berry asked him if he had seen anything. 'Yes, that was the ghost,' he told her. Did he feel frightened? 'No,' he said, 'I'm standing by you.'

Greatly touched by this expression of confidence, Mrs Berry always remembered 'the little fellow's calm quietness. He would have shamed many a man or woman, for it is no trifling ordeal to go through to those who have never witnessed a spirit out of the flesh.'

When, on another occasion soon afterwards, Charles Williams came to join in the fun with Herne, there was bound to be mischief, and, sure enough, he was 'brought through the roof of the studio', falling lightly, but 'sadly frightened'. The rafters proved to be intact, and it was made known that 'John King' had put him through the roof bodily as a punishment for disobedience. Spirit photography was of no interest to Herne and Williams but they were happy to use the studio as an extra stage.

Herne and Williams continued their séances until the late 1880s. Romance came to Herne in 1878, when he married Caroline Elizabeth Bassett, who was also a medium, and not at all bad at it. She was ten years his senior. Sometimes they gave joint performances, even at the hallowed premises, 61 Lambs Conduit Street, she styling herself Mrs Bassett-Herne. Before she had the support of Herne, she was not of commanding presence, being seen in October, 1872 to be in a 'timid nervous state' at a big séance at a grand address, Countess Paulett's house at 20 Hanover Square. However, in 1872, the *Spiritualist* (November 15th) commented that, 'Miss Kate Fox is the best medium for spirit raps in this country, but of London mediums, Mrs Bassett, of Thornham Grove, Stratford, is one of the best. She, however, gives most of her time to dark séances. Mrs Mary Marshall the younger used to be the best medium for raps and daylight manifestations, and she was always very sure of getting good results under the very worst conditions. We wish that Mrs Bassett and her spirits would cultivate daylight séances for raps and physical manifestations; there is a want of such a medium at the present time in the movement.'

By 1881, Frank Herne was a 'coach painter', and he and Caroline, aged respectively 31 and 42, were living at 24 Buckingham Road, Forest Gate, West Ham. The marriage failed, and she had separated from him before his early death on December 8th, 1887. His doctor said that he had died of a broken heart. The cause of death was 'Paralysis, 3 weeks,' and the address was 8 Albert Road, West Ham. He had been 'ailing very much for some time,' according to a friend, Mr Havers, who had known him many years, sat up with him to the last, and was with him when he passed away in a quiet sleep at 9.30 pm. He was buried at West Ham Cemetery, aged 36.

James Burns gave a lecture in 1892, in which he stated that 'the late Mrs Herne saw four husbands in the grave.' Caroline died in October, 1891, at the age of 60.

The Guppys' had known Mrs Bassett in 1873, years before she married Frank Herne, when she had come in the February with her current husband to a first séance at Highbury. Mr Guppy was impressed by her, and also enjoyed an intelligent conversation with Mr Bassett, who held his own in an assessment of the objective components of psychic manifestations. He said that he had given great attention to the subject, and that, when thoroughly traced, the whole of the phenomena were objective. He was, of course, being loyal to his wife and her powers.

Unlike Mrs Guppy, protected by her lofty, private status, 'the boys' did not lead charmed lives, although they began their careers with youthful *joie-de-vivre*. There were shocking exposures. Mr Charles Blackburn, spiritualist patron, who had been giving Frank Herne financial assistance, felt it his painful duty to report in the *Spiritualist* (December 31st, 1875) that, at a sitting at the Spiritual Centre in Russell Street, Liverpool, the spirit, 'John King', had been discovered to be Herne, with his scarf wrapped round his neck to look like a turban. He was severely beaten up in Liverpool.

The other famous shaming – of Charles Williams, this time, in concert with a new partner, one Mr A Rita, took place in Amsterdam, in September, 1878. 'Charlie', the materialised spirit, was found to be Rita himself, and when both men were searched by angry Dutch spiritualists, muslin, false beards, wigs and so on, rather grubby and worn, were secured. As was usual, 'evil spirits' were blamed, but the cause of spiritualism suffered, if only to some extent.

These were not Mrs Guppy's battles, but for some time, her husband had been anxious to protect her from any fallout.

Around the November of 1872, Miss Houghton noted with considerable chagrin that Mr Guppy had listened to 'unwise talk' and had forbidden Elizabeth to accompany her – Miss Houghton – to the photographic sittings. Samuel, the second Guppy son, had been born on September 28th. Occasionally, Mrs Guppy allowed her husband to be the master, but when a journalist, knowing there was trouble afoot, turned up at Highbury to ask for their views, and Mr Guppy was as courteous as ever, and discreet, she did not hold back: 'I at first was very indignant, I believed that Hudson had cheated, on the authority of a person whom I now know to be utterly unworthy of credit. I am now satisfied that these photographs are genuine, and that some of us will have to eat a good deal of dirt over this business.'

Her husband was standing beside her as she kept up her double bluff, and it is a good moment for us to draw back and look at the hypocritical position in which she found herself. The husbands of false mediums usually, probably always, knew, or found out, the nature of their wives' activities, and kept the secrets, like (presumably) Mr Bassett. Since Elizabeth was still carrying on with the pretence, it seems obvious that she was not confident of keeping her husband if he lost the illusion of having his own gifted medium. He had put his whole reputation and intellectual endeavour into spiritualism, as Wallace had done. If she had been tempted to confess, as to some adultery, and been revealed as a trickster, and he knew that he had been duped and gulled, she must have reasoned, he would have rejected her, and, at the very least, they would have separated. She guessed that he would not forgive her, whatever her charms and the love that he undoubtedly felt for her. There was no dilemma. She did not want to lose everything. She did not know where it would all end. Anyone could betray her – Hudson, unintentionally, or, especially, Herne and Williams and their associates – but there was a spark in her mind that would not let her rest and live blamelessly in the daylight.

She soon made her way back to the magic studio, the vibrant venue for mediums, and stayed until it collapsed. Miss Houghton, devoted to Hudson, had never left, and she had even contributed to his expenses. Later, at the Guppys' house, in April, 1873, there was a 'painful scene', when a 'Mrs B' was exposed in some fraud involving spirit faces, and Mrs Guppy was 'sadly distressed' that it had happened at her own home. Of course, she did not want to incur guilt by association. The miscreant could have been Mrs Bassett and that would have been the end of the relationship.

Frederick Hudson had been through a martyrdom of stones and arrows. Suspicion had been attached to his spirit photographs *ab initio*, and it came from convinced spiritualists. Discussion was rife about the technical methods of interfering with the plates and the process. He suffered recurrent real illnesses, and Job's comforters suggested that his powers were failing. His reign lasted until the spring of 1874. The winter had been long, foggy and damp; the studio had a tendency to flood, and his health deteriorated. He had to attend the ophthalmic hospital and he took to his bed. Then bailiffs entered the house of wonders.

Mr Guppy rose to the occasion, and on May 2nd, he sent a circular to friends of spiritualism: 'A week ago Mr Hudson's effects were seized for rent. For some time past he had been in difficulties, but had struggled on, hoping that the coming photographic season might bring a change for the better. He has abandoned all his effects to the landlord, as their value is not a third of the arrears due. His family consists of his wife, two daughters, and a son. Several friends, and I might say some (not personal) enemies, have come forward with small donations to relieve him in his present distress. My wife has kindly offered her services as cashier, to receive and pay over to Mr Hudson any sums sent to her.'

Elizabeth bore off one of the Hudson girls to live *en famille* with her for a while. The appeal brought in the useful sum of £92, but it was only enough for Hudson to take a studio in a side street, remote from passing trade, at 2 Kensington Park Road, Notting Hill Gate. His new, zinc-lined studio was at the top of the house, and supporters helped him, but he was failing again, in spite of a Benefit Soirée. Once, at his brief zenith, sitters had petitioned for appointments, and travelled in from places such as Liverpool, especially to patronise him. If someone had persuaded him to try spirit photography, that person had done him a grave disservice. He died on January 10th 1900, at 18 Barmeston Road, Catford. After 250 visits to his two studios, Georgiana Houghton was heart-broken.

7

Vitriol

A BLIGHT HAD BEEN CREEPING over the spiritualist houses in Bloomsbury, Highbury, and the grand squares of the West
End in 1873. The atmosphere was changing to one of bitter contention. The innocent times were being tarnished, the evenings
of family séances, when the table turned in the drawing-room,
good old Mrs Marshall was a legend, jolly psychic pictures were
on display, maiden aunts were scribing their experiences,
naughty Herne and Williams were capering around, people were
laughing at Mary Jane, Mrs Guppy soared over the roof tops, and
bearded professors discussed the finer points. All was contaminated by an evil influence from America, when Mr and Mrs
Nelson Holmes, a double-act of professional mediums, came
over to London from Philadelphia to try their luck, and took up
residence at 16 Old Quebec Street, off Oxford Street, by Marble
Arch.

It was going to be a bad year for Mrs Guppy. Poisonous
rumour and scandal were diffused, and it emanated from the
Holmes's. At first, the pair were kindly received by the Guppys,
and visits were exchanged several times. Elizabeth was still recov-
ering from childbirth, and she stayed at Norwood on a private
visit in part of the January before arranging a séance or two at
Highbury. Obviously cognisant of some adverse commentary
concerning her dear friend, Miss Houghton wrote off to the mag-
azines on February 14th:

> I was present at a séance at Mrs Guppy's on
> Thursday week, with a young lad as the medium,
> who will, I think, develop into great psychical pow-

ers. Mrs Guppy was not herself in the room, so that I might be the better able to appreciate his strength, as he spends much of his time at her house for the purpose of development, and I am led to mention the subject because I am rather indignant at the accusation I so frequently meet with in the publications of the day, i.e. 'the jealousy of mediums,' which I look upon as utterly groundless. Who are so anxious to develop fresh ones as mediums themselves? Indeed, to take Mrs Guppy for instance, she has been quite a nursing mother to many young beginners, who have often drawn from her to such an extent that her own vitality has sometimes suffered.

In fact, there are scarcely any among our English mediums who have not willingly given time and efforts to help others onward in the same course; how, then, can they reasonably be accused of jealousy? Simply because some gentleman had been foolish enough to reject the joys that spiritualism brings, in consequence of having heard A speak against B – two mediums who were considered by their friends to be equal in gifts. His was the loss, and perhaps ere now he may have learned better, also that one swallow does not make a summer, and that one person's harsh judgement of another ought not to be taken without enquiry as a final decision upon a point of such infinite importance.

These were strong words for Georgiana Houghton, who did not like to speak ill of anyone, but she had a sense of justice. Of course she did not realise what Mrs Guppy was teaching her protégés to do. The young lad was the previously mentioned 'JC', actually James Clark, who was to play a very important part in a frightful drama that ensued. Stirring events tended to follow one another swiftly in the spiritualist world. Mrs Margaret Fisher, of Theberton Street, is the best eyewitness:

I went to the séance of Mrs Holmes on Thursday, February 27th. They placed the visitors in different seats. I turned round and saw Mr J.C. there. I sat by him. Some lady who had never been there before asked me to sit by her. Some gentleman in a velvet coat whispered to Mrs H. and then they sent some little boy who they said was there every day to sit between us. Then Mrs Holmes was tied by a gentleman, and the lights were put out – previously the holding hands being particularly insisted on. Then the guitar and tambourine were carried about the room touching several persons. When the light was struck, Mrs Holmes's hands were still tied. Before striking the light, the Spirit's order was waited for. Lights being again extinguished, there was an awful noise of guitar, tambourine, and people saying they were touched, in the midst of which J.C. struck a very bright light (a Bryant and May patent safety), which revealed Mrs Holmes dancing about the room like a fay, with the guitar in her hand (of course, free from all ties). She immediately threw down the guitar and rushed back to her seat, from which she was about six feet distant, and placed herself as though in a trance, and commenced speaking in a cracked voice: 'O, de blackguard, de blackguard, to break the conditions by striking a light – turn de blackguard out,' when Mr – said, 'Make him stay here till the séance is over, and then we will pitch him out of the window.'

I did not see what Mr Holmes was doing when the light was struck, as my eyes were fixed on Mrs Holmes. Mr Holmes then locked the door; then Mr – went up to Mr J.C. and tried to persuade him to sit the séance out, and said that if he did not sit the séance out, he would expose him before the company present. Mr J.C. said to the effect, 'You can expose what you please – I defy you.' Then a gentleman got up and said that he had seen quite sufficient, and that he objected to see any one kept in the room against his will, and that he would not stay. Then they hesitated a little, and Mr Holmes unlocked the door, and Mr Edwin Ellis and Mr J.C. went out. After the gentlemen were gone, Mrs Holmes, in a cracked voice, said, 'De two black-guards haze been sent here by de squaw Guppy, dey were sent here to detect something, and I thought I would humour them, and I got up to go and take his matches away, but only got as far as de middle of the room.'

The spoiled séance faltered, but resumed, with Mrs Holmes 'chanting'. Mask-like faces appeared at a hole in a screen. One was like an old man with a pink face and a small screw of white hair on the top of its head. The mysterious little boy who was ever present turned out to have a helpful, supporting role: a face wearing a kind of crown emerged. 'Who are you?' asked Mr Holmes, and the child said that it had whispered, 'Mary Stewart'.

When the séance was over, Mrs Margaret Fisher's narrative went against James Clark, but it was typical of Samuel Guppy that he did not censor it, or omit it. She heard a certain Mr — say, afterwards, 'I was at a séance at Mr Guppy's, and there was a terrible racket and things flying about the room, and I caught Mr C. in the act of throwing pepper, soot, and birdseed.' Then he said, 'They are a pair of blackguards (alluding to the two gen-tlemen who were gone), although he was so fast in asking for my address, he did not give his – perhaps he had none to give.' Then a gentleman got up and said, "He has an address to give, he is a friend of mine, and I will give you his address." Then Mrs Holmes gave me a winning smile for the 5s.'

The Guppy-Holmes relationship had obviously deteriorated disastrously. Mrs Holmes, quick as a barrister on her feet, with adrenaline running, caught bang to rights, had a succession of excuses for her conduct, but blaming Mrs Guppy went beyond a mere extempore improvisation. It was of the nature of a vindic-tive tit-for-tat. She saw and recognised the perpetrator who had lit the match and broken the rules, and she may have sincerely believed that Elizabeth Guppy was behind the act. Mr Guppy was horrified. His wife had been traduced beyond all endurance. As he himself realised, the incident was strongly suggestive that Elizabeth had indeed incited the unsporting revelation, set her vassal on while she and her husband were elsewhere. To save his wife's reputation, he had to convince everyone, if he could, that it was entirely the lad's enterprise of his own, that James Clark, who was thought by Miss Houghton to be of a fragile nature, had unaccountably performed the dangerous and embarrassing exposure out of genuine motives for the cause of truth. He could have argued that James was overwrought with his psychic studies, but he preferred to emphasise the nature and extent of the Holmes's manifestations.

He hurried around, interviewing the sitters who had been present at the event, taking down what he called 'depositions', always liking to assume a lawyer-like attitude, and brought out, privately, in March, 1873, a pamphlet, which was his last publication. Entitled *Imitations of Spiritual Phenomena with Comments Thereon*, it is peppered with anecdotal and inappropriate passages, as if to defuse the awkward state of affairs with humour and urbanity. He always thought that his best weapon was his pen. Still under Elizabeth's spell, he cuts a rather pathetic figure. It was not a good idea to make mortal enemies of the Nelson Holmes's. They were rough, from a different culture. In just one session, James Clark had been falsely imprisoned and threatened with violence. Mr Guppy, too, was going to be menaced with a grievous bodily harm. Red Indians had invaded the drawing-rooms.

When Mr Guppy came to taking James Clark's 'deposition', the young man had perfected an explanation of his behaviour: he was *impressed to act as he did*. The spirits, not Mrs Guppy had sent him on his errand. This is what he stated:

> On Thursday, February 27th, I was impressed to go to Mr Holmes's. On my way there I bought a box of Bryant's patent safety matches. On arriving there, I was seated next to Mrs Fisher (whom I had met at

Mrs Guppy's) and another lady, a stranger. When the séance began, under some pretence or other, I withdrew my hand from Mrs Fisher's, and took out of my pocket the box of matches, but my hand some-how appeared restrained from striking them. Soon after, a light was called for to show that Mrs Holmes's hands were tied. The restraint on my hands removed, and I struck a light, which revealed Mr Holmes with the banjo in his hand, rapping upon the knees of a gentleman who I since find to be Mr Edwin Ellis, and Mrs Holmes standing in the middle of the room with her hands untied, having in her hands a guitar, with which she was touching a lady's knees.

Mr Holmes, when he had recovered his self-posses-sion, asked if it was I who had struck the light. I replied, 'Yes.' He told me to leave the room. I replied that I should certainly do so after what I had wit-nessed. Upon this, a gentleman present suggested that I should be made to sit out the séance. Mr Holmes then locked the door and pocketed the key. A gentleman present (Mr Edwin Ellis) then got up, declaring that he was perfectly satisfied – that he had seen enough to make him wish to leave the room. After some parleying, Mr Holmes unlocked the door, and allowed us to make our exit. Mr Ellis allowed me to refer to him, either in print or other-wise. There were nearly twenty persons at the séance, seven of whom were Mr E.'s friends.

Edwin Ellis (1841-95), who had adroitly extricated young James Clark from danger of harm, was a successful marine and land-scape painter. Born in Nottingham, he settled in London in the 1860s, but died back in Nottingham. Good examples of his work were 'The Harbour Bar', and 'Fishing Boats at Staithes'. He had been drawn to spiritualism in about August, 1870, after seeing some of Mrs Berry's spirit drawings in the window at 15

Southampton Row. He had sought an introduction to Mrs Berry and she had enlightened him on the whole subject. Interestingly, he judged that from an artist's point of view, her drawings were 'inimitable for technical manipulation.' He and his wife, Alice, became enthusiastic visitors at the séances. He was a sound person to corroborate the 'depositions' of the other eyewitnesses. Indeed, only a fanatic would dispute what actually happened at the failed séance.

Giving his address as 29 Devonshire Street, Queen Square, Ellis's contribution on February 28th, 1873 was, (in part):

> While the sitters were saying, 'Thank you, dear spirit, come and touch me, etc., etc.,' a very bright light was struck (quite unexpectedly to me) by a gentleman sitting nearly in the centre of the circle; this revealed to me Mr Holmes on one knee, reaching forward with his disengaged right hand, in which was a guitar, tapping the knee of my wife who sat next to me, and Mrs Holmes, untied, away from her chair, in the centre of the circle, similarly occupied. Mrs Holmes immediately dropped the guitar or instrument, and rushed back to her seat, appearing immediately in a state of trance; Mr Holmes for a few seconds seemed flabbergasted, and in full light still continued tapping with the guitar; recovering himself, he threw the guitar violently from him and recovered his seat. Then Mr Holmes approaching the gentleman who struck the light (while the light was still burning and also having lighted a candle) asked by what authority he had done so. Mr Holmes immediately ordered him to leave the room, and, without demurring, the gentleman prepared to comply, when Mrs Holmes and several gentlemen present said, 'He shall not go, he shall stay it out,' Mr Holmes going to him and saying he had a mind to throw him out of the window. It was proposed that he should be forced back to his chair and his hands

held. Up to this I remained perfectly quiet, but on hearing the threats I immediately rose and said I would leave the room, daring Mr Holmes or any person present to lay a finger on me or attempt to prevent my leaving. Several persons present requested me to say why I was leaving. Mr — said, 'I want to know who you are,' and gave me his card. I wrote my address for him on the blank leaf of my pocket book, telling him at the same time that I declined any argument with him. By this time Mr Holmes had opened the door, and I followed the gentleman who had struck the match out of the room, out of the house, leaving my wife and party there. I speak for myself, leaving my party to speak for themselves.

Mrs Alice Ellis, abandoned for good cause, but not unprotected, stated:

After my husband left the room, Mr — got up, saying he was well acquainted with the young man who struck the light, that he had met him at Mr Guppy's séances, where he himself had detected him in the act of producing manifestations, throwing pepper etc. The spirit Rosie then, through Mrs Holmes, echoed what had been said – said she knew him well, also that she knew my husband, and that he was one of Mrs Guppy's friends; also that on the preceding Thursday their séance had been disturbed by Mrs Guppy's friends. Mr — said that if he had seen the fellow, he would have exposed him at once as a humbug, but he kept his coat buttoned up to his chin, so that he could not be recognised ...

The spirit Rosie then said that she was much pleased with us all, and that all present were at liberty to come again for nothing to a séance. She explained why Mrs Holmes was on her feet, that she was going to take the matches from the humbug; she

scolded the lady who sat next to the said 'humbug'
for letting loose his hand, and said she ought at once
to have told the medium that his hands were loose.

Mr Guppy took off his magisterial garb and entered the witness
box himself:

> After J.C. dined with us – an early dinner – we
> retired to the drawing-room. Only J.C. and I there. I
> was reclining on the sofa, J.C. on a fauteuil. He said
> he had lights on his fingers ... He went into the dark
> room and called out to me that he had the lights. I
> told him that it was a sign that he had phosphorus
> in excess in his system. He then said, 'How do peo-
> ple feel if they are going to be carried away – I feel as
> though I should be carried away.' I said, 'That is very
> possible, as your body is in a very phosphorescent
> condition.' I thought it very possible he might be
> carried from one part of the room to the other,
> which would have been of no consequence.

[Mr Guppy's reaction here reinforces the genuine nature of his
phlegmatic response to the news that his wife had vanished from
the kitchen before her aerial flight to Bloomsbury. It also
demonstrates only too damningly that Mr Guppy was being used
on that occasion as a stout shield to shelter Mrs Guppy.]

> Had I thought of his going to the Holmes's, I should
> have absolutely prevented him, as I should have felt
> myself culpable to have allowed him to go.
>   As I knew we were going to have a séance, and that
> I should not get to bed till 12 or 1 o'clock, I com-
> posed myself to get an hour's siesta. Between waking
> and sleeping, I thought I heard him go out of the
> room, but thought he might be gone up to billiards.
> I have some faint recollection of hearing the street-
> door shut – but fell asleep. He did not return to tea,

nor to the séance. We did not know where he was gone. At last Mrs G. and Mrs — sat at the table, and the Spirit said that it knew where he was, and that he was all right, but would not tell us where. At last the Spirit, after many questions, told us that the last letter of the person's name he was gone to was 's' – but would not tell us more. We held our séance. There were present Mr J. Traill Taylor [*bona fide* photographer, editor of the *British Journal of Photography*], two Mrs Pearsons [relatives of Georgiana Houghton], Mr Volckman, Miss — , and Miss Houghton. Our guests all went away, except a relative of J.C. We had not the slightest idea of where he was – a séance at the Holmes's, or anywhere else, was the most remote thing from our ideas – as he well knew we were going to have a séance at home. At last, a little before eleven, he came and related his adventures.

Samuel Guppy was unable to resist the exercise of his creative powers: 'I have now given you the particulars of this very remarkable séance, but it would take an able painter, aided by a description by the ladies present, to give you the scene as it was when J.C. struck the light. The light given out was nearly like a magnesium light. J.C. calm, motionless, with his mouth half open, holding the light steadily as it burnt down. A dead silence at first. The ladies who were in the blissful state of being touched and recognised by the spirits of their dear departed relatives – they all of them assured me that up to the moment of the light being struck, they fully believed in the reality of the Spirit communion so taking place. The ablest painter could hardly do justice to such a subject ... Calm as a marble statue, he held up the brilliant match, his mouth partly open, perhaps like a Tam-o'-Shanter suddenly throwing a light on a witches' festival, except that the witches at the Holmes's séance were young and pretty ... ' As for what he thought of James Clark, he knew nearly as much of him as he knew of his little boy, Tommy, and 'He is a good son of an excellent father, and a young man of the highest principle. I believe he would let his hand be cut off rather than do a thing his conscience disapproved of.'

Mr Guppy holds back about the accusation against Elizabeth: one would have expected an efflorescence of words. He contents himself with saying that, 'I don't think it is worth my while to take any notice of anything Mrs Holmes has said about my wife. She very naturally thinks that we sent J.C. and that we intended doing her an injury. It would therefore, be unreasonable for us to expect any "winning smiles" from her.' He does not, however, disapprove of exposures, although it has been put to him that they damage the cause of spiritualism. 'If spiritualism is to be kept afloat by imposture, the sooner it sinks the better; but I say it will not; scientific spiritualism is the highest of all sciences.'

An anonymous postcard was sent to Mr Guppy as he scribed his 'depositions' and wandering thoughts. The sender must be presumed to be on his side, because he has abstracted from the Vagrancy Act, 1824, already perused by Mr Guppy in his defence of Mrs Tranter, the section which runs: 'Any persons using any subtle craft, means, or devices, to deceive his Majesty's subjects, are to be deemed rogues and vagabonds, and to be punished with imprisonment and hard labour.'

There was an uncomfortable atmosphere in the separate camps. Mrs Guppy's private séances continued to be closely monitored by invitation and the expectations of friendship. She was not vulnerable as she had been when she was starting out and enduring large sittings of people not all known to her, but never for payment. The Holmes's, taking payment virtually from all comers, were open to attack. Soon after the solitary sortie by James Clark, there was, on March 6th, another hostile incursion into Old Quebec Street, by Mr AL Henderson, with three supporters. Mrs Guppy was well distanced from the action in her Highbury stronghold, with witnesses to her neutral position. Samuel Guppy, including this new incident towards the conclusion of his *Imitations*, was inclined to make light of it, with his own brand of jokes, but the joint 'deposition' that he took in the immediate aftermath was decidedly lacking in humour:

At a quarter to eleven last night [he related in his preamble] I was with two friends dividing our time between billiards and chat. My wife was in the drawing-room with a lady who dissects incidents and characters as she would carve a fowl, when a rat-tat-tat came at the door as though Her Majesty in a carriage-and-four had come to see us. 'Who on earth can that be at this time of night?' said I, going to the landing, and looking over the balusters. The sound of many footsteps was heard, and then my wife's voice. 'What is it?' said I. 'Come down,' said she, 'they have spotted the ghost.' Spotted the ghost! We came down to the drawing-room, and there found six or seven gentlemen just like what men look after a race is concluded. I begged them to sit down, and take it easy, and tell us all about it; and my wife (impressed I suppose) made her appearance in less than no time in the mode in which, I think, she shows off to the best advantage, bringing in a large bowl of punch – for our visitors looked like hunters who have run their quarry down.

The visitors, refreshed, deposed that, 'at the part of the [Holmes's] séance called The Spirit-face Manifestations, the first face shown appeared as an elderly gentleman with a grey beard. At the appearance of the second face – an elderly lady – Mr AL Henderson, who was present, rushed forward, tore down the oil-cloth screen, in the aperture of which the faces appeared, and thereupon declared, supported by the three gentlemen whose signatures are appended with his that he distinctly saw a short, stout female move away from the aperture. Mr Henderson then remarked, "Gentlemen, are you satisfied that this is an imposition? Do you see that woman retreating?" but, before he could enter the room, the half-door was closed from within, from the inside and ingress thereby prevented, while Mr Holmes was standing at the table, preventing anybody from entering the room.'

Seeking in some measure to defuse an explosive situation, Mr Guppy finished his effusion on an ameliorative note: 'I, for my part, do not feel at all out of temper with Mrs Holmes, though I do not suppose she would give me the "winning smile" she gave Mrs Fisher. I am – that is, I feel quite sure, that she is a very powerful medium; and if the public asked for more than her conditions enabled her to give, she did what she could to satisfy them. Henceforward, I hope no one will disturb her séances by striking a light, or tearing her screen. There will be no deceit, for the public know what they pay for. As a lawyer, who for the nonce we made our judge, remarked, "You went there to be touched with musical instruments in the dark, and you were touched." The opposing counsel said, "We bargained to be touched by spirits." "The law does not recognise spirits," said the judge.'

Then Samuel Guppy spoils the somewhat ironical affect of his soothing words by a final bombshell: 'P.S. How came it that Mr Holmes did not carry out on Mr Henderson his written threat in his letter to me of the 27th ult.? "We promise to return him to Mrs G. minus the top of his head." So Mr and Mrs Holmes, from America, make known that investigators who break through the rules they lay down at their séances will be either thrown out of the window, or scalped, or perhaps both. After this announcement, I think they may calculate on their rules not being infringed upon.

'There are many who would wish to stifle this exposure, or, failing that entirely, to "amend it in committee", to use a political expression – that is, publish it in their manner; but I feel it would be suffering my friend J.C. (let alone what has been said about me and my wife) to remain unjustified under a torrent of Yankee abuse. Besides, I am bound to do justice to the heroic conduct of Mr Henderson, who faced the anger of fourteen spirits in Mr Holmes's back drawing-room (for in the evidence there is a relay of spirits each Thursday.)'

Although the situation in 1873 was obviously a seething cauldron, laced with scandal, gossip and hearsay, Mrs Guppy had lived out her life before, decades later, in 1964, the Society for Psychical Research released two unpublished documents from the archives, which, ever since, have been received virtually without question and fundamentally damaged her reputation. In an important paper, largely devoted to other matters, to which there are connections, which was contributed to the Proceedings of the Society, the leading members, RG Medhurst and KM Goldney, remarked on 'the jealous hatred directed by the medium Mrs Guppy against certain of the more newly arrived mediums who threatened to outstrip her in popularity. This is one of those facts of the psychic scene which were apparently well known to contemporary spiritualists, but for which it is not now easy to find evidence, just as it is surprisingly hard to find recorded impressions of the personalities of the various protagonists. Apart from eulogies by Miss Georgina [sic] Houghton ... the only personal comment on Mrs Guppy we have seen appears in a letter from Lord Rayleigh to Sidgwick [Henry], dated June 7th, 1874 [reproduced in the biography by his son]. He says: "Mrs Guppy I don't think I could stand, even in the cause of science and philosophy!"'

To buttress this vague figuring of Mrs Guppy and her attitude, they cite a private note by Stainton Moses (v. infra) in an account of a séance held on February 17th, 1873: 'The medium [Florence Cook] had been upset by an unsatisfactory séance with Lord Arthur Russell and had also been greatly vexed by some reports spread about her by Mrs Guppy. She was unfit to sit, and never ought to have gone into the cabinet.' This must have some weight. Additionally, referring to Charles Blackburn, Florence Cook's patron, Medhurst and Mrs Goldney state that, 'A man in Blackburn's position was sure to have been informed of the "Guppy plot" and, in fact, one undated fragment torn from a letter by Florence to Blackburn, now preserved in the Britten Memorial Library, reads: "Mrs Guppy will be surprised when she sees the papers. It will stop her nonsense. I believe she is saying all sorts of horrid things about me".'

The main 'evidence' adduced by the writers comes from the 'two unpublished documents from very different sources on what one might call the "Guppy Plot".' The first is extracted from the private notebooks of the Revd Stainton Moses, the medium:

Thursday, 27th Feb. 1873. Séance at Mrs Holmes's. Present 18, including Mr Ashman, and James Clark (Mrs Guppy's medium) and a Mr Ellis of Devonshire Street, Queen Square.

The manifestations commenced very favourably, and were proceeding in the usual manner when we were startled by a light being struck by J.C. The instruments were floating and being played in the air, and I saw the guitar fall to the ground from near the ceiling. Two other instruments were in the air, and I saw one of them fall. The other I did not see, but I looked at once to Mr Holmes who was in his usual place, and the medium was tied as she had been at first, and under control by Rosie. Mr Holmes immediately walked to J.C. who sat in the centre of the circle holding the match which he had struck and looking with a fixed gaze before him. He said 'I think that is satisfactory.' His face was the most unnatural one I ever saw – the face of a maniac, or of one under possession by an evil spirit. I do not think that he was responsible for his actions. Mr Holmes told him to leave the room asking him 'Who told him to strike a match.' He said 'I told myself.' Mr H. again told him to go, but afterwards at the suggestion of some person, locked the door, and refused to allow him to go. This brought me up, and I denounced J.C. as a person whom I had detected in cheating. I said publicly that he was a person whom I had proved to be unworthy of credence ...

J.C. is a dangerous and unscrupulous person, instigated, as I believe, by Mrs Guppy to molest Mrs Holmes. Mrs G. is now engaged in an attempt to bedaub the character of Miss Cook and Mrs Holmes. She is a jealous woman, and will stick at nothing. J.C. is her unscrupulous tool.

We are not disputing the actions of James Clark, but the discrepancy between Moses' version of what the Holmes pair were seen to be doing when the match flared up and the 'testimony' of Mr Guppy's deponents is very striking. We can only assume the mantle of the magistrate and decide which account we prefer. Moses was writing as it were to himself, but we cannot know what plans or mere hopes for the future of those notebooks he cherished. William Stainton Moses (1839-92), aka 'M.A. Oxon.' a man of the cloth, an intellectual, a leading figure in the movement, was a very private medium in every sense. He had resolutely chosen to prefer young Florence Cook and her pleasing manifestations rather than Elizabeth Guppy and her passé apports – a speciality of his own, to boot.

Frank Podmore, writing in 1902, was troubled by Stainton Moses: 'If we leave out of the account for the moment the difficulties involved in the supposition that a man of his character and antecedents should lend himself to trickery, there is nothing in the manifestations produced in his presence to suggest any other explanation. All that was done has been done again and again by fraudulent mediums and naughty children, and done under conditions much less favourable.' (*op. cit.*, Vol. 2, p.280)

Wondering about Moses' mental state, Podmore described him as utterly conventional in his day-to-day activities, but concluded that, 'To me it seems frankly impossible to construct a working hypothesis on the premise that Stainton Moses was of normal mind, and actuated by motives which appear to normal men.' (*op. cit.*, Vol. 2, p.288)

The second previously unpublished document, set out in all its lurid, excitatory glory, a favourite of modern commentators, is the Nelson Holmes letter to DD Home, written not contemporaneously, but three years after the events:

614 So. Washington Sq.,
Philadelphia, Penna.
16th Sept., 1876.

DD Home, Esq.

Dear Sir,

Our mutual friend, JM Roberts, Esq., of Burlington, NJ, incidentally mentioned that he had received a letter from you wherein you cite Mrs Guppy as an enemy of ours and who instigated the persecution against us in London. The purpose of this letter is to post you more fully in relation to that matter.

It is seldom that an opportunity is afforded a medium to set himself right before the public, but having every reason to expect that you will do us justice, I take this method of introducing myself and giving you the details of what was known as the 'Guppy Warfare on the Holmeses' in London in 1872-1873.

In January 1873, Mrs Guppy called at our residence, 16 Old Quebec Street, London, W, and endeavoured to enlist our cooperation in a plot whereby a certain Mr Clark, Mr Henderson, and one Vlockman [sic] were to be hired to attend a séance at Miss Cook's, and watching their opportunity, at a favourable moment, while the manifestations were in progress to throw *vitrol* [sic] *in the face of the spirit*, hoping thereby to destroy for ever the handsome features of Miss Florrie Cook, and thus at one fell stroke to effectually remove from further use a medium who, Mrs Guppy claimed, had and was taking all her, Mrs Guppy's, friends away from her and upon whose patronage Mrs G had long depended.

While reciting this horrible scheme to us, she seemed fairly possessed by a legion of fiends, and her rage at Miss Cook and her 'doll face' as she termed it, was fearful to behold. When I realised the full import of this loathing [sic] affair, I immediately ordered her from the house, and the next day wrote to Mr Samuel Guppy, her husband, and gave him notice that his wife could never again enter our house.

The day following, the poor old man called and tried to reconcile the matter and with tears in his eyes earnestly pleaded that the affair should go no further. This I could not promise, as I felt it my sacred duty, let the consequences be what they might, to notify Miss Cook and her friends. This we, Mrs H. and myself, did at Mr Luxmoore's immediately following the interview with Mr Guppy.

To many, whom we thought it our duty to inform, the story seemed to [sic] horrible for belief, and a general desire prevailed on all sides to hush the matter up.

From Miss Cook, Mrs Guppy now turned her rage against us, and soon after sent a party headed by Henderson, the photographer, to tear down our cabinet and otherwise break up our séances in London, in which scheme, however, they were signally foiled.

The foregoing will suffice to prove to your mind the cause of the 'Guppy Warfare on the Holmeses'. If necessary, I can give you the details of the infamous transactions of Mrs Guppy with Miss Emily Berry, 1 Hyde Park Place, also why Mrs Guppy used her pretended mediumship for base purposes, and gave séances solely for assignation meetings to better enable certain disreputable parties to further carry out their lewd propensities.

Hoping your health may improve and many days yet added to your lot.

I am most
Sincerely yours
Nelson Holmes

That one letter transmogrified Elizabeth Guppy into a bogey woman, like Mrs Webster, who boiled up her mistress, or Mrs Dyer, who threw dead babies into the River Thames. But we do not have to believe a word of it. There is no case to the criminal law standard of 'beyond reasonable doubt'. Where is the corroboration? There is only Holmes's word for the accusation of a serious criminal threat, and Nelson Holmes was a man of bad character: when he came to England, according to Nandor Fodor in his *Encyclopaedia* (*op. cit.*, p.171) he was charged with dishonourable attempts to obtain money. Back in America there was a great scandal when the Holmes's landlady confessed that at one of their séances she had impersonated 'Katie King'. The matter was disputed, of course. The vitriol charge, no doubt, led to comments such as Ruth Brandon's rather appealing characterisation, 'She was at once grotesque, comical and more than somewhat sinister, the kind of person who confirms that, even in his wilder flights of imagination and what one might take to be exaggerations, Charles Dickens never strayed far over the edge ... '

If many people had been told about the threat, as stated by Holmes, there should be written verification somewhere to be found, as in Moses' private notebooks. Medhurst and Mrs Goldney had unrivalled access to the Society's archives, but obviously found nothing germane, or they would have said so. There was no fear of libel, because Mrs Guppy had left this world by 1964. They present the two 'Guppy Plot' documents without analysis or their own valued expert opinion. At a guess they *do* believe every word of it, in spite of Holmes's bad reputation. If they had secret information, then it has remained so.

Why did Holmes feel the sudden need to communicate with DD Home, then in London? His letter itself provides the marker to his intentions: 'It is seldom that an opportunity is afforded a medium to set himself right before the public, but having every reason to expect that you will do us justice, I take this method of introducing myself and giving you the details of what was known as the "Guppy Warfare on the Holmeses' in London in 1872-73".' By recourse to Peter Lamont's probing modern life of Home (*The First Psychic*, 2005) Holmes's motivation becomes abundantly clear. In 1876, Home's projected exposé published in 1877 as *Lights and Shadows of Spiritualism* was causing consternation in the parlours of the mediums. 'Concerned potential targets' were attempting to ingratiate themselves with him and deflect his unwelcome attention. Holmes suggested that Home should focus on Mrs Guppy. Not on Holmes and his wife. Here, then, is the rationale for the vile allegations. In the event, DD Home abstained from any gross or indeed libellous references to Elizabeth, but he did parody the activities of an unnamed medium whose ample dress afforded opportunity for concealment.

As for the allegations themselves, in order to put forward a defence of Elizabeth Guppy, we may look to her circumstances and her character. Holmes's God was money. Elizabeth's was her reputation. Her respectability was hard-won. Her middle-class husband was her rock, and their two children were emblems of the strength of her marriage. She would not have jeopardised everything that she had achieved. Holmes had not realised that she was of higher, if acquired, social class than he had understood. He did not know about her Hull-ish background. Vitriol throwing did happen at that time, in desperate back-alleys, but not in polite drawing-rooms. She had given birth only three months earlier than the supposed threat of violence, and the only explanation with any feasibility might have been that she was in the throes of a puerperal psychosis, but there is no evidence of that. In fact, she is documented as having returned quietly to her séances. She depended upon her lawful husband for money, not her spiritualist friends.

Does the vivid description of Florence Cook's 'doll face' belong more to Elizabeth's vocabulary than to Holmes's? American dictionaries of slang do not show 'doll face' but the *OED* certainly does show its usage in the 19th century. Of course this is not definitive but it is fair to mention it. A further textual point is that the clause, 'she seemed fairly possessed by a legion of fiends' could have been derived from any sensational literature, but is curiously reminiscent of Stainton Moses' private comments on James Clark – 'His face was the most unnatural one I ever saw – the face of a maniac, or of one under possession by an evil spirit.'

The substantive part of the allegations is unbelievable. Only if she were insane would Elizabeth have proposed the vitriol attack. Otherwise, the notion is the product of Holmes's cunning and inventive mind. Hiring means employing for a fee or remuneration. You could not 'hire' William Volckman. Elizabeth knew that, but clearly Holmes did not. Made to sound sinister, like an anarchist, as 'one Vlockman', he was in fact a gentlemanly figure, rich from trade, well-educated, and respectability was as important to him as it was to Elizabeth. The Guppy couple had certainly become friends of his, through their séances, but he would not have become a party to a plot which would have brought swift and condign punishment from the criminal courts of England. Nor would William Henderson, an established, successful photographer, married, have been a person to approach. There is no reason to suppose even young James Clark to have been capable of such a crime. Serious crime was foreign to the spiritualist scene. A mob-handed attack in an enclosed space with Florence Cook's band of male protectors ever present would have provided small chance of escape. If Holmes had as he claimed, told many people about the 'conspiracy', Mrs Guppy's séances would have failed, her family life would have suffered, she would have been shunned and her career would not have proceeded grandly, as it did, with important sitters flocking to her home.

The absurd notion of Mrs Guppy as a kind of madam is a malicious, unsupported invention, further intended to discredit her, and bearing no relation to the pattern and flavour of her life. Carelessly and endlessly repeated without reflection, or background, it has become a staple of the harridan image of Mrs Guppy, second only to the comical 'Flight'. DD Home, who was fully in touch with the spiritualist world, would have known if the tale were indeed true, and that was why Holmes was driven to present it to him as secret, confidential information. It may be that a similar rumour was set up in 1891, when, on October 24th, the *Liverpool Mercury* reported that a Mr and Mrs Elizabeth Guppy had been named in the Liverpool Police Court in connection with the keeping of a brothel in Bayhorse Lane, Liverpool. Elizabeth Guppy had already been fined for the offence.

The linked reference by Holmes to Mrs Guppy's 'infamous transactions with Miss Emily Berry, of 1 Hyde Park Place' has not received attention, because as it stands it is meaningless. It cunningly evokes a courtesan. But we know that name, Berry, as borne by Mrs Catherine Berry, spiritualist author, whom we have cited throughout. She makes a number of references to her niece, Miss Emma Berry, sent away to school in Hanover when she is not in London for the holidays, attending her aunt's séances, becoming entranced, and receiving tasteful gifts from Mrs Guppy as visiting medium.

If we use the Census of 1871, Mrs Berry is living at 242 Oxford Street, with (as already noticed) her full complement of five servants. Next on the census schedule is 1 Hyde Park Place, close by, the first of a row of mansions overlooking the Park and built on the right and left of the entrance to Great Cumberland Place. And there, at 1 Hyde Park Place is Miss Emma Berry, aged 14, a scholar, and a niece, but not with the same name as the other residents at no. 1. Perhaps it is a coincidence that Holmes has chosen the address of a young girl who is very probably Mrs Berry's niece. Moreover, Emma and Emily were often used interchangeably. Why would Nelson Holmes pluck out of the air the 'Berry' name, known to him from spiritualism? Perhaps, as an American living in 1873 remarkably near the Berrys', with Old Quebec Street running up northwards from Oxford Street, and being the next road along eastward from Great Cumberland Place, he delved in his memory for people and places previously known to him which sounded all right. Of course he is not casting aspersions against an innocent schoolgirl.

The disputed year of 1873 culminated in a spectacular exposure of Florence Cook, undertaken, of all people, by William Volckman. Mr Guppy had found himself honour-bound to try to defend his wife against the suspicion of having incited her protégé, James Clark, to expose Mr and Mrs Holmes, and now Volckman was in the predicament of claiming that his bold action was his alone, and that he was not Mrs Guppy's puppet. What he did is quite famous. It was called 'ghost grabbing'. Unlike James Clark, he had proceeded to the séance in question from his own home, not slipping off mysteriously from Mrs Guppy's side. Of course, he wanted to be seen as his own man.

He was investigative, and attended as many séances given by different mediums as he could get to. It is obvious that he had been a party to warm discussions in Highbury over the punch bowl about the epidemic of false materialised spirits that were giving spiritualism a bad name. Volckman was as quick as Samuel Guppy to reach for his pen in justification of his behaviour, although he was not so popular, so affectionately regarded as Mr Guppy. Nor was he so well known. He was eloquent, spirited, sharp as a knife, and he bitterly resented being castigated. Also, he had been assaulted, and he had medical evidence to prove it: that was the crime committed at the séance. He was angry and unrepentant. A torrent of words poured from him:

> I have to state, that having for forty minutes carefully observed and scrutinised the face, features, gestures, size, style, and peculiarities of utterance of the so-called spirit, the conviction irresistibly forced itself upon me that *no ghost*, but the medium, Miss Florence Cook, herself, was before the circle. I perceived also an occasional tip-toeing by the young lady as if to alter her stature, and was much struck by the utter puerility of her remarks throughout the séance. I am confirmed in my conviction, as above stated, by the facts that the *struggling* ghost had to be forcibly extricated by my grasp, and afterwards to be 'aided' into her cabinet by a Justice of the Peace.
>
> I may add that no third-parties had any knowledge of my invitation to, or presence at, the séance in question.

Determined to establish that Volckman's crime against spiritualism was premeditated, that he had arrived at 6 Bruce Villas, Eleanor Road, Hackney, on December 9th with full *mens rea* (guilty mind), WH Harrison, editor of the *Spiritualist*, a staunch supporter of Florence Cook, stated that, 'His uneasy looks and his abrupt remarks had been the subject of comment in the early part of the evening; he was himself told of his unusual manner.'

William Volckman had a plausible explanation for his mood, which he did not deny: 'to reach the haunted house in time I had to grope my way on foot, for an hour and a half, through four miles of the densest fog it has ever been my misfortune to endure, – hence my "uneasy looks and abrupt remarks" which elicited from Mr Harrison some such natural "comment" as "how tired I looked," and upon which he has ingeniously founded a theory of "premeditation", – forgetting that the "conditions" were not favourable to that cheerful and easy demeanour which henceforth I hope will be my "usual manner" in Ghost society.' His manner of writing increasingly resembles Mr Guppy's.

Born on June 3rd, 1856, Florence Cook was then aged 17 and Volckman was obviously not susceptible to her immature charms, celebrated so embarrassingly by William Crookes in hymning her *alter ego*, 'Katie King': 'But photography is as inadequate to depict the perfect beauty of Katie's face, as words are powerless to describe her charm of manner. Photography may, indeed, give a map of her countenance; but how can it reproduce the brilliant purity of her complexion, or the ever-varying expression of her most mobile features ... ' Unimpressed by the apparition, Volckman saw his opportunity when. ' "Katie", assured [as he told us] of the harmonious character of the circle, deigned to take some of us by the hand. My turn came; and by no means to my surprise I found that her Ghost-ship could not release her fingers from my hold [as he had himself found with genuine spirits such as Charles Williams's 'John King']. Apprehending the situation, she quickly made a step backwards towards her cabinet, endeavouring to tug away her hand. But, not to be thus evaded, I with *equal* promptness "rose up and grasped her with both arms round the waist".' Volckman was very anxious to challenge the claim that he had tried to throw the spirit down with his feet, an ungentlemanly act, which, we know, Mr Guppy would never have attempted. Thus, 'My only object was gently to hold the Angel in my arms, until it should melt away, or until all present might be as convinced as myself that the "angelic visitant" was Miss Florence Cook.' It is not inconceivable that he did use his feet.

Deflecting the attention to his own vulnerability at the séance, Volckman pleads his physical inferiority to the medium's enraged protectors: 'The reader will excuse the egotistical details I am obliged to infuse into my narration. Mr Harrison says I "should be made" to confine my remarks to myself. No compulsion, however, is required to induce me to supply any items of importance to this discussion; on the contrary, I am happy to volunteer relevant testimony even at the expense of my own constitutional sensitiveness. My present weight then is 11st. 0lb. 14oz. in my clothes. – (I fancy I must have lost quite "a pound of flesh" lately. Is this owing to Mr Harrison?) My height is 5 feet 6 and five eighths in my boots, – (fashionable heels). In bulk and inches I am less than either of the three Ghost champions, one or both particulars considered ... As further evidence of a struggle I may not omit to mention the two blunt scratches which for a few days after the event adorned my nose – somewhat prominent feature, friends, of Grecian order. How I came by these marks of conflict I will not pretend to state with absolute certainty. But, reader, "remember the poor Ghost" is a young, impulsive woman, and, although some "three hundred years old", may not have quite forgotten the use of nails in emergency ...

'Students of psychology inform us – that in moments of peril the mind with lightning rapidity is enabled to take a comprehensive view of past life and all its events. – I had regained my feet. But pinioned by stalwart arms, and the object of angry cries and fierce gesticulation – the thought flashed through my brain "no one knows of my invitation to, or presence at, this eventful séance," – when, O horror!!! O despair!! – O "OUTRAGE" OF OUTRAGES!! THE GAS WAS EXTINGUISHED.'

It appeared that his beard had been torn. Five minutes had passed before Florence was revealed, *sancta innocenta*, in her cabinet. Even her coloured, wadded winter underwear, investigated by those of her own gender, had failed to reveal evidence of ghostly white cerements.

William Volckman was reviled, excoriated, a cad, a rotter, not a real gentleman. He could have killed the young lady, they complained, and he had broken the fiduciary bond between private medium and invited sitter. The example of the Earl of Caithness, who was present, but not an avowed spiritualist, was held up to him as an example of perfect, noble decorum. That will have hurt, and he dug deep for arguments of justification and tasteful quotations to demonstrate that he was a man of culture, a moral being.

'I could state,' he said, 'how for five years I have been examining many phases of the phenomena alleged to be spiritual, dating my first practical acquaintance with the subject from my appointment to the investigating committee of the London Dialectical Society. I could prove that during the whole of this period my conduct towards mediums has been of the most considerate character, and entitles me to the utmost confidence and fairness; and I could show that all this was well known to many of the "Ghost" party, not withstanding their polite designation of me and attempt to ignore my identity.'

It was no good; he was regarded as an outsider. The Cook faction had always harboured suspicions about him. He had already attended two other séances in the same household which were obviously not impressive because (said Volckman) the Cook family members themselves declared them to be very inferior. There had been no complaints then about Volckman's behaviour. It is curious that in order to gain entrance to the more important séance with full spirit form he had had to cough up a substantial bauble for the privilege. Perhaps that venal gleam prejudiced him against the haunted Hackney house and its cluster of frequenters from aristocrats to a ship's officer. That is the background behind his comments that, 'I could show that Miss Cook, if not a *professional* medium, is none the less a paid one, and that in my offer to that young lady of a piece of jewellery I was but following a "kindly" fashion indulged in by many another visitor, as Mr Cook had several times previously informed me. I could say something about my invitation as a standing promise for nine months, – a promise most reluctantly fulfilled; and I could state that such invitation followed, at last, quickly upon my present – came, be it understood, direct from the Ghost itself (as Mr Cook also informed me.) – and was politely unencumbered by any conditions.'

Whatever Volckman's protestations, the stubborn belief has persisted that he returned as a hero to Mrs Guppy's hearth. She did not disapprove of what he had done, or cast him away as a liability. However, especially since the revelations of 1964, misunderstanding and lack of knowledge have fostered untruths. William Volckman was not affianced to Elizabeth Guppy at the time, nor was he carrying on a special relationship with her. The Guppy marriage was strong and continuing. Their second son had recently been born. As a matter of fact, Volckman was still married to his first wife, although separated from her. Samuel Guppy was in good form and a third child would seem to have been perfectly feasible in a year or two. What happened *later* is a different story. Death changes everything.

8

The Last Séance

SAMUEL GUPPY SEEMED TO BE in the midst of life, hale and hearty, full of intellectual fire, and enjoying family life. In the September of 1874, however, possibly feeling that something was not quite right, he took Elizabeth, their two infants, and a nursemaid, for a cure in Ireland, at St Ann's Hill Hydropathic Establishment, near Blarney, seven miles from Cork.

Mr Guppy already knew Dr Richard Barter (1802-70), the proprietor, who had successfully abandoned the cold water douches of orthodox hydrotherapy in favour of the hot dry-air bath – the British version of the Turkish bath. 'Hot' was the operative word, and ventilation was not always exemplary. Perhaps the treatment was too rigorous for Mr Guppy, more used to pottering in clubs and billiard rooms, doing justice to his wife's hearty cuisine, smoking his Havanas, tinkering with his chemical experiments, and striving to distil spirit photographs out of the ether.

After a month, he sent Georgiana Houghton a splendid photograph of Elizabeth and himself, taken in Dublin. He looked 'as full of power and vigour as if he were at least ten years younger,' and that was how she remembered him. He died unexpectedly, at St Ann's, on January 18th, 1875. Miss Houghton was told that he passed away quietly, in his sleep, but, sadly, that was not so. He fought hard for life. An Irish death certificate has been obtained, and the given cause of death is a surprise: 'Epileptic fit. Probably a few hours.'

William Sack, MD, resident physician at the spa, and in attendance at the last illness, was the certifying informant. The bare words are probably misleading. As far as we know, there was no history of epilepsy. *Status epilepticus* is the condition of continuous convulsions likely to end in death if not interrupted, but in the case of Mr Guppy it is more probable that the fits supervened after some kind of cerebrovascular accident.

As soon as was decently possible, Mrs Guppy, an unexpected widow, dressed in her only too appropriate black, with her now fatherless boys, sailed across the Irish Sea for England. It was an image fit for a Victorian genre picture. At first she stayed in a Knightsbridge apartment at 27 Montpelier Square, never returning to live in Highbury, although the lease had not expired. Then, by no means in decline, she took a 'pretty little house' at 43 Victoria Road, expressly nearer her many friends. Her instinct was good. Previously named 'Love Road', Victoria Road was a rising and lucky address. In 2011, it was the most expensive in England and Wales. Here she moved into the ornate villa her crates of magic *materia*, her beloved menagerie of white dog, white cat, fancy birds, new-fangled aquarium, Tommy's box of white mice, but maybe not the famous billiard table.

After only three months of mourning, she took up her séances again. In the May of the year of her bereavement, she began quietly in the new setting of the Kensington house. Then, on June 28th, she launched her new campaign, climbing into a train to Brighton, to see Mrs Catherine Berry, from whom she had been estranged, no doubt seizing the opportunity for reconciliation when Mrs Berry wrote a letter of condolence. Even if there had been no such letter it would have been difficult to turn away a grieving widow's overtures.

As she chugged through the countryside, a large, lonely figure in her gloomy weeds silhouetted against the window, her carpet-bag did not, like Mrs Dyer's, hold a murdered baby, but a crumpled conjurer's puppet, which she wanted to try out on her old enemy, away from town. She was going to produce a 'materialisation'. At 9 o'clock in the evening, they took their seats in Mrs Berry's back drawing-room. 'A spirit-voice, which I think was Katie's,' Mrs Berry informed the *Medium*, 'told us to open the folding doors so as to admit just a little light. That being done, in a few minutes a white form appeared over the empty chair. We both saw it, for Mrs Guppy was not entranced then, or at any other time during the sitting. At first it was of an indefinite form, but very soon it assumed a human form, and became very distinct. The full face was towards me, and the profile to Mrs Guppy, and she asked me to lay my cheek to hers, that I might get the same view. But that I felt disinclined to do. A voice then said, "Take the wreath from the spirit's head." I took the wreath from his head, and I now have it in my possession, but I became exceedingly nervous, as also did Mrs Guppy. The spirit, however, seemed determined that I should see him to more advantage, and asked that the door of the room might be opened and a light put in the passage. I rang for my maid, who carried out the instructions. The light then fell directly on the face of the spirit, and I had a most perfect view. I had seen the Sultan of Zanzibar on the previous day, and the spirit's face somewhat reminded me of him. He had a handsome copper-coloured face, and a large black beard. On his head he had a white turban, such as worn by the spirit "John King" ... For several minutes the spirit was distinctly visible to us, but I felt so exhausted by the loss of magnetism, and so nervous as well, that I begged him to leave us. I shall never forget his sorrowful expression of countenance as he reluctantly passed away – evaporated into the atmosphere.'

Elizabeth must have stayed the night, even if Mrs Berry could not bear to place her cheek to hers, because, the following evening, William Gill, a fellow spiritualist, was invited to join them, and the same marvel was achieved. The 'column of cotton wool rose up and developed as before, the white turban, the exquisitely chiselled olive-coloured face, his age of 25.' 'The ghost,' Gill said, 'did not creep from some mysterious cabinet in which the medium had been placed – personation was entirely out of the question. The medium was with us and talking to us – she was not even entranced as mediums invariably are during the production of such a phenomenon, but was herself a witness. The séance was in every respect remarkable, and will be heard by many spiritualists with considerable surprise, the materialisation of spirit-form being a new development of Mrs Guppy's marvellous mediumship.'

So there it was - Elizabeth's own version of the desired feat. The spirit was mute, and the face rigid, not pliable. It was not ambulant in the Katie King mode, but it was palpably separate and co-existent with the medium. It was not so striking as Florence Cook's stage play, but no doubt it had its own strength, and it certainly bowled over Mrs Berry, who could be difficult. The *Medium*, apprised of these events, hastened to Brighton and investigated the scene. There was actually very little to see, as Mrs Berry could only point to the furniture and the direction of the light. 'Now,' the editor wrote, ' we have Mrs Guppy paying a visit to Mrs Berry, and obtaining a form of manifestation which we understand to be quite new even in her wonderful experience. We believe she has had it repeated in the absence of Mrs Berry.'

Elizabeth was in no hurry to let the 'Sultan of Zanzibar' out of his box again, because she had a more splendid project in the planning stage, at which she would shine in a glittering social setting in her own delightful house in Kensington. The argument that mediumship satisfied her social aspirations is fully validated by the 'brilliant reception' which she held on the evening of July 28th, 1875. Samuel Guppy, as ever, had provided the wherewithal. He could not be at her side, but we must suspect that her tender-hearted friends such as Miss Houghton were more affected by his absence than she was. All her best spiritualist friends and connections, some titled, the odd foreign prince, thronged the drawing-room - about 40 of them. There were lavish refreshments and beautiful flowers. Two tables accommodated the expectant sitters. Darkness reigned. The services of Mrs Mary Hardy, the successful American medium, on her first visit to England had been engaged and the two mediums could pool their resources and double their powers. They were both 'floated', with their dresses brushing against the sitters' faces, but the principal thrust of the manifestations came from the eructation of spirit hands through the previously cut hole in the table. It was scarcely earth-shaking, but the atmosphere was good, and the company were satisfied, even Edward William Cox, Serjeant-at-Law, probably the most challengingly intellectual of Mrs Guppy's guests. He gave her no trouble, even though he did not believe in materialised spirit forms and thought that 'psychic force' or 'virtue emanating from the soul' was active at séances.

Gratifyingly, the *Medium* gave full coverage to the gala evening, naming Prince Albert of Solms, Countess Poulett, Count and Countess Von Wimpffen, and Count Bastogi among the sitters. It was remarked that, 'Mrs Guppy's recent receptions have been much sought after, and have been amongst the most interesting events of the London season.' Elizabeth had conspicuously not respected the ritual year of mourning. Samuel stayed in the minds of his friends. The spiritualist, JD Gledstanes, who had been a guest at the 'brilliant reception', loyally reported to the *Spiritualist* on June 2nd, 1876, that Madame De Veh, the writing medium, had been receiving messages purporting to be sent by the late Mr Guppy. An attempt was made to reproduce the style of his public effusions, but it cannot be said to be successful:

> Well, I feel honoured and monstrously obliged by your delicate attention in recalling me to the tender memories of those I left behind me, whether enemies or friends, and I hope that if I have said anything worth repeating or listening to, it may not be without fruit ...
>
> Am I in a house? Well, house is not the expression. I am where others are. I am in a hall, as it were, without roofs or walls. How can I describe it? There are no limits, no beginning, no end, no top, no bottom. No words can express my meaning, so it is useless trying ...
>
> [Upon reference being made to something he had said when in the flesh]: Pray, my dear friend, do try and forget my double-dyed asinine remarks. Good God, when you say these things it is like a stab, as I feel that I was an ass. I feel now so thoroughly small, so idiotic, so to say, that you must not be astonished at my recurring so continually to my ignorance. It is such a shock to feel that one has passed for a cunning sage, when one has been a perfect empty-headed fool ...

After a very short interval, Samuel Guppy's will had been proved on February 23rd, 1875. His widow was the sole executrix, and she took all the estate and effects after a legacy of £100 to Sarah Maria Gibbon, Mr Guppy's niece. Nothing at all went to his poor, deranged son, Samuel Henry, soon (in 1880) to be incarcerated. Arrangements were put in place for the care of the infant son, Thomas, in the event of Elizabeth Guppy's dying before him. The will was executed on January 9th, 1872, before the birth of the baby, Samuel, later in that year. It turned out that Mr Guppy was not the fabulously rich man of popular belief. His effects were under £3000. The National Archives currency converter gives the 'spending worth' today of that sum as £137,100.

Elizabeth was free, and alone, aged 37, with no masculine support, and that was not a state of affairs that she was happy to tolerate. She was displaying herself at what she did best, and she was most likely to attract an admirer from the ranks of spiritualists who attended her séances. William Volckman was the chosen one. It did not matter to her that there was a cloud over his name in spiritualist circles. Nor, obviously, did it matter to him that she towered over him in size, and was burdened with two infants.

The Volckmans came from an old and influential family in Bavaria. They emigrated more to America than to Great Britain. In 1851, there were only 14 Volckmans living in the broad area of Middlesex. Volckman's father, also William, was born in 1860 at Stratford-by-bow, East London. He was a confectioner. Volkman's mother, Jane, was born in Scotland. William was their eldest child, born in Bishopsgate in 1836, and there were at least seven more children born of the union: John, Jane, Francis, Lidia, Helen, Anna and Adelaide. Volckman's prose style, although tending to the impassioned and excitable rather than witty and urbane, evidences an English education at good centres of learning. Following his father, he was a confectionery manufacturer and wholesale provisioner with vast factory premises extending to 1½ acres at 370 High Street, Stratford. A very wealthy man, he was the senior partner in the firm of William & Charles Volckman, and they employed 300 workers.

His first marriage, which failed unpleasantly, was to Elizabeth Yeomans, who was of prosperous, mercantile background. Her father, James, born in Whitechapel in c.1805, was a contractor for the government in connection with the East India Company. Her mother, also Elizabeth, was born in Northamptonshire, and she gave birth to Elizabeth, James, Jessie, Mary and William. In the year of 1851, when Elizabeth was 18, the Yeoman family were living in style at Oak Hall, Whitechapel, attended by a footman, a gardener, and four female house servants.

When they were married, William and Elizabeth set up house in Dalston, and then at 12 King Edward Road, Hackney, near the confectionery business in Stratford. A line of children were produced: Ronald, Florence, Bernard, Edwin, Mabel and Christabel. Bernard and Edwin both read medicine. William also looked after his widowed mother-in-law under the same roof.

In 1875, the year of Samuel's death, Elizabeth Volckman divorced William Volckman, on the grounds of his adultery and cruelty. Although divorce was a very last resort in those days, the grounds cited are not an indication of exceptional bad behaviour: until 1923, a wife had to prove her husband's adultery, *along with some other offence*, to gain a divorce. Mrs Volckman was so embarrassed by the stigma of divorce that she dared to supply the wrong entry for the census of 1881: 'Mutually separated.' By then, she had moved out to Croydon. Later, she lived with Florence and Mabel in Bridlington, and in 1901 she was in the Lake District, at Kendal, with one servant.

It was not until August 8th of 1875 that the Court of Probate and Divorce approved the maintenance arrangements. Mrs Volckman was to be allowed £400 a year for herself, and £95 a year for the education of the children. If she should marry again, the £400 would be reduced to £200 a year. The portion for the wronged wife was substantial, and considered to be very equitable. The decree absolute was granted, and, bearing this financial burden, Volckman married Mrs Guppy forthwith – on August 12th, 1875, unceremoniously at Kensington Register Office.

Elizabeth's marriage address was her new home, 43 Victoria

Road, and, for the registrar, she confessed to her real father, Charles Taylor White, gentleman, deceased. William gave the address, 7 Danes Inn, Strand. The plainness of the venue was redeemed by the splendour of the witnesses: Henry Emile, Count of Wimpffen, Camilla, Countess of Wimpffen, Margaret Fisher and Hannah Warrilow. Surely, at least Mrs Fisher, Samuel Guppy's finest deponent, felt a pang of sadness for him at this hasty ceremony, lacking scrupulous propriety? There was bound to be gossip. The *Belfast News-Letter* commented on August 20th that Mrs Guppy, 'became a widow a few months ago, and has now once more become a wife. The partner of her choice is a gentleman of Anglo-Teutonic extraction, named Volckman. He is a wholesale confectioner in Bishopsgate Street.' Yet again the surname is used against Volckman, engaged unbecomingly in trade, in the East End of London, to boot.

Twelve months later, the newly married couple produced a male child, the only one of their respective second marriages. He was born on August 11th, 1876, at 43 Victoria Road, and, with admirable generosity, Volckman allowed him to be called William Guppy Volckman. Moreover, from this time onwards, Elizabeth took to styling herself Mrs Guppy-Volckman. The furore over the Volckman 'outrage' gradually died down, but was never entirely extinguished from the collective spiritualist mind. Victoria Road was the marital home for some years, and Elizabeth's séances continued there when she was well enough, but by 1881 the family, with their three boys, had moved eastward from Kensington to 338/340 Stratford High Street, close by William's great factory at 370 High Street.

The birth of Elizabeth's third child was followed by a severe illness. Miss Houghton is our informant here. She had attended an afternoon séance at Mrs Guppy-Volckman's on New Year's Day, 1878, 'But it was not for the exercise of her own mediumship, for she had long been very seriously invalided, partly the result of rheumatic fever, when her life had been almost despaired of, and nothing but the tenderest and most devoted nursing could have restored her to her friends. Although then to a certain extent convalescent, her system had nothing to spare of superfluous aura, so that her powers were completely in abeyance as far as regarded manifestations in circle, but she is always liberal-hearted, so she often engaged professional mediums, to satisfy the prejudices of those persons who prefer séances at other persons' houses rather than their own.' Charles Williams was the medium.

Miss Houghton confessed that she preferred a more select circle: 'I do not mean as to worldly position, for in that respect it was composed of rather the élite, but I mean as being more spiritually minded, for the larger proportion of those present only seemed to look upon it as a variation in their usual course of worldly dissipation, without any higher thought whatever, and I really should not have felt surprised to have heard any of those very mundane enquiries propounded that one hears suggested by outsiders whose minds do not rise above the level of the stock exchange and the race-course. A lady sat near me whose first experience it was of a spirit circle, and the flippant style of the chief part of the converse with the gone-beyond ones rather shocked her, but I assured her that most of those present were not to be termed spiritualists or even enquirers, so that she must not let it deter her from seeking more deeply into this grandest of all subjects.' The difference in the motivation of Elizabeth and Miss Houghton in the grand psychic enterprise could not be better illustrated than in these reflections. Elizabeth was very happy to sit in state in company that she could once only have dreamed of, while her loyal friend was a refined Christian Spiritualist with her mind focussed on unworldly matters.

Florence Marryat (1837-99), the daughter of Captain Marryat, herself a popular writer, was a committed spiritualist from 1873 onwards. She was undoubtedly taken advantage of by American and English mediums, being especially vulnerable after the death of a deformed baby daughter. She attended many of Elizabeth's séances, including the reception of 1875, and she saw her as 'taking a great private interest in spiritualism, which all media do not. Her means justify her, too, in gratifying her whims.'

Elizabeth told her about a 'Green Lady', whom, she said, she had seen in an empty house in Broadstairs, reputed to be haunted. After easily obtaining the keys from the landlord, she had gone to investigate, although she was on crutches, having 'barely recovered at the time, from a most dangerous illness, which had left a partial paralysis of the lower limbs behind it.' She had sat down on the bare boards of the drawing-room to recover from the stairs. 'It was on a summer's evening towards the dusky hour, and she sat on, virtually helpless, waiting to see what would come.' The apparition wore a long, green satin robe.

Apparently, Elizabeth bought the lease, and the Volckmans moved into their newly furnished house. A party of friends was invited down to stay at Broadstairs and the scene was set for a 'Green Lady' séance. There was a circle of 12. William Volckman was the host, and Charles Williams was there. During the day, Florence Marryat remembered, the refurbished house, with its large rooms and windows facing the sea looked cheerful enough, but the drawing-room at seven o'clock had a different atmosphere. There was a full moon, and the sparkling waves were quite visible through the interstices of the venetian blinds. The Green Lady rose up from the carpet and stood between Mrs Guppy-Volckman and Charles Williams. Her face was white and cold as a corpse and her eyes were closed. She leaned over the table and brought her face close to each in turn before she left by the same route, sinking down into the carpet. She made no sound, but everyone saw her.

In 1878, Elizabeth, with her husband, attended a séance at which she did not shine. Although she was not the medium, it would have been better for her if she had not attended, and, in fact, the Volckmans did not return to the next, similar occasion.

Around that time, the Society for Psychical Research was despatching members to evaluate the work of a number of mediums. At this particular séance, Mrs Henry Sidgwick's sister, probably Alice Balfour, was the investigator, and her account was later read as part of a paper by Mrs Sidgwick delivered to the 20th

General Meeting of the Society in 1886 and duly printed.

The medium, undoubtedly one of Elizabeth's protégés, was William George Haxby, a rather pitiful figure, who sickened and died in 1882. A fund had been raised for him in his long, deteriorative final illness. His day job was respectable – clerk at the General Post Office. He was born in about 1857, at Hunmanby, near the Yorkshire coast, where his parents ran a grocer's shop. The family moved to 8 Sandall Road, Kentish Town, where they took in lodgers, and William George, at the age of 13, found work as a law stationer's clerk before entering the Post Office. He was noticed by Alfred Russel Wallace, (who attended some of his séances and was not critical of him,) to be a small man. That made him an agile performer, like a conjurer's assistant.

The venue was the house of some friends of the Sidgwicks'. Serjeant Cox was among the sitters. Elizabeth sat primly beside her rich, new husband, not a participant, both dressed to the nines in evening apparel. Some present may not have been aware that she and Haxby were well known to each other. 'Abdullah' was the materialised spirit. The investigator noticed that the last time Abdullah vanished, he did so close to the wall, between Mrs Guppy-Volckman and the wall. 'We saw him go down on his knees, and then all of a sudden he was gone.' Elizabeth, disposed to argue, spoke up and declared that 'He was not close to the wall, and that he disappeared through the curtain and not at the opening, and that the curtain had never moved.' The account continued, 'Most of the circle saw the curtain move, and I saw him make a rush into the cabinet close to the wall, and saw his white drapery trailing behind.'

Worse was to come: 'After this an indistinct black object came out from the cabinet, close to the wall near Mrs Guppy-Volckman, where there was a deep shadow, and disappeared under the train of her voluminous black velvet gown. Others in the circle thought the black object disappeared, but did not see how or where to. Soon after Abdullah materialised from under the gown. As the white object first appeared it was obvious to me that it was the head and shoulders of a man lying on his right side. I was sure that his legs were concealed behind Mrs Guppy-

Volckman's chair, and this Mrs H. made sure of, as she stretched out her hand and felt the cloth of his coat there.' Mrs Sidgwick summed up Haxby's 'Abdullah' as a 'miserable personation.'

Elizabeth was beginning to show to better advantage as a support to her husband. Always capable, she interested herself in the lucrative business, a respected, commanding figure around the premises. She was not a litigious person, but situations cropped up, as with the earlier abusive cabman, when she had no alternative but to proceed in court. There was a horse involved again. In 1881, a new van horse was required, and when a bay gelding that sounded quite suitable was advertised for sale in a daily paper, accompanied by a clerk and a stableman, she went to Bolt Yard, Whitechapel to examine the animal, and found it 'a perfect beauty'. He was trotted up, and Mrs Guppy-Volckman offered the owner, Henry Brown, the owner, £20, fully warranted sound and returnable. The offer was accepted, and the poor animal was led away to his new home, but he was found to be a 'roarer', gone in the wind, and absolutely incapable of work. Henry Brown had vanished from the stable, of course, and the horse was said by the police to be an 'old friend' used for the trick more than once, kept groomed and well-fed for his part in the crime. Elizabeth may not have been a clever judge of horse-flesh, but Brown was a professional horse-coper. He was sentenced to 12 months imprisonment with hard labour, for false pretences.

Slander and libel seemed to pursue her, and she was forced to defend herself, not least because of her husband's public status. In April, 1891, when Volckman was engaged in a contest for the office of president of the West Ham (North) Liberal and Radical Association, 'a man living at Osborne Road, Forest Gate,' had uttered slanders by spreading rumours that she was not actually married to Mr William Volckman. Elizabeth applied to the magistrate for a summons against him, producing the certificates for both her marriages. Her lawyer, Mr T Willis, said that the person complained of was a man of straw, and it would be useless to bring an action against him in the High Court: Mrs Guppy-Volckman was anxious for a summons. Mr Baggallay, the magistrate, said it would be practically useless for him, and it would be improper for him to grant a summons when there was not a reasonable probability of its being supported by evidence. He thought he would be sorely tempted himself – but he would not advise that – to go to the man and say to him fairly that if he repeated the slander he should have a thrashing. Throughout the hearing, incidentally, Elizabeth was referred to as Madame Volckman, a dignity which made her appear foreign. Her case had failed, but there must have been some satisfaction in hearing the magistrate castigating 'those creeping reptiles, who find their greatest enjoyment in life in telling dirty tales about other people.'

In 1892, Elizabeth had to bring a very serious action for slander. The case of 'Volckman and wife v Waring and wife' was heard in the Queen's Bench Division on January 12th before Mr Justice Mathew and a special jury (as required for such an action). The parties had been introduced five or six years previously, and had become friendly. In 1890, negotiations had been entered into for the Volckmans to let their house to the Warings, but the agreement fell through. Ill-feeling had arisen, and, it was alleged, Mrs Waring had uttered slanders against Mrs Volckman, in particular to a Mrs Turner, at the Victoria Hotel, Liverpool, where the Warings were indeed staying in 1891: he was aged 51 and she was 41.

The sensational slanders were that Mrs Guppy-Volckman had murdered her first husband; poisoned a Mrs Stewart, whom she had induced to make a will in her favour; kept a house of ill-repute in Paris and been hounded out of that city by the police; and that she was a procuress. Elizabeth went into the witness box to deny all these allegations. Mrs Waring's own counsel, Mr Bankes, told the jury that the charges were so extravagant and so wholesale that no one could have believed them. He was on firmer ground when he proposed that the claims were the utterances of a woman who was suffering from delusions. The Volckmans were strongly represented by a team of three – Mr Lockwood, QC, Mr Horace Avory and Mr Robert Wallace. William Volckman said that he was a town councillor at West

Ham; he had read through all the slanders, and one and all were pure inventions. He considered that Mrs Waring was an excitable person, but not nervous.

The jury found against the defendants and ordered damages of £100 from Mr Waring and £300 against the separate estate of Mrs Waring. There *had* been gossip about the short space between Elizabeth's marriages, but the cause of Samuel Guppy's death in Ireland has been laid open in these pages, and it does not support murder.

Some light was shed on this ill-conceived friendship, when, nearly a decade later, Elizabeth again found herself in the witness box. This was a criminal case, in the lower court. *The Times* (November 9th, 1900) reported that Gertrude Waring, who described herself as 'Lady' Waring, of Torrington Square, was charged on remand before Sir Franklin Lushington with obtaining on credit from Fabian de Jacowicz £23 worth of jewellery on the alleged misrepresentation that she was a lady of title, and that she had £10,000 standing to her account in Parr's and Gosling's banks. She also owed £21 to Caroline Spalding, the keeper of the boarding house in which the prisoner was arrested, where she claimed that she was Lady Waring and had just made £6,000 on the transfer of her house.

Mrs Guppy-Volckman was called by the prosecution: her husband was now a magistrate for West Ham. She said that she had known the accused for about ten years. She had taken her out of Rainhill Pauper Lunatic Asylum [Liverpool] to live with her for two years. Her family would have nothing to do with her and abused Mrs Guppy-Volckman for removing her. She was not, in fact, discharged as cured, and after a great deal of trouble with her, she was admitted to the private asylum, St Luke's, London, where Mrs Guppy-Volckman had to pay for her keep and clothe her. It now appeared that she had not acted irresponsibly in liberating Mrs Waring from Rainhill, because she had taken her, on her discharge, to be seen by Dr Wallace, of Harley Street, and he had certified that she was of sane mind. The Lunacy Commissioners, however, advised Mrs Guppy-Volckman that she took her out at her own risk.

The magistrate came to an unusual decision. He said that as it was clear that the accused was not discharged as cured from Rainhill, and Fabian de Jacowicz appeared to have been intimately connected with her for many years, he must have known that she was not responsible for her actions. He discharged 'Lady' Waring forthwith, and made no order for the restitution of the jewellery, which she had pawned, anyway, three days after receiving it.

These are obscure events, the bare facts covering over a pit of dire upheavals. Elizabeth must have had her husband's consent. She had been in the habit of taking in lame ducks. Did she want to groom this excitable person for mediumship? Perhaps she was already a spiritualist. Her husband seemed to have disappeared. Why was Elizabeth so very determined to persist with the rescue? Perhaps we should give her the benefit of doubt and admire her kindness to an old friend, even though she had accused her of crime and infamy.

In the 1880s, the Volckmans moved out of town to the White House, a picturesque, not grand, country dwelling at Knotts Green, Leyton, Essex. There were quietly comfortable holidays. In 1911, the Census caught them at Miss Mary Jane Walker's apartment house, Belle Vue, Beacon Hill Road, Hindhead, Surrey. William was 75, and Elizabeth was 70. She had brought with her 23-year-old Rose Ethel White – her own ladies' maid. She had come a long way from Hull, although she dutifully gave her birthplace as 'Lanes, Horncastle.'

In 1888, Young Tommy – Thomas Guppy – Elizabeth's eldest son, died in his 19th year, on March 15th, at Sydney, New South Wales, where he had gone for his health. Samuel Guppy, the second boy, did not die young, but he had no luck. On August 18th, 1897, at the parish church, Cranleigh, Surrey, he married Septima Durrant, youngest daughter of the late Revd David Robinson Durrant, MA, of Yiewsley, Uxbridge, and previously of 4 Rutland Gate, Hyde Park. This would seem to have been exactly the kind of match that his father, in his lifetime, would have expected for his son, but it was not like that at all.

Yseult Bridges knew the story well, because her parents were very fond of Samuel, and, as a family, they always saw him when visiting England. Septima, who was older, had a considerable fortune, with land near Malden, in Surrey, which Samuel, an outdoor type, was happy to farm, while she went hunting. They lived in a good, Georgian house. She was a difficult woman, domineering and possessive. Unable to have a child, after a hunting accident, she tried to adopt Yseult Bridges, and when her offer, which was generous, was rejected, she became unpleasant, and would have nothing to do with the family. In due course, Samuel wrote from Canada: he had left Septima and was more than happy without her. She adopted three children from an orphanage. Elizabeth must have known about her son's misfortunes.

Elizabeth's last child, William Guppy Volckman, seems to have fared better and he had the distinction of serving in the Royal Flying Corps in the First World War. In 1899, at Portsea Island, he had married Bertha Cadman, from Nottingham. A daughter, Florence, was born, and in 1901, the family of three were living in South Hammersmith. William and Bertha were described as 'Actor' and 'Actress'.

A disaster that altered their lives came to the Volckmans in 1893, with the great fire of their confectionery factory at Stratford. The whole of the East End of London was brilliantly illuminated, and the flames cast reflections for miles around. It was the second big fire that had broken out in the area that week, and there were suspicions of arson. It originated mysteriously in the main building, before the midnight of June 16th. The blaze spread to every building across the site, and eight engines could not contain it. A room containing rare essences for flavouring and colouring sweets, valued at £500, exploded like a fireworks display and rained down an incendiary shower. William was not ruined: he was far too astute not to be insured. The damage was estimated at £50,000, but premises and stock were covered. The following April, the entire stock-in-trade, machinery and plant were put up for auction. The Volckmans' private victoria carriage and light, well-built pair were included in the disposal. William called it a day, and by 1901 the Volckmans had retired and were resident in Market Street, Brighton.

Despite her lasting poor health, Elizabeth continued to reign over a circumscribed number of séances for friends, never losing the need to be admired for her powers, influencing others and being an extraordinary person. *Light* periodical of May 29th 1897, in a respectful reminder that she was still active, recorded a recent séance, equipped with the familiar, holed table. One of her pop-up materialisations, a mute, white figure, rose over the table, and raps indicated that it was the spirit of a victim of the notorious Bazaar fire of Paris, in which 126 people, mostly women of the Catholic aristocracy, were trapped and burnt to embers.

Elizabeth became a widow again, when, on May 2nd 1913, William Volckman died at the Nightingale Nursing Home, Strafford Road, Twickenham. He was 77. Two homes were listed for him; The Cabin, Beacon Hill Road, Hindhead, Surrey, and 40 Twickenham Road, Teddington, Middlesex. He left the considerable sum of £17,964 and probate was granted to his widow and the Public Trustee. He had been a pillar of the community, with many public offices. When the will was proved in the September of 1913, it was revealed in the press that it included a touching tribute to his wife: 'I desire hereby to place on record my heartfelt appreciation of the devotion and constant affection of my generous-minded, unselfish, and very dear wife, Elizabeth Guppy-Volckman, whose loving companionship has been to me the greatest of solaces, and whose graciousness generally to all and sundry has suffered no diminution during the many years of painful illness she has so courageously endured.' Both Samuel and William had always wanted to protect her.

Elizabeth's last day in this world was in the winter of 1917, on December 9th, at 3 Norfolk Square, Brighton. She had reached the age of 79. The cause of death was 'Senile Decay', certified by W Barrington Prowse, MRCS. Her usual attending physician had been Dr Abraham Wallace, both a friend, and a spiritualist. Her son, William, of Hurst Park, Molesey, was the informant. Her will apportioned her effects of £13,908 between her two surviving sons, Samuel Guppy and William Guppy Volckman. By a codicil, she left £100 to John and Jane Priestley, who had been looking after her. Both husband and wife, William and Elizabeth Volckman, lie together in Teddington Cemetery, Shacklegate Lane, Richmond (Grave 33, Section CY) near the chapel, not in unconsecrated ground.

* * *

After five long years a widow, a lonely old woman, had died in Brighton, cared for by strangers. As she sat and watched the seasons, her stream of consciousness was strikingly different from those in a similar position. Once she had been famous Mrs Guppy, with counts and princes flocking to her drawing-room. Her best moments were in the darkness, strewing flowers like wheat until the revelation of the plenty heaped on the table. Her swirling dreams brought streaks of light, like phosphorus, and shooting stars in velvet blackness. The spirits awaiting her were poor old Samuel Guppy, handsome William Volckman, young Tommy lost in a foreign land, and reproachful members of her forgotten family in Hull.

Notes to Chapters

1
The Sculptor's Apprentice

The First Psychic ... 2005, p.279, n.2.

Incidents in My Life ... 1863, Chapter 1.

Mind over Space ... 1962, p.138.

The facts are that she was born Elizabeth ... Birth and family certificates obtained and correlated.

Metheringham ... A large, improving village, nine miles SE of Lincoln, according to *Whites 1842 Directory of Lincolnshire*, with a population of 1194, scattered farms, heathland and a long tract of cultivated fen. Charles Chaplin was lord of the manor. A market was held around the village cross on Saturday evenings. A steam engine drained the parish and dried the old Holywell spring. St Wilfrid's Church was a large, ancient structure, and there was a Wesleyan Chapel, a school, a Sick Club and a Cow Club.

William Grinsell Nicholl ... often as executant rather than designer ... view the website of Bob Speel at: www.speel.me.uk/sculpt/nicholl.htm.

Horncastle, her birthplace in 1838 ... At the corner of the Market Place, there stood, then, the fine house belonging to Henry Selwood, a prosperous attorney, whose daughter, Emily, after long wait and pining, became the devoted wife of Alfred Tennyson.

This dubious establishment was the Hamburgh Tavern ... view the website of Richard Hayton at: www.yorkshirehistory.com

an insolvent, James White ... v. Insolvent Debtors' Court cases in the *Hull Packet*, July 3rd, 1840.

In 1849, a direful strain of Asiatic cholera was brought into Hull ... v. Recollections of Hull, Revd James Sibtree, cited in Hullwebs History of Hull. (www.hullwebs.co.uk)

... Charles was a commercial traveller, the metier which he kept up at least until 1871, when he reached seventy ... In 1871, Charles White's son, George Henry, was a shipsmith and his son-in-law, William Mawler, married to Mary Jane, was a ship steward. All, with Charles and Sarah White, Elizabeth's parents, and Charles White Mawler, aged three, were living together at 37 Walker Street, Hull. In 1881, Sarah, aged 70, widowed, was in Grimsby, living with her now widowed daughter, Sarah, the basket maker, aged 37 and her six children at 165 Kent Street.

Henry Walter Bates ... Naturalist, (1825-92) praised and encouraged by Darwin, friend of Alfred Russel Wallace and embarked with him in 1848 on a joint expedition to the Amazons where he stayed for 11 years, to the detriment of his health. He published his *Naturalist on the Amazons* in 1863. Needing a job, he was famously pipped for a post in the Zoological Department at the British Museum by the poet, Arthur O'Shaughnessy. In 1864, he was appointed assistant secretary to the Royal Geographical Society.

Mrs Emma Hardinge Britten ... (1823-99) She was right out of Mrs Guppy's league; an inspirational trance speaker, an orator, travelled the world to promote spiritualism, a successful author. However, there were similarities about the early life of both mediums. She was born in the East End, and when her sea-captain father died early she was forced to earn her own living and support the family. At the age of 11 she taught music, and later acted. As a girl, she was very good-looking. There was a given history of childhood psychic experiences. She married well. In America, she embraced theosophy, with Madame Blavatsky. There is still a shade of mystery about her, a suspicion that she was a deep occultist, learned in the Black Arts.

Lady Lyell, wife of the geologist, found him 'unimpressive' ... My Life, 1905, p 433, where Wallace reflects on his youthful shortcomings.

2

Into the Dark

' ... *four hours before the flowers appeared.*' ... *Miracles and Modern Spiritualism*, p164

'*A large mass of earth about its roots.*' Although silence generally preceded the revelation, there were exceptions. The naturalist, the Revd JG Wood, told Newton Crosland (*op. cit.*, pp. 156-8) who had brought him to spiritualism, that at a séance with Miss Nicholl, immediately after the door was locked and the gas-jet lowered to a point, 'there commenced an astonishing rustling of leaves and branches' before a pyramid of shrubs and flowers was found.

... *apports* ... *appear on the table intact and as it were reconstituted.* Others, such as Cesare Lombroso (1836-1919), psychiatrist and anthropologist, rejecting the explanation of disintegration and reintegration, sought meaning in the concept of a fourth dimension.

' ... *a mind like yours, which I have always considered to be of so superior a quality.*' *My Life*, vol 2, pp.278-9

Mental Magic, 1884. Fuller title: *Mental Magic: A Rationale of Thought, Reading, and Its Attendant Phenomena, and Their Application* ... Thomas Welton, George Redway, York Street, Covent Garden, 1884.

... *dentist, Theodosius Purland* ... *My Life*, vol 2, p.75.

... *hysterical patients at the Salpêtrière Hospital in Paris.* See for vivid enlightenment, *Medical Muses: Hysteria in Nineteenth-Century Paris*, Asti Hustvedt. WW Norton, 2011.

The visitors to Mr Home or Mrs Guppy all see whatever occurs of a physical nature. Miracles and Modern Spiritualism, pp 123-4

' ... *a crinoline which would fold inwards when the wearer was seated.*' Grateful use has been made of *The History of Underclothes*, C Willett and Phillis Cunningham, Michael Joseph, 1951, p.165, *et passim*. Also note that in 1867, the year of Elizabeth's marriage to Mr Guppy, a trousseau costing £100 included '12 nightdresses, 12 chemises, 12 drawers, 6 camisoles, 6 vests, 2 French corsets, 2 crinolines, and a great many petticoats.'

In the darkness ... blood flowed. Experiences in Spiritualism, Catherine Berry, p.34.

3
Netting Mr Guppy

'*One evening I accompanied the Davenports to Mr Guppy's residence in Great Marlborough Street.*' Although no date is given for the parlous performance, it is not difficult to substantiate. The 'stomping story' as remembered by the Revd Davies was historical – ten years old, in fact. The Davenport brothers, Ira Erastus and William Henry, had arrived in England in 1864, and had given their demonstrations from that October to the end of the year. In the New Year, they visited the provinces, disastrously, and left for the continent. In 1868, they did return to England, but the Guppys, having married in 1867, were living abroad by then, and when they finally came back, Mr Guppy had taken a new house, at 131 Holloway Road.

... an anonymous tome, ludicrously entitled Mary Jane. Samuel Guppy was incontrovertibly the author of *Mary Jane*. There is no scope for doubt; there are too many veridical references. For instance, Mrs Britten refers to him as the author (*op. cit.*, p.160) and the title page with the dedication to Miss Houghton (*v. ante*) is definitive. The full title is no more appealing than the short one; viz, *Mary Jane; or, Spiritualism Chemically Explained with Spirit Drawings. Also Essays By, and Ideas (Perhaps Erroneous) of "A Child at School."*

One journalist thought it was fiction. See 'Metropolitan Gossip', a column in the *Louth and North Lincs Advertiser*, August 8th, 1863.

... the device of a wife with psychic powers would be more persuasive. Samuel Guppy might even have implanted a deliberate clue in the text. Why did he refer, twice, to his 'wife' as 'the Marchioness'? *Prima facie*, he is joking that he is married to a stately dragon. However, the Victorian reading classes were all familiar with 'the Marchioness' as a memorable character in *The Old Curiosity Shop*, where she is a very thin, ill-treated maidser-

vant. Elizabeth was famously the opposite in build: was this the joke? Or could he have been thinking of his own influence on Elizabeth? In Dickens' story, Dick Swiveller educates the maid and eventually marries her.

Of course, he would be interested in phrenology ... Alfred Russel Wallace also believed in phrenology.

... his old friend, W., whom he had known intimately for many years ... Not Wallace! Not William Grinsell Nicholl! Might be James Wason, habitué at séances, appears in Mrs Berry's *Experiences in Spiritualism* (p. 79) attending a séance in 1871 with Mrs Guppy. A table cover was placed on his head in the darkness. He was a Liverpool solicitor.

' *... I found Elizabeth, as her family knew her, a most warm and kindly person.'* She includes without critical comment the lengthy passage from Wallace's *Miracles and Modern Spiritualism* (p. 164) on the apport of flowers 'covered throughout with a most beautiful coating of dew,' and it is possible that her reverence for her naturalist father might have predisposed her to accept Wallace's statements unreservedly.

Isambard Brunel was his more flamboyant partner ... A partner in spirit, if not attested to in formal documentation. *v. Brunel,* Angus Buchanan, 2002, p.201.

4
The Medium Abroad

... Mrs Guppy put it that she had asked Mr Herne to agree to the test ... By spiritualist definition, a test was a request demanded of a medium to convince a sitter that the medium had genuine psychic ability. Just giving correct factual information about a departed person could suffice as a successful test. Not by any means were all tests passed, even when there was a strong expectation of success.

Her attitude was rueful, but accepting. Miss Houghton believed that she was attended by 70 guardian angels, coming to her in septs of seven.

The duping of Miss Houghton by Mrs Guppy was not attended

by malice. Remarkable gifts from the spirits came to good Miss Houghton *via* Mrs Guppy. At a Whit Sunday séance in 1868, a dove, received as a symbol of The Comforter (The Holy Spirit) was given to her and lived for eight years in perfect harmony with her mistress. She laid 58 eggs, all preserved. When the gentle bird died, Miss Houghton took her body to a taxidermist, and, be it noted, Elizabeth paid for the work to be done.

Preston, the cook, who was a good needlewoman ... Preston had been with Miss Houghton and her mother for some 30 years, and was a confidential servant, often chatting to her mistress on her way up to bed, but also a household tyrant, upsetting the maids with her bad temper. It was also discovered that she had been robbing Miss Houghton in every way she could. She died shortly after being dismissed. *v. Evenings at Home* in *Spiritual Séance.* (p. 344).

5
The Flight of the Enchantress

... publicity may have exceeded her expectations. On February 29th, 1872, *Nature* carried some points by EB Taylor (Sir Edward Burnett Taylor, 1832-1917, leading anthropologist) in response to a review by Alfred Russel Wallace of his important book, *Primitive Culture.* In the matter of werewolves, Wallace had argued that, 'were-wolves were probably men who had exceptional power of acting upon certain sensitive individuals, and could make them, when so acted upon, believe they saw what the mesmerist pleased; and who used this power for bad purposes.' Tylor now proceeded, with tongue-in-cheek, to apply that idea somewhat further: 'Granting that a were-wolf, in virtue of being a person capable of exerting mesmeric influence, can delude people, and even assemblies of people, into fancying that they perceive monstrous unrealities, the question arises, was anyone with this were-wolf-faculty in the room when Mrs Guppy made her celebrated aerostatic entrance? Is Mr D. D. Home a were-wolf?' He was not seriously suggesting that Mrs Guppy was a were-wolf.

Lyon v Home ... Notorious case which dented but did not hole

the vessel of spiritualism. It was a very discreditable story. DD
Home met a wealthy widow in her sixties, Mrs Jane Lyon, who
took a fancy to him and wanted to adopt him as her son. She settled large sums of money on him but then changed her mind
and sued for the return of around £60,000. The trial was hard
fought. She claimed that, as a medium at séances, Home said
that the spirit of her dead husband was instructing her to give
him the money. Scientific witnesses testified that Home's abili-
ties were genuine. The Vice-Chancellor, Sir George Giffard
found for the plaintiff, although he was not impressed by Mrs
Lyon and her tendency to contradict herself, and ordered the
return of her money. He delivered the opinion that spiritualism
was 'mischievous nonsense, well calculated, on the one hand, to
delude the vain, the weak, the foolish, and the superstitious;
and, on the other, to assist the projects of the needy and of the
adventurer'. This was all happening in the April and May of
1868, when Mrs Guppy was on her triumphant tour abroad with
her new husband, and Home himself, after brief setback, was
going on to higher effects, such as, most famously, floating into
a window from outside.

    ... *the unhappy gentleman who had to pay £500 because he
would make a wager that the world was flat.* In 1870, John
Hampden, a flat-earther, offered £500 to any person able to
prove that the world was round. Alfred Russel Wallace took up
the challenge and, after contention, the stake was awarded to
him. However, through appeal to the betting laws, Hampden
managed to recover the money, and thereafter pursued Wallace
with scurrilous invective for nearly 20 years – yet another
instance of his bad luck.

    Mr John Bright. Leading Liberal statesman, (1811-89) famous
orator and reformer, a man after Samuel Guppy's own heart: in
its non-spiritualist part, *Mary Jane* is all about reform, even if
skewed towards eccentric dialectic.

    *The magistrate was the well-known Frederick Flowers (1810-
86).* 'He possessed kindness, tact, and discrimination, and a
strong sense of justice, especially towards those who were poor
and weak.' *Dictionary of National Biography.*

6
A Cast of Extras

This commentator, John Beattie ... v. Georgiana Houghton's *Chronicles of the Photographs* ... (*op. cit.*, pp.151-2).

... a fact, too, of deep significance, dependent on the laws of a yet unknown chemistry. Miracles and Modern Spiritualism, p. 198.
Wallace ... was not against spirit photography, nor did his enthusiasm for it wane. As late as 1891, he 'challenged the S.P.R. properly to investigate' because the images were 'evidence that goes to the very root of the whole inquiry and affords the most complete and crucial test in the problem of the subjectivity or objectivity of apparitions.' *v. On Spirit Photographs: A Reply to Mr A. R. Wallace.* Proceedings of the S.P.R. Vol. 7, part 19, 1891-2, pp.268-289.

... little Frederick might have been schooled for his part in the drama. Frederick was a warehouseman at Somerset House in 1881, and, ten years later, he was a civil servant. Alice Hudson, the last-born daughter, became an 'artist/sculptor'.

Herne and Williams continued their séances until the late 1880s. For amplification of an apparent split in the Herne-Williams partnership, and other interesting material on them, *v. PsyPioneer Electronic Journal,* ed. Paul J. Gaunt, Vol. 7, No. 1 and No. 3.

Caroline Elizabeth Bassett, who was also a medium ... Medhurst and Goldney state without compromise that Mrs Bassett was a private medium (*Proceedings of the Society for Psychical Research,* Volume 54, Part 195, March, 1964, p.49) but Frank Herne was definitely not a private medium, so there must have been an adjustment when they married.

7
Vitriol

Mr AL Henderson, with three supporters. Henderson was 'a well-known photographer ... a skeptic, *a Saul among the spiritualists'* (Nandor Fodor, *Mind over Space,* p. 153 *et seq.*) On November 2nd, 1873, he was 'carried' from Mrs Guppy's séance room to a stable at 29 Kingsdown Road, one-and-a-half to two miles distant. He was suddenly missed. He woke as from a dream in a stable yard, with a horse. There were rumours then that the transportation was a trick, with the implication of a hoax, but he was still denying that in 1895. If it was a hoax, bravo! If it was a simulated psychic transport, connived at with Mrs Guppy, who had indeed asked the spirits to carry someone out of the room, then he was not a sincere spiritualist and he knew all about false mediumship.

In an important paper ... RG Medhurst and KM Goldney remarked 'on the jealous hatred ... v. *William Crookes and the Physical Phenomena of Mediumship*, Proceedings of the S.P.R., Volume 54, Part 195, March, 1964.

The first [document] *is extracted from the private notebooks of the Reverend Stainton Moses* ... v. *Proceedings of the S.P.R.,* (op. cit., p.58).

The second document is a remarkable letter from Nelson Holmes to DD Home ... v. *Proceedings of the S.P.R.,* (op. cit., pp. 58-59).

Vitriol throwing did happen at that time ... i.e. sulphuric acid, hideously corrosive, introduced internally or externally. Sexual jealousy was known to fuel the desire to mutilate and death could follow. By section 29 of the Offences against the Person Act, 1861, it was laid down as an offence imprisonable for life, for any person unlawfully and maliciously ... to throw at or upon or otherwise apply to any person, any corrosive fluid ... with intent in any of such cases to burn, maim, disfigure, disable or do grievous bodily harm to any person, whether any bodily injury be effected or not.

If we use the census of 1871, Mrs Berry is living at 242 Oxford Street ... As previously stated, by the middle of 1873, Mrs Berry had moved to a house in Connaught Square, a little further to the west of Marble Arch, but this point does not invalidate the discussion about Miss Berry.

A torrent of words poured from him. A full coverage of the contentious correspondence which followed the incident, taken from the spiritualist press, interspersed with lively discussion, is usefully provided in the *PsyPioneer Journal*, as previously cited. It is unusual for Volckman's 'defence' to be shown in full.

8
The Last Séance

Dr Richard Barter. He had previously treated Mr Guppy's constitutional gout, and therefore this was not likely to have been his first visit.

Elizabeth was in no hurry to let the 'Sultan of Zanzibar' out of his box again ... The late Dr Eric Dingwall, of the Society for Psychical Research, told Richard Whittington-Egan, when a member of that same society, that he was in possession of a letter from JN Maskelyne (author of *Modern Spiritualism*) stating that Mrs Guppy went to see him to enquire about some conjuring tricks. (Notes of conversation between Dr Dingwall and RWE dated February 3rd, 1966.)

... part of a paper by Mrs Sidgwick delivered to ... the Society in 1886 ... Mrs Sidgwick, Principal of Newnham College, President of the S.P.R., was a strict and ingenious investigator, but kind and respectful to the mediums, v. *Mrs Henry Sidgwick a Memoir by her niece*, Ethel Sidgwick, Sidgwick and Jackson, 1938, p. 93.

... Septima ... adopted three children from an orphanage. Her eccentricity continued. Under the heading, 'Comedy of Resistance to Insurance Act,' the *Western Times* (August 15th, 1912) reported that, 'Mrs S. D. R. Guppy, of Broadlands, New Walden, Surrey, has, in consequence of threats to burn down her house, asked for police protection. Mrs Guppy, on the advent of the Insurance Act, discharged all her servants and engaged either girls under 16 or men over 70, each of whom were exempt from the Act. Now she wants a coachman of 70 or over, and has received hundreds of applications for the post. Scores of letters have reached Mrs Guppy, some sympathising and others blaming her for her action. One of the writers said he had the plans of her house and would burn it down'.

... the entire stock-in-trade, machinery and plant were put up for auction. The following lots were specified: 10 tons jams, 5 tons sweets, 2 tons sugar, 1 ton peel, 1 ton biscuits, ¾ ton spices, 4 tons fruit pulp. There were steam engines, cranes, pulpers, pressers, boilers, furnaces, tanks galore.

Bazaar fire of Paris ... On May 4th, 1897, a terrible fire destroyed the annual charity sale of Notre Dame at Rue Jean-Goujon on the banks of the Seine. The victims panicked in the large wooden shed, and charred remains were identified by early use of dental records.

... probate was granted to his widow and the Public Trustee. Presumably the Public Trustee had been invoked because the sum involved was large, and the widow was in poor health.

When the will was proved ... it was revealed in the press ... i.e. in the *Western Times*, September, 1913.

The cause of death was 'Senile Decay' ... Not necessarily senile dementia as we know it, but gradual deterioration of the organs. www.ancestry.co.uk, *The Volckman Name in History*, The Generations Network, Inc. Utah, 2008

Select Bibliography

Berry, Catherine, *Experiences in Spiritualism: A Record of Extraordinary Phenomena Witnessed through the Most Powerful Mediums, With Some Historical Fragments Relating to Semiramide, Given by the Spirit of an Egyptian who Lived Contemporary with Her*, James Burns, 1876

Brandon, Ruth, *The Spiritualists: The Passion for the Occult in the Nineteenth and Twentieth Centuries*, Weidenfeld and Nicolson, 1982

Bridges, Yseult, *Child of the Tropics, Victorian Memoirs*, Collins and Harvill Press, 1980

Britten, Emma Hardinge, *Nineteenth Century Miracles; or Spirits and their Work in Every Country of the Earth: A Complete Historical Compendium of the Great Movement Known as 'Modern Spiritualism'*, William Britten, 1884

Buchanan, R. Angus, *Brunel: The Life and Times of Isambard Kingdom Brunel*, Hambledon and London, 2002

Crosland, Newton, *Rambles Round My Life: An Autobiography (1819-1896)*, EW Allen, 1898

Davies, Revd Charles Maurice, DD, *Mystic London: or, Phases of Occult Life in the Metropolis.* Tinsley Brothers, 1875

Fodor, Nandor, *Encyclopaedia of Psychic Science*, Arthurs Press, 1933
Mind over Space, Citadel Press, NY, 1962

Guppy, Samuel, *Mary Jane; or, Spiritualism Chemically Explained with Spirit Drawings. Also Essays By and Ideas (Perhaps Erroneous) of, 'A Child at School'*, Printed by John King and Co., London, 1863
Imitations of Spiritual Phenomena with Comments Thereon, Penfold and Farmer, 1873

Hall, Trevor H, *The Spiritualists: The Story of Florence Cook and William Crookes*, Gerald Duckworth, 1962

Home, DD, *Incidents in my Life*, London, 1863
Lights and Shadows of Spiritualism, GW Carleton, NY, 1877

Houghton, Georgiana, *Evenings at Home in Spiritual Séance: Welded*

Together by a Species of Autobiography, EW Allen, 1882

Houghton, Georgiana, *Chronicles of the Photographs of Spiritual Beings and Phenomena Invisible to the Material Eye Interblended with Personal Narrative*, EW Allen, 1882

Jolly, Martyn, *Faces of the Living Dead: The Belief in Spirit Photography*, The British Library, 2006

Lamont, Peter, *The First Psychic: The Peculiar Mystery of a Notorious Victorian Wizard*, Little, Brown, 2005

London Dialectical Society, *Report on Spiritualism, of the London Dialectical Society, Together with the Evidence, Oral and Written, and a Selection from the Correspondence*, J Burns, 1873

Marryat, Florence, *There Is No Death*, Griffith Farran, 1891

Maskelyne, John Nevil, *Modern Spiritualism. A Short Account of its Rise and Progress, with some Exposures of so-called Spirit Media*, Frederick Warne, 1876

Melechi, Antonio, *Servants of the Supernatural; The Night Side of the Victorian Mind*, Heinemann, 2008

Open University, *An Introduction to the Humanities, Religion and Science in Context*, Block 4, 1998

Owen, Alex, *The Darkened Room: Women, Power, and Spiritualism in Late Nineteenth Century England*, Virago Press, 1989

Podmore, Frank, *Modern Spiritualism: A History and a Criticism*, (2 Volumes), Methuen, 1902

Price, Harry, *Poltergeist over England: Three Centuries of Mischievous Ghosts*, Country Life Ltd., 1945

Rowlands, MJL and Beavis, IC, *Tunbridge Wells in Old Photographs*, Alan Sutton, 1991

Wallace, Alfred Russel, *Miracles and Modern Spiritualism. Three Essays*, James Burns, 1875
My Life: A Record of Events and Opinions, (2 Volumes), Chapman and Hall, 1905

Illustrations

1. The Lanes, Horncastle: the birth-place of Mrs Guppy.

2. The Hamburgh Tavern, Hull: childhood home of Mrs Guppy.

4. Thomas Sims: Alfred Russel Wallace's brother-in-law.

3. Mermaid: chunky sculpture by William Grinsell Nicholl.

5. The Davenport brothers from America

6. Msida Bastion Cemetery, Malta: burial place of Georgina Guppy.

Left: 7. Miss
Georgiana
Houghton.

Above: 8. Mrs Thomas
Everitt: medium.

Right: 9. Mrs Elizabeth
Guppy, with baby.

10. The Transport of Mrs Guppy.

11. Frederick Hudson: spirit photographer.

12. Alfred Russel Wallace and 'spirit' of his mother.

13. Mrs Tebb, Mrs Guppy, and Miss Houghton (seated).

14. Alfred Russel Wallace and 'spirit'.

15. Mr Guppy with medium and 'spirit'

16. Frank Herne, with 'double'.

17. Charles Williams: medium.

18. Mrs Guppy with flowers and a 'spirit'.

19. St Ann's Hydropathic Establishment, Blarney.
(Samuel Guppy's place of death)

20. The White House, Leyton.
Home of Elizabeth and William Volckman (street view).

21. The White House (garden view).

By the Same Author

Khaki Mischief: The Agra Murder Case

Murder on the Bluff: The Carew Poisoning Case

Scottish Murder Stories

Classic Scottish Murder Stories

Doctor Forbes Winslow: Defender of the Insane

The Stockbridge Baby-Farmer and Other Scottish Murder Stories

Jack L'Éventreur (Translation from Jean Dorsenne)

Frank Miles and Oscar Wilde: "Such White Lilies"

Arthur O'Shaughnessy: The Music Maker

The Execution of Mary Ansell (forthcoming)

With Richard Whittington-Egan

The Story of Mr George Edalji (Ed.)

The Bedside Book of Murder

The Murder Almanac

Murder on File

Index